Modernist Cooking Made Easy:
Sous Vide

The Authoritative Guide to
Low Temperature Precision Cooking

By Jason Logsdon

For more information please contact Primolicious LLC at 12 Pimlico Road, Wolcott CT 06716.

ISBN-13: 978-0-9910501-7-8
ISBN-10: 0991050177

Other Books By Jason Logsdon

Modernist Cooking Made Easy: Getting Started

Modernist Cooking Made Easy: Party Foods

Modernist Cooking Made Easy: The Whipping Siphon

Beginning Sous Vide

Sous Vide: Help for the Busy Cook

Sous Vide Grilling

To my Mom,
who from an early age
gave me the confidence
to do anything I set my mind to

TABLE OF CONTENTS

FORWARD: WHY SOUS VIDE? 1

UNDERSTANDING THE SOUS VIDE PROCESS

INTRODUCTION TO SOUS VIDE 2
How Sous Vide Works 3
Sous Vide Technique 4
Recommended Sous Vide Setups 6

PRE-SOUS VIDE PREPARATION 9
Salting 10
Seasonings, Spices and Herbs 10
Bagging with Sauces 10
Brining 11
Pre-Searing 11
Smoking 12
Marinating 13
General Pre-Sous Vide Tips 13

SOUS VIDE SEALING 15
What Does Sealing Do? 16
Types of Sealers 16
Plastic Safety 20
General Sealing Tips 20

SOUS VIDE TEMPERATURE CONTROL 23
What to Look For 24
What I Recommend 24
Circulators 24
Water Baths 27
Temperature Controllers 27
Beer Cooler Sous Vide 28
Sous Vide on the Stove 28

DETERMINING TIME AND TEMPERATURES 29
Sous Vide Time 30
Sous Vide Temperature 32
Checking Core Temperature 34

SOUS VIDE FINISHING 35
Searing 36
Smoking 39

Breading and Frying 39
Cook, Chill, and Hold 39
Using Sous Vide Juices 39
General Finishing Tips 40

SOUS VIDE RECIPES

A WORD ABOUT THE RECIPES 42
What Should I Sous Vide First? 43
Modernist Notes 45
Why the Range 45
Recipe Considerations 47
Converting Existing Recipes 50

BEEF, LAMB, AND OTHER RED MEAT 53
Filet Mignon with Creamy Blue Cheese 56
Ribeye with Herb Butter and Broccoli Raab 59
Flank Steak with Argentinian Chimichurri 61
Sirloin Steak with Lime-Ginger Slaw 63
Asian Skirt Steak with Bean Sprouts 65
Chuck Steak with Deep Fried Brussels Sprouts 66
Raspberry Salad with New York Strip Steak 69
Hanger Steak with Peach Salsa 71
Top Round with Orange Sauce 73
Flat Iron Steak with Pancetta Asparagus 75
London Broil Beef Fajitas 77
Chuck Pot Roast with Roasted Vegetables 79
Chuck Roast with Bacon and Kale 81
Prime Rib Roast with Horseradish Cream 83
Short Ribs with Feta and Beet Salad 85
Beef Carnitas with Tangerine-Chipotle Sauce 87
Top Round French Dip Sandwiches 89
Easy Corned Beef 91
Tri-Tip with Roasted Fennel and Orange Salad 92
Memphis-Style Beef Ribs and Spicy Lime Corn 95
Thick Cut Pastrami Reubens 97
Rogan Josh Spiced Lamb Loin 100
Rack of Lamb with Quinoa-Mint Salad 101

PORK 103
Honey-Chipotle Glazed Country Style Ribs 104
Cuban Pork Chops with Frijoles Negros 107

Bourbon Glazed Tenderloin with Pea Pesto 109
Pulled Pork with Pineapple Chutney 111
St. Louis Ribs with Bourbon BBQ Sauce 113
Prosciutto-Wrapped Pork Loin Roast 115
Pork Rillettes 117

SAUSAGE AND GROUND MEATS   119
Beer Brat Grinders with Guinness Mustard 120
Italian Sausage with Acorn Squash Puree 123
Bacon, Pineapple, and Poblano Cheeseburger 125
Spaghetti and Meatballs 127
Chicken Sausage with Caprese Salad 129

CHICKEN, TURKEY, AND POULTRY   130
Chicken Parmigiana 132
Fried Buttermilk Chicken 135
Chicken Wings 137
Shredded Chicken Thigh Enchiladas 139
Chicken Thighs with Chile-Cheddar Polenta 141
Turkey Breast with Cranberry Chutney 143
Shredded Duck Legs with Sesame Noodles 145
Duck Breast with Port Reduction 147

EGGS   149
Soft Boiled Egg on Cheddar Hash Browns 151
French-Style Scrambled Eggs 153
13 Minute Egg on Wilted Spinach Salad 155
Chocolate Chip Cookie Dough Balls 157

FISH AND SHELLFISH   159
Shrimp Cocktail with Chipotle Sauce 161
Salmon with Apple and Jalapenos 163
Mi-Cuit Salmon 165
Halibut with Honey-Roasted Beets 167
Sea Bass with Microgreens and Mustard Oil 169
Monkfish in Dashi with Snow Peas 171
Red Snapper Tostadas with Mango Salsa 173
Sesame Crusted Tuna with Avocado Salad 175
Scallops with Orange and Chile Strips 177
Calamari with Asian-Flavored Vegetables 179
Cod Chowder with Sourdough Croutons 181

FRUITS AND VEGETABLES   182
Asparagus with Dijon Mustard Vinaigrette 183
Broccoli with Parmesan and Lemon 185

Sweet and Spicy Glazed Carrots 187
Butter-Poached Beet Salad with Pecans 189
Corn on the Cob with Basil 191
Orange-Saffron Fennel Confit 192
Poached Cherry Tomatoes 193
Preserved Lemon Confit 194
Butternut Squash Salad 195
Butter Poached Turnips 197
Dual-Cooked Creamy Potato Puree 198
Rustic Roasted Garlic Mashed Potatoes 199
Chipotle Sweet Potato Salad 201
Spiced Cabbage with Apples 202
Bourbon-Maple Apple Chutney 203
Vanilla Pears with Rosemary Caramel 205

INFUSIONS   207
Cherry-Infused Rye Old Fashioned 208
Creamsicle with Orange-Vanilla Vodka 209
Chile-Tomato Infused Vodka Bloody Mary 211
Raspberry Infused Vinaigrette 213
Tarragon, Lemon, and Shallot Vinaigrette 215
Rosemary and Sage Infused Oil 217
Chile Pepper Infused Oil 219

SWEET AND SOUR   220
Sous Vide Yogurt 221
Sous Vide Creme Fraiche 223
Lemon Curd 224
Cinnamon-Vanilla Creme Brulee 225
White Chocolate Creme Brulee 227
Dulce de Leche 229

REFERENCES

SOUS VIDE TIME AND TEMPERATURE   231
Beef - Roasts and Tough Cuts 233
Beef - Steak and Tender Cuts 234
Chicken and Eggs 235
Duck 236
Fish and Shellfish 237
Fruits and Vegetables 240
Lamb 241
Pork 242
Turkey 244
Fahrenheit to Celsius Conversion 245

SOUS VIDE THICKNESS TIMES   **247**
Beef, Pork, Lamb Thickness Chart   249
Chicken Thickness Chart   251
Fish Thickness Chart   253

INGREDIENT TABLES   **255**
Ingredient Techniques   256
Ingredient Temperatures   257

SOUS VIDE AND MODERNIST RESOURCES   **259**
Modernist Resources   260
Ingredient and Tool Sources   262

RECIPE INDEX   **263**

DID YOU ENJOY THIS BOOK?   **267**

ABOUT THE AUTHOR   **269**

FORWARD: WHY SOUS VIDE?

I initially got my start in modernist cooking when I began exploring the sous vide process. I was fascinated with the process and hooked on learning more about the new types of cooking. Since then I've expanded into other modernist techniques and worked with everything from whipping siphons to pressure cookers and blow torches; created foams, gels and spheres; made barrel aged cocktails and brewed beer.

But the one technique
I use on a daily basis is sous vide.

Although sous vide cooking is not as "sexy" as some of the other modernist techniques it has two huge advantages for both the novice and experienced cook. Most importantly it will allow you to significantly increase the quality and consistency of the dishes you create on a daily basis. And for those of you whose lives are harried, the sous vide technique also allows you to create remarkable meals while working around your hectic schedule.

Over the last five years I've cooked hundreds of sous vide meals and written four cookbooks on the subject that have brought sous vide cooking into tens of thousands of home kitchens. I've used it for fancy modernist dishes, simple everyday post-work meals, food for parties and barbecues and everything in-between. With the introduction of several low-cost circulators, sous vide is more accessible than ever to the home cook. I decided it was time to take another look at sous vide and write a comprehensive primer for cooks of all experience levels.

This book uses my years of experience to demystify the sous vide process, serve as a reference for more than 80 cuts of meat and vegetables, and provide a collection of inspiring recipes to get you on your way to sous vide success.

Sous vide is a simple and extremely effective way to cook. This book covers every step of the sous vide process, from seasoning, sealing, and temperature control to how to determine the times and temperatures needed to turn out great food. There are also extensive write ups for the main types of food including steak and red meat, pork, fish and shellfish, eggs, fruits and vegetables, and more.

After reading this book you will be able to consistently prepare great food with a minimal amount of effort.

The bulk of this book is the more than 85 recipes it contains. Feel free to skim the recipes looking for something that inspires you, or turn to a specific recipe to learn all about how to cook the cut of meat it features. I have provided images of many of the dishes but for larger, full color images you can go to:

MCMeasy.com/SVGallery

To stay up to date with sous vide, modernist cooking, and what I am working on please:

Like my Facebook page at: www.facebook.com/ModernistCookingMadeEasy

Join my monthly newsletter at: MCMEasy.com/Newsletter

Follow me on twitter at: @jasonlogsdon_sv

If you enjoy this book I'd love it if you took the time to leave a review on Amazon.com, the reviews always help other people decide if they want to purchase the book or not.

Most importantly of all, remember to have fun!

SECTION ONE

UNDERSTANDING THE SOUS VIDE PROCESS

INTRODUCTION TO SOUS VIDE

If you have any questions you can ask them in the Sous Vide Forums on my website. Just post your question and other cooks will weigh in with their answers.

You can find them on my website at:
MCMEasy.com/Forums

Sous vide is one of the most popular modernist techniques and one that is pushing modernist cooking into the mainstream. From world class chefs like Thomas Keller and hit television shows like Iron Chef America and Top Chef to everyday restaurants like Panera, sous vide is popping up everywhere.

Sous vide can initially be an intimidating type of cooking and conceptually it can be very difficult because of its differences with traditional cooking. The various types of sous vide equipment, questions about vacuum sealing, and the science of the safety of sous vide can all play a part in confusing new cooks.

However, once you understand a few basics, sous vide cooking is one of the easiest and most foolproof ways to cook. In this book I'll give you the foundation you need to get started with sous vide including the basic process, the important safety information, and recommended setups you can use.

How Sous Vide Works

Sous vide, or low temperature precision cooking, is the process of cooking food at a very tightly controlled temperature, normally at the temperature the food will be served. This is a departure from traditional cooking methods that use high heat to cook the food, which must be removed at the exact moment it reaches the desired temperature.

The core tenant of sous vide cooking is that food should be cooked at the temperature it will be served. For instance, if you are cooking a steak to medium rare, you want to serve it at 131°F (55°C).

With traditional cooking methods you would cook it on a hot grill or oven at a minimum of 400°F to 500°F (204°C to 260°C) and pull it off at the right moment when the middle has reached 131°F (55°C). This results in a bulls eye effect of burnt meat on the outside turning to medium rare in the middle.

The same steak cooked sous vide would be cooked at 131°F (55°C) for several hours. This will result in the entire piece of meat being a perfectly cooked medium rare. The steak would then usually be quickly seared at high heat to add the flavorful, browned crust to it.

Sous vide was first used as an upscale culinary technique in kitchens in France in the 1970s and traditionally is the process of cooking vacuum sealed food in a low temperature water bath. This process helps to achieve texture and doneness not found in other cooking techniques, as well as introducing many conveniences for a professional kitchen. Sous vide has slowly been spreading around the world in professional kitchens everywhere and is finally making the jump to home kitchens as information and inexpensive equipment has become more prevalent.

As sous vide has become more popular and moved to the home kitchen the term now encompasses both traditional "under vacuum" sous vide and also precision low temperature cooking of any kind. Some preparations rely on the vacuum pressure to change the texture of the food but in most cases the benefits of sous vide are realized in the controlled, low temperature cooking process, not the vacuum sealing. This means that fancy vacuum sealers can be set aside for home sealers or even Ziploc bags.

SOUS VIDE TECHNIQUE

The actual process of cooking sous vide is very simple. You determine the temperature you'd like to cook your food to, say 131°F (55°C) for a medium-rare steak. Then you heat some water up to that temperature, seal your food in a vacuum bag or Ziploc bag and place it in the water until the food is heated through to the temperature of the water.

For foods that aren't tender (think pot roasts, short ribs, briskets, etc.) you can continue cooking it once it comes up to temperature until the food has been tenderized (sometimes up to 2 or 3 days!). Then just finish your food with a sear and you're all set!

I go into much more detail in the the subsequent chapters but here is a brief look at each step.

Pre-Sous Vide Preparation

Just like many traditional methods, you often will flavor the food before cooking it. This can be as simple as a sprinkling of salt and pepper or as complicated as adding an elaborate sauce, spice rub, or even smoking the food. Depending on the type of seasoning it can either be rubbed directly onto the food itself or added into the bag with the food.

For a detailed look at flavoring the food and other preparation techniques please see the "Pre-Sous Vide Preparation" chapter.

Seal the Food

Once the food has been seasoned and is ready to cook it is added to a sous vide bag, the air is removed, and the bag is sealed closed. Removing the air results in closer contact between the food and the water in the water bath. This helps to facilitate quicker cooking since water transfers heat more efficiently than air. Sealing also keeps the flavor of your food contained and keeps the food from getting into you sous vide machine.

The most effective method of sealing food is with a chambered vacuum sealer but those are expensive and usually overkill for home use. I normally use regular Ziploc Freezer Bags, which work well for most foods, and sometimes I'll use a FoodSaver Vacuum Sealer for longer cooking foods or for higher temperatures. More information about sealing can be found in the "Sous Vide Sealing" chapter.

Heat and Maintain the Water
To cook the food you heat a quantity of water up to the temperature you will cook the food at. This temperature will normally be the same that you will want your food to end up.

There are many ways to heat up the water for sous vide cooking, ranging from your stove to expensive laboratory circulators. Luckily, there are more low-cost options available than ever and you can easily get started with sous vide cooking without spending a lot of money.

The temperature you cook the food will depend greatly on what it is. A detailed discussion of temperatures can be found in the "Determining Time and Temperatures" chapter and different equipment options are found in the "Sous Vide Temperature Control" chapter.

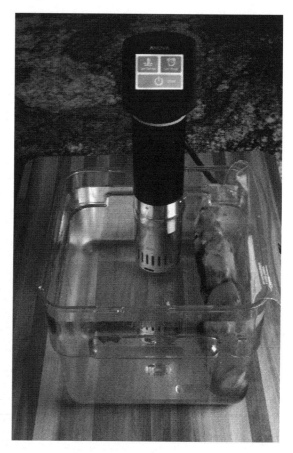

Cook the Food

Put the sous vide bag containing the food in the water and let it cook for the amount of time needed to either heat the food through, or to fully tenderize it. Depending on what you are cooking, this time frame can range from 15 minutes for some fish up to 3 days for short ribs and other tough cuts.

The "Determining Time and Temperatures" chapter looks closely at the different methods of determining cooking times.

Finish the Dish

To get a good finish and texture on your food, especially meats, it is almost always advisable to quickly sear it. This is usually done in hot pan, on a grill, or with a culinary blow torch. Some meals also call for other methods of finishing the food, such as breading and deep frying for chicken, or smoking for brisket.

You can also quickly chill the food in an ice bath which is ½ ice and ½ water and then refrigerate or freeze the food for later re-heating. More details can be found in the "Sous Vide Finishing" chapter.

RECOMMENDED SOUS VIDE SETUPS

There are many different options when determining your sous vide setup and what you decide on will depend a lot on your situation.

Trying It Out

If you are just getting started with sous vide and want to see if it's right for you, I'd recommend trying beer cooler sous vide or sous vide on the stove first. They are both great ways to try out sous vide with minimal financial commitment. I go into more details in the "Sous Vide Temperature Control" chapter.

Recommended: Ready to Take the Plunge

If you know you are ready to really use sous vide cooking, then this is the set up for you. I'd recommend one of the new low-cost immersion circulators, they range from $150-$300 and can do almost anything you'd want to do at home. I would start out using Ziploc Freezer Bags but a FoodSaver vacuum sealer is always nice if you don't mind spending the extra money. This is the system I usually use at home.

Professional Setup

If you are using sous vide constantly or are in a professional kitchen you'll want to go with a higher-end circulator. I highly recommend the PolyScience Chef Series. A chambered vacuum sealer will also help with prepping and storing foods in a working kitchen.

PRE-SOUS VIDE PREPARATION

Like most traditional cooking, the first step in sous vide is to prepare the food for cooking. There are countless methods you can use, from a simple sprinkling of salt and pepper all the way to pre-smoking, marinades, and complex spice rubs.

SALTING

When cooking meat with almost any traditional cooking method the first step is to salt it. This is also true for items cooked sous vide for shorter amounts of time, less than 4 or 5 hours. I always salt short-term meat using about the same amount I would when grilling or pan searing.

However, for longer times there is more disagreement about what is the correct method. Meat that is cooked for longer amounts of time that has been salted loses a little more moisture than unsalted meat. Salting the meat also subtly changes the structure of the proteins on the outside, making the meat a little tougher and more "cured" tasting.

I personally find the flavor of salted meat beefier and richer tasting. Because of this, I usually lightly salt longer cooking items, using about a quarter as much salt as I would normally. Many people prefer the unsalted, slightly moister meat so they refrain from salting until after the meat has been cooked sous vide.

The difference between the two methods is very minor and you can't go wrong either way. I suggest trying it both ways and see what you personally prefer.

SEASONINGS, SPICES AND HERBS

The addition of seasonings, spices, and herbs is another common method of adding flavor to both traditional and sous vided foods.

Dry spice rubs work great and can be used in the same quantities they are in traditional cooking methods. Woody herbs such as rosemary, thyme, sage, and bay leaves, also work great with sous vide. Dried herbs can also be used well in almost all sous vide cooking.

Pungent spices like fresh garlic and ginger are best not used in sous vide cooking. The lower temperatures the food is cooked at isn't enough to mellow out the flavors, so they retain their sharp bite.

Softer herbs like basil and parsley work fine with shorter cooked items but don't hold up as well over longer cooking times.

BAGGING WITH SAUCES

A great way to add flavor to your sous vide foods is through the addition of various sauces to the sous vide bag. The sauce will add flavor and permeate the food, similar to a flavor-based marinade.

This technique can be used to add strong flavors to the food. Using several tablespoons of BBQ sauce, hot sauce, teriyaki sauce, and other strong sauces is a great way to ensure the flavors transfer to the food.

Base flavors can also be introduced this way. I'll often use a tablespoon of soy sauce, Worcester sauce, or other strong condiment to add base flavors to foods.

Brining

In traditional cooking, brining is a great way to maintain the juiciness of food, as well as to firm up the texture and introduce flavors. This is still all true in sous vide cooking, though it isn't as apparent because the sous vide-only result is so good by itself.

Any food you usually brine will benefit from brining before cooking it sous vide, it is especially beneficial to pork and chicken. Brining fish is also a great way to firm up the flesh and to draw out the albumin - the weird white stuff sometimes found on fish.

There are several ways to brine food and you should use the one you are most comfortable with. The easiest for me is a simple brine Michael Ruhlman made from ½ cup sugar, 1 cup salt, and 1 gallon of water. To this brine you can add spices and seasoning such as peppercorns, cloves, garlic, herbs, or any other flavorful aromatics.

Combine these ingredients over medium heat until the salt and sugar are dissolved then let them cool fully. You can also heat only half of the water initially and add the other half as ice to more quickly cool down the brine.

Once the brine has fully cooled, submerge the food in it and let it soak in the refrigerator for several hours. The length of time depends on the size and type of meat. In general:

Pork chops - 1 to 3 hours
Pork roast or loin - 12 hours
Chicken Breast or thighs - 1 to 3 hours
Whole chicken - 5 to 10 hours
Fish - 15 minutes to 3 hours, depending on preparation style

Remember not to reuse the brine, it will be full of impurities from the food.

Pre-Searing

It's common knowledge that sous vide foods need a sear after cooking to crisp up the exterior and add the wonderful Maillard reaction. Some people feel that doing a pre-sear of the meat will also help flavor it and allow the seared flavors to penetrate the meat. However, this is one of the more controversial questions around sous vide.

The undisputed benefit of pre-searing food is to sanitize the outside of the meat. A quick sear will kill any bacteria present on the surface. Another way to do this is to dip the sous vide bag into boiling water for a few seconds after bagging the food. This is more useful for items with longer cooking times where there may be time for bacterial growth.

Pre-searing also helps the food brown more quickly during the post-sear, though searing time usually isn't too large to begin with.

The downside of pre-searing is that it adds another step to the process. Many people also feel that the pre-sear flavors do not penetrate the meat or add any additional flavors, making the additional step irrelevant to the final outcome.

There is no consensus on this issue, Modernist Cuisine and Serious Eats both say not to pre-sear while Chef Steps and The French Culinary Institute both recommend it. However, with the large amount of people looking into the issue and experimenting with it, I think it's pretty clear that the flavor benefits, if there are any, are very minimal.

If you work in a Michelin starred restaurant where this minor flavor change is important, then running your own blind taste tests makes a lot of sense. For the rest of us cooks, doing a pre-sear probably won't make a noticeable difference, so feel free to skip the step, unless you are trying to pasteurize the surface. And if you feel strongly that the pre-sear makes a flavor difference and don't mind the extra step, by all means,

give it a pre-sear!

SMOKING

Smoking food is a great way to add additional flavor and it can easily be used in conjunction with sous vide. Just remember that you are adding smoke flavor to the food, not replacing a traditionally smoked food. These methods will work great if you want to add some great flavor to your food, though it's still best to smoke it in a traditional manner if you want a super-smokey pork shoulder with a red smoke ring.

A key point to remember during smoking is to make sure the temperature of the food stays below the temperature you will be sous viding it. Otherwise the benefits of the sous vide process will largely be negated.

There are several good ways to keep the temperature down. The first is to use a cold smoker. Either a more professional setup or something like the PolyScience Smoking Gun. These methods only heat the food a minimal amount, if any. The Smoking Gun is usually better suited to post-sous vide smoking but it works well with more tender proteins such as fish.

The other way to keep the temperature down is to only smoke the food briefly. Because most smoking occurs around 200°F (93°C) you can usually smoke the food for at least 15 to 30 minutes before cooking it sous vide, especially if you start the smoking process with the meat taken directly from the refrigerator.

Using high quality liquid smoke is another way of adding a smoky flavor to your foods. When I'm in a hurry I'll often put some directly in the bag before sealing it. It can't replace traditionally smoked foods but it's great in a pinch!

MARINATING

Marinating foods before cooking them is another wonderful way to introduce new flavors. The traditional method of marinating a food then removing it from the marinade and cooking it works great with sous vide. However, I often get asked if you can sous vide a food while it's still in the marinade.

While cooking a food in the marinade isn't dangerous, there are several potential negatives.

A big issue is the question of timing. Many marinades call for specific amounts of time that meat should be in them. These times rarely line up with the amount of time the meat should cook for. This means something has to give time wise on either the marinade or the sous viding, and the end result won't be as good.

To further complicate the matter, most marinades and brines are designed to

work on raw meat. Once the food goes into the sous vide bath it quickly comes up to temperature and is fully cooked. A 1" (25mm) steak will be cooked through in about 50 minutes, meaning the marinade will be trying to work on cooked meat for most of the marinating time. The outside 0.4" (10mm) will be cooked in only 8 to 10 minutes. Once the meat is cooked, the protein has been changed and will be affected differently by the marinade or brine.

A final issue is that due to the sealed environment there is no evaporation, compared to braising, for example. This means alcohol based marinades, or marinades with high acidity don't reduce during cooking and can take on bad flavors.

I usually just marinate my food ahead of time to be safe, but if you are in a hurry you can give it a shot and see how it turns out.

GENERAL PRE-SOUS VIDE TIPS

Cut Meat Down to Size
Because of the amount of time it takes for the heat to penetrate, large pieces of meat don't cook as evenly. The outside layers might come up to temperature, and start tenderizing, 4 to 5 hours before the middle heats up.

For longer cooked items this isn't as big of a problem because the middle will still be cooked for a long time. If the middle of a chuck roast only cooks for 32 of the 36 hours the difference will not be noticeable. However, it can be very apparent in shorter cooked items, especially the more tender ones. If a beef tenderloin is sous vided whole, the outside might be cooked for 2 to 3 times longer than the middle, resulting in an overly tender outside around a perfectly cooked middle.

Unless I need the whole piece of meat for presentation purposes I'll cut roasts into 2" to 3" slabs (50mm to 75mm). This will help them cook more evenly while still allowing me ample room for post sous vide searing, slicing, and serving.

Remove the Fat

Since sous vide cooking does not get up to high temperatures, about 145°F to 150°F at the most for meats, it does not render fat nearly as well as other cooking techniques. When it comes to dishes cooked over a long period of time, such as short ribs or a roast, be sure to remove any extra fat from the meat before cooking it. This will result in a much leaner and more tender meat with a lot better texture.

Easy on the Fresh Spices

Because of the length of time sous vide cooking requires, especially for the tough cuts of meat, and the effects of the vacuum seal, fresh spices can come across much stronger than they would in a normal piece of meat. It's better to err on the side of less and re-season after taking them out of the sous vide bath than to try and eat a dish that only tastes like rosemary or garlic.

Turn to the Powders

Using fresh herbs and spices instead of dried ones is normally a good idea when cooking. However, with sous vide it can be better to use the dried powders in some cases. This is especially true for things like garlic, onion, and ginger because the raw form of these can sometimes create a bitterness in the final dish.

Pre-Sous Vide Bacterial Control

While sous vide kills most of the dangerous bacteria present in beef, some people like to be extra cautious, especially for longer cooking items. They will first sear the meat or seal it and dunk it into a pot of boiling water for 15 to 20 seconds. This fully pasteurizes the outside of the meat and ensures nothing will grow during the sous vide process. I personally skip this step but many people swear by it.

SOUS VIDE SEALING

New vacuum sealers and other sous vide sealing devices come out often
and you can find up to date reviews on the latest equipment at
MCMeasy.com/Sealers

One of the more common questions I am asked is "What is the best way to seal your food for sous vide cooking?" There are so many options for sealing your food that it can get confusing figuring out exactly what you need.

There are several ways of doing it, ranging from large chambered vacuum sealers costing over a thousand dollars all the way down to Ziploc bags from the grocery store. Here's the low down on what you'll need to master the art of sealing your sous vide food.

WHAT DOES SEALING DO?

Since sous vide means "under vacuum" people understandably believe that the vacuum sealing process is critical to sous vide. However, this actually isn't the case. With a few minor exceptions, getting a vacuum seal isn't nearly as important to the sous vide process as just removing most of the air. There are a few things accomplished by sealing the food, as well as by removing the air.

Keeping the Flavors In
You don't want the food directly in the water or the water leaking into the sous vide bag. Sealing the food traps all the juices and flavor in the bags instead of losing it to the water bath.

Preventing Bags From Floating
Bags with air in them float, leaving parts of the food out of the water and potentially at dangerous temperatures.

The more air you pull out, the less chance there is of floating.

Air Transmits Heat Poorly
Air is a really poor transmitter of heat compared to water (you can stick your hand in a 400°F (200°C) oven for a few seconds but sticking it in much cooler boiling water will scald you almost instantly). So removing all the air from the sous vide bag will result in a faster and more evenly cooked food.

Increased Holding Time
The biggest advantage vacuum sealing has over other types of sealing is that you can store the food for a longer time before and after cooking it. This is especially helpful in restaurants but usually doesn't come into play for most home kitchens.

TYPES OF SEALERS

There are many different ways to seal your food for sous vide cooking. I personally use normal Ziploc Freezer bags for 90% of my sous viding, with a smattering of FoodSaver bags for longer cooking times. Here's a look at several of the options, from most expensive to least expensive.

Chambered Vacuum Sealers
Chambered vacuum sealers are the best, and most expensive, method of sealing food for sous vide cooking. They are large devices that can suck out the air even if there are liquids in the bag. They usually have a variable vacuum strength you can

set, which is great for other modernist techniques like compression and infusing. However, they are usually overkill for home cooks.

Chambered vacuum sealers also come with downsides. They tend to run at least $500 and up to more than $1000. They are also big and heavy, most weigh between 50 to 85 pounds (22 to 39kg) which makes them hard to move from the counter top.

The most consistently highly rated chambered vacuum sealers are the VacMaster brand sealers. The two most common models are the VacMaster VP210 and the less powerful VacMaster VP112 but most of their models are highly regarded. The cost of bags is also pretty small for chambered sealers, running about $0.14 per bag.

Edge Sealers

Edge sealers are a good intermediate step if you want the power of a vacuum sealer but don't want the bulk or expense of a chambered vacuum sealer. They are much less expensive, usually around $100 to $200 and are small and portable. They are also great if you often pre-package food at home since they help it last longer in the freezer without getting freezer burn.

The biggest downside to edge sealers is that they can't effectively seal bags with liquids in them. The pump will pull the liquids out with the air, preventing the bag from sealing well and potentially damaging the sucking mechanism. Edge sealers also can't get as great of a vacuum as chambered sealers and are usually not adjustable.

Another negative is that the bags themselves are very expensive, usually about $0.75 per bag, or 5 times what a chambered sealer or Ziploc bag costs. I know several people who use Ziploc bags and set aside the $0.50 difference every time towards saving up for a chambered vacuum sealer.

The most common brand of edge sealer is the FoodSaver brand. Both the FoodSaver V2244 and FoodSaver V3240 models are highly regarded.

Ziploc Bags

Many people are surprised when I tell them that the type of sous vide bag I use most often is a standard Ziploc Freezer Bag, usually in the gallon size. They are inexpensive, easy to find, and very easy to use. They get almost as good of a seal as the edge sealers if you use the Water Displacement Method. They also handle liquids better than edge sealers so you can use sauces and marinades in your sous viding. And of course, the upfront cost of $5 for 20 of them is hard to beat!

Another thing I really like about using Ziploc bags is that they are easy to open and re-seal. Many foods like sirloin, brisket, and pork shoulder have a lot of variety in the toughness of the meat and need different lengths of cooking time, which can be hard to determine before actually cooking them. The same holds true for many vegetables which require different cooking times based on their ripeness and the season they are picked.

With Ziplocs I can open the bag after the minimum amount of cooking time has passed and check the tenderness. If it needs more tenderizing I just re-seal the bag and put it back in the sous vide machine for a few more hours. When it's tender enough, I'll pull it out and it's ready to serve whenever I want. It really helps prevent under- and over-cooking foods.

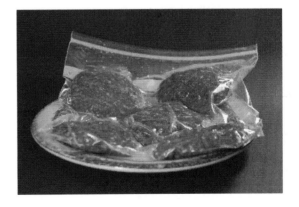

Opening and re-sealing the bags is also helpful if the food has given off some gas and is starting to float. This often happens during longer cooks and it can be a pain to try and weigh down the bags.

With Ziplocs, you can release the gas, re-seal the bag, and the food will easily stay below the water again.

The downside to Ziploc bags is the occasional leakage of water, especially for longer cooks at higher temperatures. If I'm cooking for longer than a day I'll often use my FoodSaver or at least double bag the food.

Water Displacement Method
Getting all the air out of Ziploc bags is critical but easy. Place the food in the bag, including any liquids or marinades, and seal all but one corner of the bag. Place it in the water bath, being sure everything below the zip-line is covered by water. You can see how all the air is forced out of the bag. Then seal the rest of the bag.

I try to seal the food before the water has heated up but if the water is hot you can use a wooden spoon to hold the bag under. I almost always use the gallon size Ziplocs, I find the extra room at the top makes them easier to seal.

Other Containers

Depending on the type of food you are cooking you can also use high-quality food-safe plastic wrap, mason jars, oven bags, and ceramic ramekins. There are also hand pump bags, sous vide-specific "zip-top" bags, and other miscellaneous sealers but I've found that unless you're doing something specific (ramekins work great for custards, saran wrap is wonderful for roulades) either a chambered sealer, edge sealer, or Ziploc bag works best.

PLASTIC SAFETY

Another common concern of sous vide is cooking in plastic and whether or not this is dangerous. Many scientists and chefs believe that cooking in food grade plastic at these low temperatures does not pose any risk, the temperature is about equivalent to leaving a bottle of water in your car, or in a semi during transport, in summer.

However, I find it hard to believe that we know everything about how plastic reacts to heat, water, our bodies, and the environment. As such, I encourage you to read up on the safety of plastic in sous vide and plastic in general then come to your own conclusions about the safety of using these techniques or consuming products packaged or shipped in plastic.

GENERAL SEALING TIPS

Don't Stuff the Bags

In order to ensure proper cooking it's important to make sure the thickness of the food in your sous vide bags is relatively even. Don't force in extra food or layer the food in the bags. It's better to use multiple bags with a single layer of food than one large bag. Most recipes assume a single layer of food when determining the cooking time.

Freeze the Liquids

If you need to seal liquids using your edge vacuum sealer one easy method is to freeze the liquids first. Then you can add them to the sous vide bag and seal it. Once the food is in the water bath the liquid will unfreeze and work its magic. Two things to remember: 1) alcohol won't freeze and 2) if there is a large amount of liquid the seal on the bag won't be very tight because liquids are denser than ice.

Need Liquids? Use the Override

Many edge vacuum sealers have an override switch to seal the bag at its current vacuum state. If you need to seal liquids in the sous vide bag and you are using a high-temperature dish or you don't want to use Ziplocs then you can use this to remove a lot of air from the sous vide bag.

Fill the sous vide bag with the food and liquid. Place it in your vacuum sealer and then hang it off of a counter, so the liquid is as far away from the sealer as possible. Be sure to support the bottom of the bag so you don't have a mess on your hands. Then begin the vacuuming process, watching the level of the liquid. As soon as the liquid nears the top of the sous vide bag hit the "Seal" button, which should seal the bag without pulling the liquid all the way out.

SOUS VIDE TEMPERATURE CONTROL

The technology behind sous vide machines is always changing and updating. You can find up to date reviews on the latest machines at MCMeasy.com/SVMachines

Controlling the temperature of the water bath is the most important part of sous vide cooking. There are many different ways to accomplish this but they all have one purpose: to keep the cooking temperature consistent. They do this in different ways and each way has pluses and minuses.

What to Look For

When choosing a sous vide machine there are a few things to look for. People will weigh each factor differently but each one comes into play when deciding on which sous vide machine to purchase.

Versatility and Ease of Use

Because of the differences in how the sous vide machines work, there are distinct trade-offs for each type. The ability to use the machine in different containers, easily control and change the temperature, and thoroughly clean and put it away are all big factors when choosing a sous vide machine.

What Does it Cost

While it doesn't affect the cooking itself, the price of the machine is important to most people. You don't want to spend $1,500 if a $200 machine will get the job done for you just as well.

Stability of Temperature

Temperature stability is the most important factor as far as the cooking process itself goes. Techniques range from a variation of several degrees to as small

as 0.1°C. Another factor here is how quickly a machine can initially bring the water up to temperature as well as when cold food is added.

What I Recommend

I personally use an inexpensive circulator to do the majority of my cooking. I have had good experience with both the PolyScience and Anova and highly recommend them. They can now be had for $150 to $300.

If you are just trying out sous vide, there is nothing wrong with saving your money and trying a few recipes using beer cooler sous vide, explored later in this chapter, until you decide you want to step up your equipment.

Here's a detailed look at the various methods and machines you can use to control your sous vide temperature.

Circulators

Immersion circulators consist of a heating element and a water pump. These combine to heat and circulate the water, keeping it a very consistent temperature. Circulators are the most reliable way to maintain your water temperature.

Immersion circulators can be used with almost any container of water, from stock pots to plastic tubs up to 5 gallons or more. This versatility often comes in handy, letting you cook a small amount of food in a small pot and only needing the larger sizes when cooking for a lot of people. This helps save energy costs and speeds up the heating process.

Immersion circulators also have the best temperature stability of all the sous vide machines. Most machines keep it to within 1°C and many are even more stable than that. The circulator pump also helps ensure the water is evenly heated, eliminating hot and cold spots. The majority of immersion circulators heat the water very quickly as well.

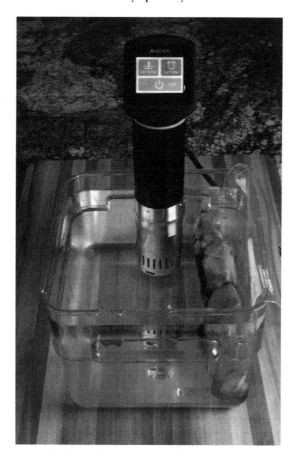

Immersion circulators used to be very expensive but lately the prices have been dropping as new machines enter the market, pushing the prices from over $1,000 down to as low as $150. Because of this, I highly recommend getting an immersion circulator if you are getting serious about sous vide cooking.

The top of the line circulator is probably the PolyScience Professional Chef Series which is used in many of the top restaurants in the world and costs around $800.

Even though the PolyScience is a great machine, many of the inexpensive immersion circulators are more than adequate for home use. I recommend the Anova or Sansaire circulators, though many people also like the Nomiku. For an in depth look at the different circulators you can see our very detailed guide to inexpensive immersion circulators at: MCMEasy.com/Circs.

Circulator Containers
When using an immersion circulator you need something to hold the water while it is heating. The most common containers are polycarbonate containers, large stock pots, and plastic coolers. As more containers come out I will continue to update the article I have at MCMEasy.com/Containers

Polycarbonate Containers
Polycarbonate containers are my favorite containers and what I almost always use

at home. They come in a wide variety of sizes, allowing me to have one bath for normal nights and a larger bath for parties or large gatherings. They retain heat well and most have lids that help prevent evaporation, though you will have to cut a hole for your circulator.

The containers are transparent, which makes it easy to see at a glance if the food is starting to float. The food also fits in the containers due to their square shape.

My main container is a 12 quart, 11" x 11" x 9" container (10 liter, 28cm x 28cm x 23cm) that works great for most foods. I also have a larger, "party container" that is 4.75 gallon, 12" x 18" x 9" (18 liter, 30cm x 46cm x 23cm). It will hold enough steak or chicken for about 20 people or several racks of ribs.

All of my containers are Cambro Camwear brand but Rubbermaid Commercial also makes some good containers.

Stock Pots

The biggest advantage to using stock pots for sous vide is that almost everyone already has one. You can also use the containers for other things, compared to the single-purpose polycarbonate containers.

Stock pots don't hold the heat in as well, and sometimes the food has trouble fitting due to the round shape. That said, many people use them and they work just fine.

Coolers

Coolers are a container many people already have on hand. They hold the heat very well and come in a variety of sizes. You can also create a hole in the lid for the circulator if it is a dedicated sous vide cooler. Food also fits in them nicely due to the square shape.

Coolers are more bulky than the other containers so they will take up more counter space. Depending on your circulator it also might have trouble attaching to the thicker walls of the cooler. Long term heating of the cooler walls can sometimes be problematic because they are designed for cold, not heat.

WATER BATHS

Sous vide water baths are basically a self-contained temperature controller and heater with a set water bath. They used to be more popular when laboratory-grade equipment was commonly used for sous vide cooking. Now the most common water bath is made by Sous Vide Supreme, which runs $300 to $450.

In general, water baths are bulkier than immersion circulators and they are more expensive than the new line of inexpensive circulators. Due to the built-in bath size you also have limited options for the size of container you will be using. Because there is no circulation mechanism in the water baths they tend to be less precise than immersion circulators but they still are good enough for most sous vide cooking. On the plus side, because they are self contained, they are very easy to use.

TEMPERATURE CONTROLLERS

Sous vide temperature controllers use a crock pot or rice cooker to heat the water while a device regulates the temperature. Basically, a temperature controller works by turning the crock pot on and off to keep the water temperature stable.

Sous vide temperature controllers are pretty easy to use, especially if you already have a good crock pot or rice cooker. They used to be the best low-cost method of trying out sous vide but the advent of less expensive immersion circulations has pushed them into the background.

Most sous vide temperature controllers are $100 to $200. I recommend either the Dorkfood or SousVideMagic temperature controllers. They both are highly thought of and have been used by many people.

BEER COOLER SOUS VIDE

If you are looking to try out sous vide at home, the easiest way is to use either beer cooler sous vide or sous vide on the stove. They both use things you have on hand so there's no cost involved in trying them out.

Beer cooler sous vide uses the insulating properties of a beer cooler to hold the water temperature stable, or at least stable-enough. It works well for short-time cooks, such as steak, fish, and chicken breasts.

Coolers are good at retaining their temperature but they still lose heat over time. For cooks longer than a few hours you'll have to periodically add more hot water to it. You can measure the temperature of the water with a meat thermometer.

Beer Cooler Sous Vide Process
Heat enough water to fill the cooler, this can usually be done on the stove using a thermometer. Make sure the water is a few degrees hotter than you want to cook at because when you add the food it will drop in temperature. Fill the cooler with the heated water, place your sealed food into it, put the lid on, and wait. That's all there is to it.

SOUS VIDE ON THE STOVE

Sous vide on the stove is similar to the beer cooler sous vide method except after you heat the water on the stove, you place the sealed food into the pot. The temperature is maintained using the stove or cold water to raise or lower the temperature as needed. It's more hands-on than beer cooler sous vide but it is ok for shorter term cooks and is a good introduction to the sous vide process.

Determining Time and Temperatures

You can also get this time and temperature information on your mobile phone if you have an iPhone, iPad or an Android.

Just search for "Sous Vide" and look for the guide by "Primolicious".

The two most important variables in sous vide cooking are time and temperature. Each one affects the end quality, texture, and taste of sous vide dishes both individually and in tandem. Learning to understand how they affect the food is one of the most important things as you begin sous vide cooking.

Sous Vide Time

There are three main goals when determining how long to cook food, whether through sous vide or by traditional means. They are to heat the food, make the food safe to eat, and tenderize the food. You will determine how long to cook your food using one or more of those criteria.

Heat the Food

The timing of fully heating the food is pretty easy with sous vide because the water bath is at a set temperature. It takes about an hour for a 1" (25mm) thick piece of meat and 3 hours for a 2" (50mm) thick piece to heat through. Unlike traditional cooking methods, with sous vide the outside layers will not be overcooked during this process. Also, except for the most tender of foods, going over the time by an hour or two will not make much of a difference. You can see a more detailed breakdown of heating times in the appendix "Sous Vide Thickness Times".

Make the Food Safe to Eat

The other big issue with food safety is pasteurizing the food, otherwise known as "killing all the icky stuff in it". This is the issue addressed with the government recommendations about internal food temperatures, such as "always cook chicken to 160°F" and "don't eat pork that is below 150°F".

The first thing to remember about these guidelines is that they are designed to ensure that if 300 million people cook 3 meals a day then none of them will ever get sick. In other words, they're pretty much overkill. There's not a single upscale restaurant that follows these guidelines, they are going to cook a good quality piece of pork to 140°F to 145°F (60°C to 63°C) and take the one-in-a-million chance someone will get an upset stomach.

That aside, the biggest problem with the guidelines, or at least as how they are reported, is that they don't take time into account. For instance, the next time you're baking and forget to stand back when you open the door you'll get hit in the face with 400°F+ (204°C+) air. However, it probably won't hurt, much less kill you. But if the outside temperature got up to even 150°F (66°C) for an entire day, there would be a tragic amount of deaths.

The guidelines are made to ensure that if your food hits the temperature for even a tenth of a second, it will be fully pasteurized. So chicken "has" to be cooked to 160ºF (71ºC) to kill everything. However, according to the same guidelines chicken will be equally pasteurized if it's cooked at 136ºF (57.7ºC), you just have to keep it there for 63.3 minutes, which is easy with sous vide.

For many foods pasteurization isn't important. Solid cuts of beef don't need to be pasteurized as long as the outside is seared. High-quality fish are also fine.

For specific times needed to pasteurize at a specific temperature please see the appendix "Sous Vide Thickness Times".

Tenderize the Food

There are many tender foods such as chicken breasts, fish, and several tender steaks like filet that only need to be heated through, but there are also many types of meat that require tenderization. While you could cook a chuck steak in an hour using sous vide, the result would be a chewy, fatty mess, even though it would be "fully cooked".

Like braising or roasting, the longer you cook food with sous vide the more tender it becomes. The main difference is that adding time to sous vide cooking doesn't overcook the outside layers of the food. Also, because the sous vide temperatures are so low, the tenderization happens much more slowly, resulting in much longer cooking times. To really enjoy that

medium-rare chuck steak, you'll want to cook it for about two days.

The time needed for cooking increases as the food gets tougher and the temperature you are cooking it at gets lower. Here are some general guidelines which will vary a little by the specific cut.

Tender Beef: 1 to 4 hours
Tough Beef: 10 to 48 hours
Tender Pork: 2 to 8 hours
Tough Pork: 12 to 48 hours
White Chicken: 2 to 4 hours
Dark Chicken: 4 to 8 hours

I have more recommended times for specific cuts in the appendix "Sous Vide Time and Temperature".

All Meat is Different
More and more people are purchasing meat from places other than the supermarket for a variety of reasons from better flavor and texture to healthier meat and more humane treatment. I'll save any lectures for another time but one thing is apparent, meat raised in different ways behaves differently when cooked. We've found that some grass-fed beef roasts only need to be cooked for about one half the time of a comparable supermarket roast before they become tender. So be aware that meat from different places cooks differently because there's nothing worse than turning an expensive cut of meat to mush.

SOUS VIDE TEMPERATURE

All sous vide cooking is done at temperatures below the boiling point of water, and normally not above 185ºF (85ºC). The food is typically cooked at the temperature it will be served at, so most settings are between 120ºF (48.9ºC) and 185ºF (85ºC), depending on the food being prepared.

As food increases in temperature, the proteins, collagen, and other components are changed. The higher the temperature used, the faster the food is tenderized, and the faster the proteins in the meat are changed during the cooking process. These changes determine the final texture of the food.

As the proteins are heated they begin to squeeze out moisture from the meat, which is why overcooked steaks are so dry. As the collagen is heated, it breaks down, tenderizing the meat, which is why pot roasts are fall-apart tender. Choosing the right heat for what you are trying to accomplish is critical to your success.

The power of sous vide cooking comes from precisely controlling both temperature and time. This is important because of the way meat reacts to different temperatures.

At 120ºF (48.9ºC) meat slowly begins to tenderize as the protein myosin begins to coagulate and the connective tissue in the meat begins to break down. As the

temperature increases so does the speed of tenderization.

However, meat also begins to lose its moisture above 140ºF (60ºC) as the heat causes the protein in the cells to shrink and wring out the moisture. This happens very quickly over 150ºF (65.6ºC) and meat becomes completely dried out above 160ºF (71.1ºC).

Many tough cuts of meat are braised or roasted for a long period of time so the meat can fully tenderize, but because of the high temperatures they can easily become dried out. Using sous vide allows you to hold the meat below the 140ºF (60ºC) barrier long enough for the slower tenderization process to be effective. This results in very tender meat that is still moist and not overcooked.

Determining Temperatures

The temperature food is sous vided at determines the end result more than any other factor.

Sous vide gives you pin-point control over the exact temperature you will cook your food. However, when getting started this is pretty much overkill. I've found it best to think in terms of ranges of temperature, as each range tends to result in pretty similar food.

For example, compare a grilled medium-rare steak to a braised pot roast. The steak is red, moist, and probably still a little chewy. The pot roast is brown, dry (except for the wonderful juices in the braise) and is pull-apart tender.

We've all had steaks with different doneness, even ones that are all "medium-rare", but they are still basically the same type of dish, especially when compared to the pot roast.

The medium-rare range goes from around 130°F to 139°F (54.4°C to 59.4°C) for beef. As long as you set your sous vide machine in that range, you'll get a great medium-rare steak. Once you've tried it a few times you can decide if you prefer 131°F or 132°F, but that's not critical to get started successfully.

Here are some of the more common ranges.

Medium-rare beef: 130°F-139°F (54.4°C-59.4°C)
Medium beef: 140°F-145°F (60°C-62.8°C)
Traditional "slow cooked" beef: 156°F-175°F (68.8°C-79.4°C)
Extra-juicy tender pork: 135°F-145°F (57.2°C-62.8°C)
Traditional tender pork: 145°F-155°F (62.8°C-68.3°C)
Traditional "slow cooked" pork: 156°F-175°F (68.8°C-79.4°C)
Extra-rare chicken breast: 136°F-139°F (57.7°C-59.4°C)
Traditional chicken breast: 140°F-150°F (60°C-65.6°C)
Mi-cuit fish: 104°F (40°C)
Traditional fish: 122°F-132°F (50°C-55.5°C)

So picking a temperature is as easy as figuring out what kind of meat you want and selecting any number in that range. I have more recommended temperatures for specific cuts in the appendix "Sous Vide Time and Temperature" as well as the "Sous Vide Recipes" section.

Danger Zone Concerns
The first thing to remember about sous vide, or any cooking, is that you can only have the food between 40°F (4°C) and 130°F (54.5°C) for a few hours before bad stuff starts to happen. That range is called the "danger zone" (cue Top Gun music) and you always want to limit the amount of time the temperature of the food is within that range.

We all know this in general, it's why we don't buy chicken at the grocery store and leave it in the hot car for the afternoon while we go to the mall. However, with sous vide you can specifically set the temperature, and many foods are good when cooked in the danger zone for short amounts of time.

For instance, many fish benefit from temperatures in the danger zone and "rare" steak is cooked in it as well. This is all fine, and most experts agree you can have food in the danger zone for up to 4 hours before it becomes unsafe. However, if you are used to eating rare steak and you decide to do a tougher cut of meat, you can't just extend the cooking time to 10 hours to tenderize it or you'll be in the danger zone for WAY too long. So you'll have to increase the temperature to at least 130°F (54.5°C) for extended cooks.

CHECKING CORE TEMPERATURE

For some more advanced applications, especially in professional kitchens, it can be helpful to monitor the core temperature of an item. I don't use this in the recipes in this book but it can be a helpful method of determining doneness for certain things.

If you are using Ziploc bags you can simply open them, take the temperature with an instant read thermometer, then reseal the bag. You can also use an oven probe thermometer, insert it into the food before sealing it, then make sure that the top of the Ziploc stays above the water line during the cooking time.

For vacuum sealed foods weather stripping tape can be placed on the outside of the bag through which the probe can be inserted. This will keep the water out but still let you view the temperature of the food.

SOUS VIDE FINISHING

Once you are done cooking the food sous vide, you have one final chance to add flavor to it. This is most often done through searing the food, though there are many ways to flavor it

SEARING

One of the areas sous vide falls short is creating that nice flavorful, brown crust on foods. Luckily there are several ways to finish foods after they have been sous vided to create the crust without further cooking the food.

The main goal of post sous vide browning is to create the crust while heating the interior of the food as little as possible. The keys to accomplishing this are dry food, high temperature, and short times.

Prepping Sous Vide Food For Searing

Moisture that is on the surface of the food will prevent it from browning, increasing the cooking time needed, and potentially heating the food further. Properly drying the food after sous viding is critical but easy.

After you take the food out of the bag pat it dry, either with paper towels or clean kitchen towels. I have a certain set of smaller kitchen towels that I only use to dry off food after sous vide, but paper towels will work as well. I tend to dry it off at least 5 to 10 minutes before I will sear it, allowing the remaining moisture

to evaporate and the meat to cool slightly.

If you want to ensure you get a deep crust without overcooking the inside of the food you can also cool the food down more before searing it. This gives you more of a leeway in your browning time before the temperature of the inside of the food is raised too much.

It is almost always a good idea to salt the food before searing it. Don't be afraid to taste your dishes as they come together to make sure they are properly seasoned. Since the food is already cooked after the sous vide process you can cut off a small piece before searing it to test for seasonings. You can also add other spice rubs at this point, or use a glaze to add additional flavor.

Ways of Searing Your Food

Maintaining a high temperature for your searing is critical to keeping the times short and preventing overcooking. There are many effective methods you can use for a post-sous vide sear.

Pan Sear or Cast Iron
Pan searing your sous vided food is the easiest method for most people. It's also especially effective if you have a heavy cast iron pan.

The process of searing it in a pan is simple. First make sure your sous vide food is completely dry. Then heat a thin film of oil in the pan over medium-high to high heat until it just starts to smoke. Add the meat to the pan, being careful of splattering, and cook for 45 to 90 seconds per side, just until the food browns.

Oven or Broiler

The oven is pretty effective for certain types of browning. The broiler can be used for steaks or thinner cuts and the oven itself can be turned up high to brown roasts.

One of my favorite meals is sous vided prime rib roasts. After the sous vide process I'll coat them with a garlic-herb mixture and put it in the oven set to 500ºF (260ºC) and let the crust brown slightly before serving it.

Grilling

If you have a high quality grill it can be used effectively for sous vide browning. For gas grills, make sure it is turned all the way up, close the lid and let the bars fully heat. Brush some oil on the meat and place on the grill, leaving the lid open. Cook for 45 to 90 seconds per side, just until it browns and grill marks form.

For charcoal grills you want the coals as hot as possible. Some people even cook directly on top of their chimney-style starter to maximize the heat. Just brush the meat with some oil and place on the grill, leaving the lid open. Cook each side for 45 to 90 seconds until grill marks form.

Torch

A favorite method of finishing sous vide is using a torch. The torch quickly browns the outside of the foods and gives you better control than searing in a pan. It is especially good for uneven foods and it gets really, really hot, sometimes exceeding 3,500ºF (1,927ºC).

There are many different torches but the most recommended are typically the Bernzomatic TS8000BT and the Iwatani Torch, both of which connect directly to propane or MAP-Pro containers. The smaller pastry-style torches usually aren't powerful enough for proper browning. For a more in-depth look at the torches available you can check out our detailed guide to sous vide torches at MCMEasy.com/Torches.

The type of gas used is not nearly as important as the technique used to perform the sear. The most important thing is to be sure that the flame produced by the torch is a fully oxidizing flame. In this type of flame the gas is being completely combusted and can be identified by the dark blue, relatively short, flame that hisses and roars.

If the flame is large, with a yellow tip, it is referred to as a reducing flame. In this type of flame there are unburned hydrocarbons from the fuel that will end up in the food giving it an unpleasant flavor.

So for optimal searing results be sure to not have the torch pointed at the food until it has been lit and adjusted to achieve the short, hissing, blue flame. Then aim the torch at the food keeping it moving so that the food sears evenly but does not burn.

Torch Taste
The phenomenon of "torch taste" will invariably be brought up whenever the torch method of sous vide finishing is discussed. Torch taste is the unpleasant "gaseous" or "fuel" flavor that is often associated with dishes that have been finished with a torch. Initially the presence of torch taste was attributed to the chemicals contained in the fuel itself. There was often discussion as to which of the more popular fuels: propane, butane, or MAPP caused the greatest amount of torch taste when used.

Recently, however, some tests run at UC Davis indicated that the primary cause of torch taste was the creation of new, unpleasant, chemical compounds on the food when the heat is too high. These results would indicate that controlling the temperature at which the sear is performed is the most important factor in reducing the presence of torch taste. Using the method I outline previously helps eliminate any torch taste.

Searzall
The Searzall is a effective addition to torches. Made by Dave Arnold from the French Culinary Institute, it's an add-on for the Bernzomatic TS8000 torch that helps to diffuse the flame, making it better for cooking with. As the Searzall site says, it works by "forcing the torch's flame through two layers of fine, heatproof alloy mesh converting the majority of the flame to infra-red, radiant heat - a cook's best friend".

Deep Frying
One method of browning that people often don't think of is deep frying the food. The whole concept behind deep frying is to quickly brown the outside of foods while keeping the inside tender...and that's exactly what we're looking for in a sous vide finishing technique.

To deep fry your food, heat a pot of oil to around 375°F to 400°F (191°C to 204°C), making sure the pot is less than half way full or it can bubble out. Make sure your food is completely dried off then place into the oil. It should take 30 to 90 seconds to fully brown the food. Remove it from the oil and you're all set.

SMOKING

Many foods benefit from the addition of a smoke flavor. For a strong smoke flavor it's usually best to smoke the food before cooking it but you can take advantage of more aromatic smoking post sous vide for a more nuanced flavor.

Using a traditional smoker to add some smoke works well, just be careful not to raise the temperature of the food above the sous vide cooking temperature or you can negate many of the benefits. Using a device like a PolyScience Smoking Gun can also add some good aromatic smoke flavor to the food.

BREADING AND FRYING

There are many foods that have coatings applied to them and it's usually a struggle ensuring the coating is cooked at the same time the food is. Sous vide solves this problem by cooking the food ahead of time.

Once the food is cooked just apply the batter or breading. Then finish it as you normally would, usually in a hot oven or by deep frying it.

This method can also help when pan frying meat as well. A light dusting of flour or corn meal will help create a crust faster and add some deeper flavors. Heavier coatings are also good for specific foods like breaded or fried chicken, beef Wellington, or herb crusted steaks.

COOK, CHILL, AND HOLD

While not technically a finishing method, cook, chill, and hold is a widely used concept in the restaurant industry and it's very easy to apply the same concepts at home. First cook the food sous vide then chill the bag in a bowl filled with ½ ice and ½ water until it is completely cold, usually an hour or so. At that point you can put it in the refrigerator for several days or freeze it for several months.

When you are ready to eat, place the bag in a water bath set anywhere at or below the original cooking temperature. It will usually be brought up to temperature in 30 to 60 minutes.

This is a great method for people who work regular jobs or who have trouble finding 2 to 5 hours of cooking time before dinner. Several days before you want to eat you cook the food sous vide, chill it, and then refrigerate it until the night you want to eat. You can also freeze it for several months with just a minor decrease in quality.

USING SOUS VIDE JUICES

Even though sous vide meat retains more of its juices than traditionally cooked meat it still releases a lot of them. Luckily all the juices are caught in the sous vide bag and they can be put to use. The juices are full of flavor and make a great sauce, dip, or glaze. However, they can be hard to work with unless you know a few tricks.

The juices can be used straight from the bag but they will be runny and will usually curdle when heated. For quick weekday meals I'll often use them as is but for anything more elegant they need to be handled properly.

Making the juices ready to use isn't very hard. Pour the juices from the bag into a pot and bring to a simmer. This will cause the proteins to coagulate. Then skim the juices or strain them through a chinois or cheesecloth. They are now ready to use like a typical beef broth.

I will often deglaze the pan I used to sear the beef in with some of the juices to make a simple pan sauce. The juices can also be reduced to a more concentrated state, though this can take 15 to 45 minutes, depending on the amount of juices and the reduction desired. A flour-based slurry can also be used to thicken the juices to make gravy.

GENERAL FINISHING TIPS

Don't Forget the Spice Rubs

Just because your food was already cooked with sous vide doesn't mean you have to omit spice rubs. Once the food is out of the sous vide bath and dried off you can add any of your favorite spice rubs to it. Once you add the spice rub

just finish the food like normal and you should be all set.

The only caveat is if you are torching the food you should be careful about using seasonings that can be easily burned. You don't want to leave a blackened taste on the meat, unless your are cooking in that style.

Paint on the Glaze

Another great way to add flavor is to apply a glaze to the food when you put it on the grill or under the broiler. Just add it to the food before you apply the heat and make sure to flip it once or twice so the glaze can take.

Throw Out Your Mops

When you finish sous vide meals you can apply spice rubs or glazes before you finish them on the grill. However, mop sauces and basting sauces don't work well since they prevent the meat from browning and will lead to overcooked meat.

To use your favorite sauces I suggest putting a small amount of them into the sous vide bag with the food before you sous vide it. This is a great way to get the flavor to permeate throughout the meat.

One caveat though, be careful with alcohol or vinegar based mops because no evaporation will occur in the bag. Feel free to experiment with different types and quantities to see what works best for you.

SECTION TWO

SOUS VIDE RECIPES

A WORD ABOUT THE RECIPES

I'm always adding more recipes to my website so for more inspiration you can check out the latest dishes:

MCMEasy.com/Recipes

This chapter contains all the information you need to successfully follow the recipes in this book and to maximize their flavor and presentation. It also gives you some hints for what to cook first, explains the time range in the recipes and discusses how to adapt your favorite recipes to sous vide.

WHAT SHOULD I SOUS VIDE FIRST?

I get asked a variation of this question all the time, even experienced sous vide cooks are wondering if they're missing out on a food they should be trying.

There are so many different things you can do with a sous vide machine that it can be hard to figure out what you want to try first. I think there's two categories of sous vide foods, things you can use sous vide to cook better, and things you can only do with sous vide. Here's some of my favorite things to do sous vide, all of which are covered by recipes in this book.

Things Sous Vide Does Better
Corned Beef
Corned beef can often turn out too dry for my liking but with sous vide you can really control the temperature and tweak the tenderness and dryness to your liking.

Pork Ribs
Not much can beat a slow smoked rack of ribs but when you don't have time to mind the smoker you can reach for your

sous vide machine. With several options for times and temperatures you can tweak the ribs to be exactly how you like them.

Chicken Breasts

One of the things that sous vide excels at is cooking chicken breasts. Chicken becomes tough and overcooked so easily and it's so hard to do properly with traditional methods. Using sous vide makes cooking chicken breasts so easy and they turn out moist and tender every time.

Pork Chops and Loin

Pork has a reputation as being bland and dry. But with sous vide you can make awesome pork and it's one of my favorite things to cook. I especially love pork chops, loin roasts, or tenderloin. I cook them at 140°F (60°C) which leaves a little pink in the middle, though my parents prefer it with no red at around 141°F (60.6°C). The pork turns out incredibly tender and moist even without brining them first.

Pork Sausages

Another food that's easy to overcook is sausage. The timing to ensure a well-cooked sausage with a nicely browned outside is very hard to hit exactly. Using sous vide takes the difficulty away and leaves you perfectly cooked sausages every time.

Chuck Roast

Another cut of meat that benefits from the long cooking times is chuck roast. You can do an awesome traditional "braised" chuck roast by cooking it at 160°F (71°C) for 24 hours.

Things Only Sous Vide Can Do

Cheap Sous Vide Steak

My favorite steak is rib eye but I can't afford to eat them all the time because they are so expensive. With sous vide you can buy a chuck roast or beef brisket for about a quarter of the cost, cook it for 2 days and you now have something that tastes very similar to rib eye for a fraction of the cost. I usually do my steaks at 131°F (55°C).

Burgers

I love a good medium-rare burger but you have to be careful where you order them from for safety reasons. With sous vide you can cook it long enough to pasteurize the meat so it's completely safe to eat. I like to do 2 to 3 hours at 131°F (55°C) then quickly sear them. They turn out a perfect medium rare all the way through and are incredibly juicy.

Salmon

Salmon is my favorite fish and I really enjoy trying it in lots of different preparations. Cooking salmon sous vide has opened up several new ways to try it. It's fun to try out the different temperatures and see what you like best.

French Style Scrambled Eggs

French style scrambled eggs are a creamy, almost custard like style of scrambled egg, a lot different than the sometimes rubbery American style ones. With sous vide they are easy to make and consistently come out super creamy.

Short Ribs

Sous vide short ribs are one of the dishes every one says you have to try when you get your machine. They turn out really tender but still not overcooked. They're really a staple of sous vide cooking.

MODERNIST NOTES

For many of the recipes I give Modernist Notes that you can follow to take the dish to another level. These notes take advantage of modernist ingredients or equipment and are a way you can slowly learn more about modernist cooking and how it is used in everyday cooking. The Modernist Notes are always optional so feel free to skip them if you are not interested.

The notes usually lay out a process to follow, plus the ingredients you will need. Just weigh the ingredients and add them as recommended. For more information on specific ingredients and techniques you can see my website or modernist books at MCMEasy.com/Easy.

WHY THE RANGE

One of the most common questions I get asked about my sous vide recipes is some variation of "the recipe says to cook it for 3 to 6 hours, but when is it actually done?"

The short answer is that anytime within the given range the food is "done". As long as the food has been in the water bath for more than the minimum time and less than the maximum time, then it is done. There isn't a specific magical moment of true doneness that can be generalized.

For those that want more information, here's the explanation why.

The How and Why

To have this conversation we first need to determine what "done" actually means. For sous vide there are two main "doneness" concerns when cooking your food. The first is to ensure that the food actually comes up to the temperature you are cooking it at (or becomes pasteurized at for some food). The second concern is making sure the food is tender enough to eat without being "over tender", mushy, or dry.

Once the food you are cooking is completely up to temperature and it is tenderized enough to eat (and not over tenderized), it is now "done". For some already tender cuts of meat like filets, loins, and chicken breasts you don't have to worry about tenderness since they start out that way. That means that these cuts are "done" once they get up to temperature.

However, despite them being "done" at the minimum time shown, they stay "done" for several hours past that time, depending on the starting tenderness of the meat. This is why I give a range. You can eat a 1" (25mm) cut of filet mignon after 50 minutes but you can also eat the filet up to 3 hours after it has gone into the bath without any loss in quality, tenderness, or flavor.

This is how my ranges are determined. They specify that for an average cut of the given meat, they will become "great to eat" tender at the minimum time given. They will continue to get more tender the longer they are in the bath but will remain "great to eat" tender until the final time given, at which point they may begin to get mushy and overcooked. In essence, they will be "done", and very tasty, for that entire span between the minimum and maximum times.

Another Way to Look at It

Another way to think about how this works is to use the following analogy. Pretend you were helping a new cook grill a steak. If they told you they wanted to cook it medium rare and asked you to tell them how to tell when it was "done", what would you say?

Most people would reply with, "when the temperature is between 131ºF to 139ºF" (55ºC to 59.4ºC).

If the friend isn't a cook they would ask "Yeah, but when is it actually done?"

The answer at this point really comes down to personal preference since to some people medium rare is perfect at 131ºF (55ºC) and others prefer a little more well done 135ºF (57.2ºC), but a medium rare steak is "done" anywhere in that range.

Other Critical Variables

One other complicating factor is that there are many variables that go into determining how fast a piece of meat tenderizes and/or becomes tender.

The most obvious variable is that some cuts of meat are tougher than others. For example, a top round roast needs to be tenderized a lot longer than a ribeye. Most people realize this and that's why almost all sous vide charts break the food down by "cut".

Another less obvious, but almost as important, factor is where the meat came from. How the cow was raised greatly impacts how fast the meat tenderizes. I've found that grass-fed meat from my local farmer needs just half the time to become tender compared to supermarket meat (this is also true when roasting or braising them). I've also talked to a reader in Mexico who eats local grass-fed beef that needs slightly longer times than normal because the cows work more.

There are then the variables in the actual cow itself. Whether the meat is a prime, choice, or other grade makes a difference in tenderizing time. As does the marbling, how old the meat is, and several other factors.

So taking all of this together it can be hard to accurately determine a range of "doneness" that will work for all cuts of meat all the time. But I have done my best to come up with a detailed range of times that the "average" piece of meat will be done in. The only way to really learn is to experiment with the types of meat in your area and see how they react. And luckily for us, sous vide allows us to have

a wide range that food is done in, helping to prevent overcooking.

In Conclusion
So while there might be one magical moment in the cooking process where a certain piece of meat is the most ideal tenderness, in practice there is a wide time range in the cooking process where the meat will be "done". As long as you take it out sometime in that range it should turn out great.

As you get more experience with your local meats, and determine your personal preferences, you can start to tweak your cook times to suit them more exactly. But as you are learning just remember that the food will be "done" anywhere in that range, and don't sweat the details!

RECIPE CONSIDERATIONS

Read the Recipe FIRST
This might sound like a no-brainer but with sous vide and cook times that can stretch into multiple days it is very important to read the whole recipe before starting. Many recipes also require marinades or other initial steps and often times you need to start working on the finishing portion of the recipe while the meat is still cooking. Just read through the recipe first, make sure you understand it, and then you won't run into any surprises down the road.

Searing Isn't Specific

In almost every recipe I have a step that recommends "quickly sear it until the meat is just browned". Any searing method you prefer will work fine unless otherwise specified. So use whatever method you find to work best and is easiest for you.

Handling Food After Cooking

Most of the recipes begin with a pre-sous vide and a sous vide cooking phase for the meat. The finishing phase is almost always later in the recipe under "To Assemble" and should be done right before serving. You can go directly from the cooking to the finishing, assuming the other components are done, or you can chill the sous vided food and refrigerate it until later, at which point you will briefly reheat it in a water bath set at or below the original temperature, before searing or finishing it.

Choose Your Own Time and Temperature

For each recipe I've tried to provide a detailed description of why I choose the time and temperature used, as well as other recommendations for that specific cut. This should allow you to better understand the difference between the various time and temperature combinations and use the one that will best meet your needs.

Sous Vide Bags

In the recipes I just say "Add the food to the sous vide bag". This can be any type of sous vide bag you feel comfortable using, from plastic wrap or Ziplocs up to industrial food bags.

It also assumes that you are using as many sous vide bags as you need for the food to lay in one even layer, usually less than 2" (50mm) thick. If spices or liquids are added to the bags then just split them evenly between all the bags.

Pre-Salting

Most of the recipes call for you to "lightly salt and pepper" the meat. As discussed in the "Pre-Sous Vide Preparation" chapter, people are divided on whether they prefer a pre-salt. If you do not want to pre-salt, then just skip this step.

Warm Your Plates

Food cooked sous vide can often seem cooler than traditionally cooked food because of the low temperatures used. One way to combat this is to warm your plates in an oven set on low before plating the food. It only takes a few minutes but it will help the food keep its temperature longer.

Mix and Match Recipes

Many of the sides, spices, and salsas can go with a variety of meats. If a dish sounds good but you have flank steak on hand instead of sirloin steak go ahead and switch them.

You can also apply recipes to other cuts of meat in the same way, like taking a steak recipe and using it for chicken. Just find the cut of meat you'd like to use in the Time and Temperature Charts and use the values given there instead of the ones in the recipe. Feel free to experiment with the meats to see what combinations you prefer.

Fresh is Better

Another way to improve your dishes is to be sure to use fresh ingredients. If a recipe calls for lime juice or orange juice, instead of using bottled juice just grab a lime and juice it for the recipe, you'll be able to taste the difference.

Substitutions Are Great

Just because a recipe calls for an ingredient doesn't mean you have to use it. Feel free to leave out spices you don't like (or use less of them), add in your favorite vegetables, use a different sauce, or just use the recipe as a general guideline and create your own dish. Cooking should be fun and experimenting with the ingredients is part of the joy.

Working Times Are Relative

To help with the planning of meals I have given time estimates for each component in the recipe. These estimates are just a guideline and also assume all the ingredients for that component are prepped before starting.

Times are hard to come up with because a professional chef can prepare food much faster than my Grandma. In general I tried to use times for a "normal"

home cook. I also did my best to be consistent across recipes. So while it might take you longer or shorter than the times say, it should be that way for all recipes and you can still use them as a general guideline.

Salt and Pepper

Most of the recipes call for "Salt and pepper" as an ingredient. Proper seasoning is critical to good cooking and you should salt and pepper your ingredients after they come out of the bag as you are searing them and making any finishing steps.

While I'd like to give you specific measurements, how much you use is in large part a matter of taste. And since studies show this likely differs across people through genetics and upbringing, I haven't given specifics. Be sure to taste your food as you go and you should be fine.

Boneless vs Bone-In

Many ingredients come either with or without the bone in them. I usually don't specify which version to use for a dish because often both work well. Just make sure if the bone is sharp you don't vacuum seal it too tightly or it could puncture the bag.

One exception to this is for sandwiches, in which case you should use the boneless version or at least remove the bone before putting it together.

Fish Doesn't Mean Whole Fish

Unless otherwise specified when I say "1 pound mahi mahi" I am referring to filets or steaks, not whole fish. Whole fish can be done sous vide but are not covered here. I'm generally assuming filets or steaks ½" to 1" thick (13mm to 25mm).

Ingredients, Ingredients, Ingredients

You want to know what the secret to good cooking is? Use high-quality ingredients. The better the ingredients you use the better your resulting dish will be. This is even easier with sous vide since you will be perfectly cooking the food every time and don't have to worry about ruining it.

More and more farmers markets are opening up in cities everywhere and if you are planning a nice meal then the extra flavor from locally grown fruits and vegetables (and even meat) is more than worth the extra money.

CONVERTING EXISTING RECIPES

Even though I provide more than 85 recipes in this book I know I can't cover it all. One of the great things about sous vide is that it is easy to convert existing recipes into sous vide recipes with just a few tweaks. This means you can quickly convert the recipes from your favorite cookbooks into sous vide meals. There are three main steps to accomplish this.

Determine the Time and Temperature to Use

First look at the type of meat in the recipe and look up the time and temperature needed to cook it in either a recipe for that cut or in the Time and Temperature Charts section.

Isolate Seasonings

The next step in converting the recipe is to isolate the seasonings. Many foods are seasoned ahead of time with a rub or glaze and then cooked. While others have a sauce or crust added during or after the cooking process.

First look at the recipe you are converting and see what these seasonings are. Once you find the seasonings you need to determine whether they should be added before or after the sous vide process.

Season Before

Many recipes will call for spice rubs, marinades, or other similar seasonings. Throughout the marinating and cooking processes these flavors will melt into the meat and flavor it, and at the end of the cooking period they won't be distinct flavors.

These seasonings are the type you want to add before the sous vide process. You can add the spice rubs to the meat before bagging it or place fresh herbs like rosemary and thyme directly into the bags. In general it's best to substitute powdered garlic, onion, and ginger for their fresh counterparts, otherwise they can impart an off flavor.

Season After

Often times a recipe, especially steaks and chops, will have some sort of crust on it. While these crusts flavor the meat they don't break down during the cooking process like many rubs or marinades do. This means when you eat the meat you still get the distinct flavor and texture of the crust. The same goes for sauces and glazes.

These are the types of seasonings to add after the meat is cooked sous vide. If you add a crust beforehand the moist sous vide process will quickly dissolve it. To get around this, once you take the meat out of the sous vide bag you can dry it and then add the crust. Once you sear it the crust will be very similar to a traditional one.

Choose Your Finishing Method

One of the key things in most sous vide dishes is the finishing method used. The different methods add their flavors and textures to the meat. Depending on what the dish is and what you are trying to accomplish you will want to choose the method that most closely matches the recipe you are converting.

Putting it All Together

Now that you know all the steps it is very easy to take a recipe you love and convert it to a sous vide recipe.

Just determine the type of meat being cooked and the time and temperature needed to cook it. Next isolate the seasonings and see if they need to be added before or after the sous vide cooking. Finally, choose your finishing method, usually pan frying or grilling but it can also be roasting or smoking.

Season your food before if it is needed. Place it in the water bath for the indicated time at the indicated temperature. Remove it from the water bath and add any post-sous vide seasonings. Then finish it with the method of your choice.

BEEF, LAMB, AND OTHER RED MEAT

In this chapter I showcase the various cuts of beef, lamb, and other red meats. I cover how to properly cook them for the best results, as well as recommendations for other common times and temperatures. The toppings and sides in each recipe aren't exclusive to the cuts they are paired with so if you want to use a certain cut of meat with different sides it should work out great.

WHAT IS RED MEAT?

There are many different types of red meat and the ones I'm most familiar with are beef, lamb, and veal. The recipes reflect this bias but most red meat behaves the same way. Because of this you can find a comparable cut of beef or lamb and tweak the recipes to handle most other types of red meat.

If you have a type of meat that is usually grilled to a medium-rare temperature, you can follow recipes for a cut of beef that is usually grilled medium rare. The same works for meat that is usually braised, you can find a beef cut that is braised and follow the recipes for them. I've seen this process work well for grilled deer tenderloin, pulled moose shoulder, kangaroo steaks, bison burgers, elk steaks, and meat from other exotic animals.

One concern is pathogens that might be present in wild game. If you are eating wild game, cooked traditionally or with sous vide, you should make yourself aware of the pathogens and what temperatures are needed to kill them as it may differ from beef.

TEMPERATURES TO USE

There are two main ways to cook beef and other red meats. The first is to a steak-like texture and the second is a more pull-apart braise-like texture. The texture you are aiming for will determine the temperature you will use.

Steak-Like Texture

I generally like my steaks cooked medium-rare, so all the steak-like recipes will call for 131ºF (55ºC) but if you prefer a less rare steak you can increase the temperature, 141ºF (60.6ºC) is a standard temperature for medium, and anywhere in-between tastes great.

If you prefer rare steaks, you can drop the temperature to 120ºF to 125ºF (49ºC to 52ºC), but remember you are now in the danger zone and shouldn't cook the steak for more than 1 or 2 hours for safety reasons.

If you are cooking for people with different temperature preferences you have a few options. You can cook the steaks at different times or fool around with the temperatures when one is done but that can start to become complicated and just adds to the cooking time. The easiest and fastest method I've found is to cook both steaks at the lower temperature, then during the searing phase just sear the one you'd like more well done for a longer period of time. This will continue to cook the steak, raising the temperature to where you want it.

Traditional Braise-Like Texture

There are many different time and temperature combinations you can use for a traditional braise-style texture. They range from around 150ºF (65.6ºC) up to 185ºF (85ºC). I tend to prefer temperatures in between, around 161ºF to 171ºF (71.6ºC to 77.2ºC) for a firmer, but still flaky texture. I give recommendations for specific cuts in the recipes as well as the "Sous Vide Time and Temperature" chapter.

TIMES TO USE

When dealing with red meat there are two broad categories of cuts. Tender cuts and tough cuts. Tender cuts are traditionally grilled and just heated through while tough cuts are traditionally roasted or braised for a long period of time so the connective tissue has time to break down. The type of cut you are using will determine the length of time you will want to cook it for.

Tender Cuts

Tender cuts just need to be heated all the way to the middle of the piece of meat and not tenderized through any longer cooking. The sous vide process is very forgiving though so most cuts can be heated for a few hours after the middle has reached the target temperature without any negative effects.

Several recipes for tender cuts call for the meat to be cooked until "heated through". The amount of time needed to do this will depend on the temperature and the thickness of the steak. There are specific times in the "Sous Vide Thickness Times" chapter but in general a piece of meat ½" (13mm) thick will be done in 20 minutes, a 1" (25mm) piece will take 50 minutes, a 1.5" (38mm) piece will take 1:45 and a 2" (50mm) piece will take 3 hours.

Tough Cuts

Tough cuts of meat need extended cooking times to break down the connective tissues. The amount of time depends on the cut of meat, the temperature you are cooking it at, and the desired texture of the finished meat. I provide recommendations for many different cuts both in this chapter and in the "Sous Vide Time and Temperature" chapter.

As I covered in the "Salting" section of the "Pre-Sous Vide Preparation" chapter, some people don't like to pre-salt meat that will be cooked for a longer time. I prefer a light salting and the recipes reflect this. Feel free to skip this step if you like it unsalted.

In-Between Cuts

Some cuts are tender enough to be just heated through but can benefit from extended cooking. Some common examples of this are sirloin and flank steak. Both cuts are traditionally grilled and then served, but cooking them for 5 to 10 hours will break down some of the connective tissue, making them even more tender than usual. Sometimes this isn't desired and I usually prefer my flank steaks to have some bite to them so I'll just cook them long enough to heat through but some people really love a super-tender flank steak.

In the recipes for these cuts I've provided suggested extended cooking times in addition to the "heated through" recommendation so you can determine which you prefer.

How to Finish

To finish red meat I will usually dry it really well, salt it and then sear it. To sear red meat I usually panfry or grill it, or use a torch. If I'm deep frying something else I'll often use the oil to deep fry the meat as well. Whatever method you use, you will want to sear it very quickly to prevent it from overcooking any more than is necessary.

FILET MIGNON WITH CREAMY BLUE CHEESE

Cook: 131°F (55°C) for 2 to 3 hours • Serves: 4

Filet mignon, or beef tenderloin, is a super tender, lean cut of beef that is often served as a fancy steak. Filet is so lean it lacks a lot of the flavor of fattier cuts so it is often complemented with a strongly flavored sauce. For this recipe I turn to a creamy blue cheese sauce and some sherried mushrooms to round out the flavors of the meal. I also cook it with Worcester sauce for added flavor.

Filet mignon is one of the best steaks to cook with sous vide because any overcooking starts to turn the filet chewy. It's the most tender cut of beef and it only needs to be heated through the sous vide process, not tenderized. You can either measure the thickness and cook it for the minimum time needed or just give it 2 to 3 hours. This recipe works just as well for a tenderloin roast as it does for steaks, just increase the time in step with the bigger width of the tenderloin.

Ingredients

For the Filet Mignon
4 portions of filet mignon,
   about 1 to 1 ½ pounds (450g
   to 700g)
Salt and pepper
1 tablespoon garlic powder
2 tablespoons Worcester sauce

For the Blue Cheese Sauce
½ cup blue cheese
¼ cup heavy cream
2 tablespoons lemon juice
3 tablespoons olive oil
Salt and pepper

For the Sherried Mushrooms
1 pound mixed mushrooms,
   cleaned and de-stemmed
2 tablespoons olive oil
¼ onion, diced
4 garlic cloves, minced
2 tablespoons diced rosemary
   leaves
¼ cup dry sherry
2 tablespoons butter
2 tablespoons lemon juice

To Assemble
Rosemary leaves, diced

For the Filet Mignon

At least 2 to 3 hours before serving
Preheat a water bath to 131ºF (55ºC).

Salt and pepper the steak then sprinkle with the garlic powder. Place the steak in a sous vide bag, add the Worcester sauce, then seal. Cook the filet mignon until heated through, about an hour for a 1" (25mm) steak or 3 hours for a 2" (50mm) steak.

For the Blue Cheese Sauce

At least 10 minutes before serving
Blend all of the ingredients together until smooth. The cheese sauce can be stored in the refrigerator for a day or two.

For the Sherried Mushrooms

30 minutes before servings
Clean and de-stem the mushrooms then cut into large pieces. Heat the oil over medium heat then add the onion and garlic. Cook until the onion is translucent, about 10 minutes. Add the mushrooms and rosemary then cook, stirring occasionally, until the mushrooms are tender. Add the sherry and cook until the sherry has evaporated. Stir in the butter until it melts. Remove from the heat and stir in the lemon juice.

To Assemble

Lightly salt the outside of the filet mignon then quickly sear it until the meat is just browned.

Place the filet mignon on a plate with the sherried mushrooms. Top the steak with the blue cheese sauce then sprinkle some rosemary leaves on top.

Modernist Notes

For an upscale modernist take you can turn the blue cheese sauce into a thick foam using a whipping siphon. Omit the olive oil and increase the heavy cream to ¾ cup. Blend everything together then pour it into a whipping siphon. Seal and charge the siphon then dispense onto the steaks. The blue cheese foam can be made a day or two ahead of time and stored in the refrigerator.

RIBEYE WITH HERB BUTTER AND BROCCOLI RAAB

Cook: 131°F (55°C) for 2 to 3 hours • Serves: 4

Ribeye is by far my favorite cut of meat. It's full of beefy flavor, has a nice amount of flavorful fat, and has a great texture. It's also probably the most contentious steak when it comes to sous vide. Some people swear by it while other people hate it, preferring to cook it through traditional methods. I have to say I fall into the latter camp, I love a ribeye cooked directly on a hot grill, but I have come to enjoy sous vide ribeye as well.

I think the key to a good sous vide ribeye is to use the sous vide to heat the meat through, then let it cool slightly before giving it a great sear. The sear is more important for a ribeye than for other cuts due to the high fat content. Letting the steak cool slightly allows you to sear it for a little bit longer, rendering more of the fat. I usually cook ribeye for 2 to 3 hours because you just need to heat it through. However, the timing is not nearly as critical as for filet mignon and it can go up to 5 to 6 hours with no problems.

Ingredients

For the Ribeye

4 portions of ribeye, 1 to 2 pounds (450g to 900g)

1 tablespoon thyme leaves

1 tablespoon chopped rosemary leaves

1 teaspoon garlic powder

Salt and pepper

For the Herb Butter

½ stick butter, softened at room temperature

1 tablespoon finely chopped parsley

1 tablespoon finely chopped basil

1 tablespoon finely chopped tarragon

⅛ teaspoon freshly ground black pepper

For the Broccoli Raab

2 tablespoons olive oil

1 bunch broccoli raab, trimmed and cleaned

4 garlic cloves, diced

½ teaspoon Aleppo or other hot pepper flakes

2 tablespoons water

Salt and pepper

To Assemble

Smoked Maldon salt

Nasturtium flowers

For the Ribeye

At least 2 to 3 hours before serving

Preheat a water bath to 131°F (55°C).

Combine the spices in a bowl. Salt and pepper the ribeye, coat it with the spices then place it in a sous vide bag and seal. Cook the ribeye until heated through, about an hour for a 1" (25mm) steak or 3 hours for a 2" (50mm) steak.

For the Herb Butter

At least 20 minutes before serving

To make the butter place all of the ingredients in a bowl then mix and mash thoroughly using a fork. The butter will last in the refrigerator for several days or in the freezer for a month.

For the Broccoli Raab

30 minutes before serving

Heat a pan over medium heat.

Add the oil to the pan and warm. Add the broccoli raab, garlic, and pepper flakes and cook for a few minutes. Add the water to the pan, cover the pan, lower the heat and cook until tender. Salt and pepper to taste.

To Assemble

Remove the cooked steak from the sous vide bag and pat dry. Let the steak cool for 10 minutes. Lightly salt the outside of the steak then quickly sear it until the meat is browned and the fat has rendered slightly.

Add the broccoli raab to a plate and top with the steak. Sprinkle with the smoked Maldon salt then add a dollop of the herb butter and some nasturtium flowers.

FLANK STEAK WITH ARGENTINIAN CHIMICHURRI

Cook: 131°F (55°C) for 2 to 12 hours • Serves: 4 to 8

Flank steak is one of my favorite cuts because it is full of beefy flavor and has a nice bite to it. Serving it with chimichurri, a flavorful garlic and parsley-based sauce, is very popular in Argentina and other South American countries. This version isn't a truly authentic Argentinian chimichurri but it comes pretty close.

Because I like the bite of flank steak I usually only cook it enough to heat it through, about 2 to 3 hours, but if you let it go for 10 to 12 hours it turns out really tender. You can make the chimichurri sauce several days ahead of time and store it in the refrigerator.

Ingredients

For the Flank Steak
2 pounds flank steak (900g)
1 teaspoons garlic powder
½ teaspoons ground cumin
½ teaspoons ancho chile powder
Salt and pepper

For the Chimichurri
1 bunch fresh parsley
⅛ cup fresh oregano
6 garlic cloves, coarsely chopped
3 tablespoons red wine vinegar
3 tablespoons lime juice
1 cup olive oil
1 teaspoon paprika
½ jalapeno, deseeded and
    coarsely diced
Salt and pepper

To Assemble
Cucumber, sliced
Carrots, thinly sliced
Cherry tomatoes, quartered
Parsley leaves

For the Flank Steak
At least 2 to 12 hours before serving
Preheat a water bath to 131ºF (55ºC).

Mix together the spices in a bowl. Salt and pepper the steak then coat with spices. Place the steak in a sous vide bag then seal. Cook the flank steak for 2 to 12 hours.

For the Chimichurri
At least 10 minutes before serving
Combine all the ingredients in a blender or food processor and process until combined well, leaving a few larger pieces of the ingredients in the chimichurri. Pour the chimichurri into a container and reserve until serving. It will last in the refrigerator for several days.

To Assemble
Remove the cooked steak from the sous vide bag and pat dry. Lightly salt the outside of the steak then quickly sear it until the meat is just browned. Cut across the grain into thin slices.

Make a small pile of the cucumber, carrots, and cherry tomatoes then place some slices of flank steak over it. Top with the chimichurri and some parsley then serve.

Modernist Notes
I will usually mix in 0.15% xanthan gum to help hold the chimichurri sauce together so it better coats the steak. Just add it in when you are blending the ingredients together.

SIRLOIN STEAK WITH LIME-GINGER SLAW

Cook: 131°F (55°C) for 2 to 3 hours or up to 10 • Serves: 4 to 8

Lime and ginger are two great ingredients that can stand up to the bold flavors of this heavily seasoned steak. I like to combine them in a vinaigrette-style sauce that is drizzled over a crispy cabbage and pepper slaw which adds texture and brightness to the dish.

Sirloin is a very popular mid-range steak with a pretty good mix of tenderness and fat. It can be heated through, usually 2 to 3 hours, or if you prefer a more tender steak it can be cooked for up to 10 hours. There is a wide range of tenderness for sirloin so you will need to determine the best time for steaks from your butcher.

Ingredients

For the Sirloin Steak
2 pounds sirloin steak (900g)
½ teaspoon ground cumin
½ teaspoon ancho chile powder
½ teaspoon smoked paprika
¼ teaspoon mustard powder
¼ teaspoon ground coriander
Salt and pepper

For the Lime-Ginger Sauce
1 tablespoon rice vinegar
2 tablespoons lime juice
1 tablespoon honey
1 tablespoon soy sauce
2 teaspoons minced ginger
3 tablespoons olive oil
1 tablespoon sesame oil
Salt and pepper

For the Cabbage Slaw
2 cups thinly sliced red cabbage
2 cups thinly sliced bok choy or
    Chinese cabbage
1 orange bell pepper, thinly
    sliced
2 medium carrots, cut into
    matchsticks
12 snow peas, cut into strips

To Assemble
Tomatoes, sliced
Sesame seeds
Basil leaves, chopped

For the Sirloin Steak
At least 2 to 3 hours before serving
Preheat a water bath to 131°F (55°C).

Combine all the spices in a bowl. Salt and pepper the steak then coat with the spices. Place the steak in a sous vide bag then seal. Cook the steak for 2 to 3 hours, or up to 10 hours for a more tender steak.

For the Lime-Ginger Sauce
At least 10 minutes before serving
Whisk together the vinegar, lime juice, honey, soy sauce, and ginger in a small bowl. While whisking, drizzle in the olive oil and sesame oil. If you have an immersion blender you can add all the ingredients to a bowl and blend them together. Salt and pepper to taste.

For the Cabbage Slaw
At least 10 minutes before serving
Combine all the ingredients in a bowl and toss well. The undressed slaw can be stored in the refrigerator for several hours.

To Assemble
Remove the cooked steak from the sous vide bag and pat dry. Lightly salt the outside of the steak then quickly sear it until the meat is just browned.

Place a few tomato slices on a plate. Add the steak and top with the cabbage slaw. Drizzle the lime-ginger sauce over top. Sprinkle with the sesame seeds and basil leaves then serve.

Modernist Notes
Adding xanthan gum and lecithin to the lime-ginger sauce will prevent it from breaking down over time. The sauce will also coat the slaw much better. I usually blend in 0.6% lecithin and 0.5% xanthan gum for a thickened sauce.

ASIAN SKIRT STEAK WITH BEAN SPROUTS

Cook: 131°F (55°C) for 12 hours • Serves: 4 to 8

Skirt steak is similar to flank steak and has a nice chewy bite to it. It is usually served thinly sliced to maximize the tenderness. You can either keep the traditional texture by cooking it for 1 to 3 hours or you can tenderize it more with a 12 to 24 hour cook. For the shorter cooking times I usually use 135°F (57.2°C) so more of the fat is broken down. For longer cooking times I stick with 131°F (55°C).

For this recipe I use an Asian marinade to flavor the skirt steak before sous viding it. I serve it with a side of Korean bean sprouts which results in a light but flavorful meal.

Ingredients

For the Skirt Steak
2 pounds skirt steak (900g)
2 cups apple cider
½ cup soy sauce
½ yellow onion, diced
5 to 6 garlic cloves, diced
2" piece ginger, diced (50mm)
2 teaspoons sesame oil
½ teaspoon freshly ground black
　　pepper

For the Korean Bean Sprouts
2 teaspoons sesame seeds
1 tablespoon sesame oil
8 ounces fresh bean sprouts
　　(225g)
1 scallion, thinly sliced
2 garlic cloves, minced
¼ cup water
Salt and pepper

To Assemble
Sesame oil
Scallion, sliced
Peanuts

For the Skirt Steak

At least 18 hours before serving
Combine all the ingredients in a bag or bowl and refrigerate for at least 6 hours, and up to overnight.

Preheat a water bath to 131°F (55°C).

Remove the steak from the marinade and pat dry. Place the steak in a sous vide bag then seal. Cook the steak for about 12 hours.

For the Korean Bean Sprouts

30 minutes before serving
Heat a pan without oil over medium heat. Add the sesame seeds and cook until just beginning to brown. Add the remaining ingredients and cook until the bean sprouts are tender and just beginning to wilt. Remove from the heat then salt and pepper to taste.

To Assemble

Remove the cooked steak from the sous vide bag and pat dry. Lightly salt the outside of the steak then quickly sear it until the meat is just browned. Cut into thick slices.

Place several slices of steak on a plate and top with the Korean bean sprouts. Drizzle with some sesame oil and sprinkle the scallion and peanuts on top.

CHUCK STEAK WITH DEEP FRIED BRUSSELS SPROUTS

Cook: 131°F (55°C) for 36 to 60 hours • Serves: 4 to 8

I love ribeye steaks but they are so expensive I tend to only have them as a special treat. Luckily for me, if you sous vide a chuck steak for a few days it comes out tasting almost as good as a ribeye, at only about a third of the cost. For this recipe I serve the chuck steak with a flavorful fresh pesto and crunchy deep fried brussels sprouts.

In order to tenderize the chuck steak enough for it to be enjoyable you need to cook it for at least a day, and sometimes up to three days. I tend to do 2 full days but it will depend on the quality of steak you use. There will still be some fat you need to cut off, but usually not too much. Because I have oil already heated for the brussels sprouts I will usually just deep fry the chuck steak to sear it. I prefer to lightly salt the chuck steak before sous vide it but some people prefer to cook it unsalted.

Ingredients

For the Chuck Steak

2 pounds chuck steak (900g), or
    chuck roast cut into
    1" (25mm) slabs
2 teaspoons garlic powder
1 teaspoon onion powder
1 teaspoon ground cumin
Salt and pepper

For the Pesto

1½ cups packed fresh basil
1 cup packed fresh parsley
¼ cup pine nuts
½ teaspoon salt
¼ teaspoon black pepper
¼ cup grated fresh parmesan
    cheese
2 tablespoons lemon juice
4 garlic cloves, minced
½ cup olive oil

For the Brussels Sprouts

½ pound brussels sprouts,
    trimmed and cut in half
    (240g)
Oil
Salt and pepper

To Assemble

Blue cheese, crumbled
Basil leaves
Lemon zest
Lemon juice

For the Chuck Steak

At least 36 to 60 hours before serving

Preheat a water bath to 131ºF (55ºC).

Mix together the spices in a bowl. Lightly salt the steak then coat with the spices. Place the steak in a sous vide bag then seal. Cook the steak for 36 to 60 hours.

For the Pesto

At least 20 minutes before serving

Combine all the ingredients into a blender or food processor and process until it forms a smooth paste. This can be done a day or two ahead of time and stored in the refrigerator.

For the Brussels Sprouts

20 minutes before serving

Fill a pot of oil one third to half way full with oil then heat it to 350ºF (176ºC). Set up a plate with paper towels on it or a cooling rack over a baking sheet.

Add the brussels sprouts to the hot oil, working in batches if necessary to prevent overcrowding. Cook them until golden brown, 2 to 4 minutes. Remove from the heat and place on the cooling rack. Sprinkle with salt and pepper.

To Assemble

Remove the cooked steak from the sous vide bag and pat dry. Lightly salt the outside of the steak then quickly sear it until the meat is just browned. Cut into thick slices.

Place the steak on a plate with the brussels sprouts. Top the brussels sprouts with the blue cheese crumbles. Add a dollop of pesto to the steak then top with the basil leaves and lemon zest. Drizzle some lemon juice over the brussels sprouts then serve.

Modernist Notes

For a fun plating change I like to make browned butter balls to serve on the brussels sprouts. Melt 150 grams butter over medium heat and lightly whisk it as it melts. The butter will begin to foam and once it settles the milk solids will start to brown. Once the butter begins to brown and smell nutty, remove it from the heat. The butter can very quickly go from browned to burned so keep an eye on it.

Let the butter cool slightly then slowly whisk or stir in enough maltodextrin for it to form a thick paste that you can easily form into balls. It usually takes around 70 to 100 grams.

Form the butter paste into small balls about ½" (13mm) in diameter. Once made, the butter balls can stay in the fridge for several days.

RASPBERRY SALAD WITH NEW YORK STRIP STEAK

Cook: 131°F (55°C) for 2 to 3 hours • Serves: 4 to 8

We have several raspberry bushes in our yard and by the middle of summer we get inundated with the tasty berries. I'm always trying to find new uses for them and this raspberry salad is a fresh way to enjoy them. The raspberries are blended into a flavorful vinaigrette for a light salad that complements the heavier steak.

New York Strip steaks, also called strip or club steaks, are one of the more tender cuts of beef. Because of their tenderness they only need to be heated through with the sous vide process, usually 2 to 3 hours, but if you want it to be extra tender you can cook it for up to 8 hours.

Ingredients

For the Strip Steak
2 pounds New York strip steak (900g)
Salt and pepper
1 teaspoon ground coriander
½ teaspoon garlic powder
½ teaspoon ground allspice

For the Raspberry Vinaigrette
2 cups fresh raspberries
2 tablespoons raspberry vinegar or rice vinegar
1 tablespoon honey
2 tablespoons olive oil
Salt and pepper

To Assemble
Mixed baby greens or the lettuce of your choice
½ yellow or red bell pepper, diced
10 cherry tomatoes, halved
¼ cup fresh raspberries or mixed berries
2 radishes, sliced
2 tablespoons sunflower seeds

For the Strip Steak

At least 2 to 3 hours before serving
Preheat a water bath to 131°F (55°C).

Mix together the spices in a bowl. Salt and pepper the steak and then coat with the spices. Place the steak in a sous vide bag then seal. Cook the steak for 2 to 3 hours, or up to 8 hours for a more tender steak.

For the Raspberry Vinaigrette

At least 10 minutes before serving
Blend together all the ingredients using a standing or immersion blender. The dressing will last in the refrigerator for several hours. For a more refined presentation you can strain the dressing.

To Assemble

Remove the cooked steak from the sous vide bag and pat dry. Lightly salt the outside of the steak then quickly sear it until the meat is just browned. Cut into thin slices.

Assemble the salad by placing the lettuce on plates. Top with the pepper, tomatoes, raspberries, and radishes. Drizzle the vinaigrette on the salad and add the strips of steak. Top with the sunflower seeds. Lightly sprinkle the salad with salt and pepper and serve.

Modernist Notes

For a more upscale presentation you can turn the raspberry vinaigrette into a froth using a whipping siphon. Omit the olive oil from the dressing and add 2 tablespoons of water. Blend it together then strain out the raspberry seeds. Blend in 0.3% xanthan gum. Pour the vinaigrette into a whipping siphon then seal and charge the siphon. When assembling the dish, drizzle olive oil on the salad then dispense the vinaigrette froth on top.

HANGER STEAK WITH PEACH SALSA

Cook: 131°F (55°C) for 2 to 3 hours • Serves: 4 to 8

In summer I eat as many peaches as I can because during that time of year they are so sweet and juicy. This salsa is very simple to put together and it really highlights the flavor of the peaches while still complementing the steak. Make sure you are using fresh and ripe peaches to maximize the flavor of the salsa.

Hanger steak is an underutilized cut of meat. It is flavorful and tender like a ribeye but at about half the price. Because it is already tender you only need to cook it long enough to heat it all the way through, usually 2 to 3 hours. Once it's cooked, be sure to slice it across the grain to maximize the tenderness.

Ingredients

For the Hanger Steak
2 pounds hanger steak (900g)
2 teaspoons ground coriander
1 teaspoon ground cumin
½ teaspoon chipotle chile
   powder
Salt and pepper

For the Peach Salsa
3 peaches, diced
¼ of a red onion, chopped
3 tablespoons lime juice
3 tablespoons orange juice
1 jalapeno pepper, diced
3 tablespoons chopped cilantro
½ of a red pepper, diced
2 tablespoons honey
Salt and pepper

To Assemble
Peach slices
Cilantro leaves

For the Hanger Steak Steak

At least 2 to 3 hours before serving
Preheat a water bath to 131°F (55°C).

Mix together the spices in a bowl. Trim any silver skin off the hanger steak. Salt and pepper the steak and then coat with the spices. Place the steak in a sous vide bag then seal. Cook the steak for 2 to 3 hours.

For the Peach Salsa

At least 75 minutes before serving
Mix all of the ingredients together in a bowl and let sit for at least an hour for the flavors to meld. This can be done up to a day ahead of time.

To Assemble

Remove the cooked steak from the sous vide bag and pat dry. Lightly salt the outside of the steak then quickly sear it until the meat is just browned. Cut across the grain into thin slices.

Place the steak on a plate and top with the peach salsa and peach slices. Sprinkle the cilantro leaves on top then serve.

TOP ROUND WITH ORANGE SAUCE

Cook: 131°F (55°C) for 1 to 2 days • Serves: 4 to 8

Top round is a very lean and relatively tough cut of meat that really needs to be tenderized by sous vide. I always cook it at 131°F (55°C) for at least a day, and up to 2 days, to tenderize it enough to be enjoyable.

I prefer to serve top round with a strong sauce because the lack of fat tends to make it drier and less flavorful than other cuts. For this recipe I serve it over rice with a sweet and spicy orange sauce that helps cover up the blandness and complement the beefy flavor.

Ingredients

For the Top Round
2 pounds top round steaks (900g)
2 teaspoons garlic powder
1 teaspoon ginger powder
½ teaspoon pepper
½ teaspoon ground cloves
½ teaspoon cayenne chile powder
Salt and pepper

For the Orange Sauce
3 tablespoons sesame oil
3 scallions, thinly sliced
1 tablespoon minced garlic
1 tablespoon minced fresh ginger
1½ cups orange juice
2 tablespoons soy sauce
2-4 tablespoons sriracha sauce
2 tablespoons honey
2 cups mandarin oranges
Salt and pepper

To Assemble
4 cups cooked white rice
½ tablespoon grated orange peel
½ cup chopped parsley

For the Top Round Steak
At least 1 to 2 days before serving
Preheat a water bath to 131°F (55°C).

Mix together the spices in a bowl. Lightly salt and pepper the steaks then coat them with the spices. Place the steaks in a sous vide bag then seal. Cook the top round steaks for 1 to 2 days.

For the Orange Sauce
At least 20 minutes before serving
Heat a pan over medium heat.

Add the oil and scallions to the pan and cook for 1 to 2 minutes. Add the garlic and ginger and cook for 1 to 2 more minutes. Add the orange juice, soy sauce, sriracha sauce, honey, salt, pepper, and a quarter of the Mandarin oranges. Cook until it thickens slightly and the flavors are combined, about 5 minutes. Stir in the remaining mandarin oranges then remove from the heat and keep warm until ready to serve.

To Assemble

Remove the cooked steak from the sous vide bag and pat dry. Salt the outside of the steak then quickly sear it until the meat is just browned. Cut into bite-sized pieces.

Put a large spoonful of white rice on a plate or in a bowl, top with some of the top round and cover with a scoop of the orange sauce. Sprinkle with the orange peel and parsley then serve.

Modernist Notes

For a more clingy sauce I will blend 0.15% xanthan gum into the orange juice before adding it to the pan. This helps hold it together and it will better coat the steak.

FLAT IRON STEAK WITH PANCETTA ASPARAGUS

Cook: 131ºF (55ºC) for 12 to 24 hours • Serves: 4 to 8

Flat iron, or top blade, steaks are becoming more popular. They are traditionally grilled, so to replicate it you can just heat them through. However, they are a tougher cut of meat so they can benefit greatly from a longer sous vide time, up to 24 to 48 hours. It really comes down to how tender you'd like the result to be.

Asparagus is a very simple side to fix but it is also very versatile. Once you blanch it in salted, boiling water you can add any number of seasonings to make the asparagus compliment the meal you are having. Here I go very simple and saute it with some pancetta and chicken stock.

Ingredients

For the Flat Iron Steak
2 pounds flat iron steak (900g)
1 teaspoon paprika
1 teaspoon garlic powder
½ teaspoon ancho chile powder
Salt and pepper

For the Pancetta Asparagus
1 bunch asparagus, ends cut off
1 cup diced pancetta
1 tablespoon thyme leaves
¼ cup chicken stock
Salt and pepper

To Assemble
Fresh parsley, chopped
Lemon zest
Parmesan cheese for grating

For the Flat Iron Steak

At least 12 to 24 hours before serving
Preheat a water bath to 131ºF (55ºC).

Mix together the spices in a bowl. Lightly salt and pepper the steak then coat with the spices. Place the steak in a sous vide bag then seal. Cook the steak for 12 to 24 hours.

For the Pancetta Asparagus

40 minutes before serving
Bring a pot of salted water to a boil. Add the asparagus and cook until it becomes tender, 5 to 10 minutes depending on the thickness of the asparagus.

While the asparagus is cooking, heat a pan over medium heat and add the pancetta. Cook until the fat is rendered and the pancetta begins to turn crispy.

Drain the asparagus and pat dry with a paper towel or kitchen cloth. Add to the pan with the pancetta along with the fresh thyme and chicken stock. Cook until the chicken stock reduces slightly and begins to stick to the asparagus, 2 to 5 minutes. Remove from the heat.

To Assemble

Remove the cooked steak from the sous vide bag and pat dry. Lightly salt the outside of the steak then quickly sear it until the meat is just browned.

Place the steak on a plate and top with the pancetta asparagus. Sprinkle with parsley and lemon zest. Shave some Parmesan cheese on the top using a microplane or grater and serve.

LONDON BROIL BEEF FAJITAS

Cook: 131°F (55°C) for 1 to 2 days • Serves: 4 to 8

Even though it's easy to find cuts labeled "London Broil" it actually isn't an officially recognized cut. It is typically a chuck steak or a top round steak and will sometimes be labelled as such, otherwise you can guess the real cut based on the marbling of the steak. Chuck steaks have a lot of marbling while top round will be much leaner. A London broil with a decent amount of marbling makes a great inexpensive steak as long as you cook it for 1 or 2 days to tenderize it.

I enjoy using London broil steaks in fajitas because it can help mask some of the blandness of the top round or the chewiness of the chuck steak. I've listed some other common fajita sides but you can use whatever you like in your fajitas.

Ingredients

For the London Broil
2 pounds London Broil (900g)
1 teaspoon pepper
1 teaspoon ground cumin
1 teaspoon ground coriander
1 teaspoon garlic powder
½ teaspoon ancho chile powder
1 tablespoon soy sauce
1 tablespoon Worcester sauce
Salt and pepper

For the Peppers and Onions
2 tablespoons canola oil
3 garlic cloves, diced
2 onions, preferably Vidalia or sweet, cut into ½" slices (13mm)
3 bell peppers - green and red, cut into ¼" strips (6mm)
1-2 poblano peppers, cut into ¼" strips (6mm)
Salt and pepper

To Assemble
10 tortilla wrappers
6 cups sliced lettuce
4 tomatoes, diced
Refried beans
Mexican rice
Grated pepper jack cheese
Sour cream

For the London Broil
At least 1 to 2 days before serving
Preheat a water bath to 131°F (55°C).

Mix together the spices in a bowl. Lightly salt and pepper the steak then coat with the spices. Place the steak in a sous vide bag, add the soy sauce and Worcester sauce then seal. Cook the steak for 1 to 2 days.

For the Peppers and Onions
20 minutes before serving
Heat a pan to medium-high heat.

Heat the oil then add the onion to the pan and cook until it starts to become tender, 5 to 7 minutes. Add the garlic, bell peppers, and poblano peppers and cook until they become tender. Remove from the heat and set aside.

To Assemble
Remove the cooked steak from the sous vide bag and pat dry. Lightly salt the outside of the steak then quickly sear it until the meat is just browned. Cut into thin slices.

You can either pre-assemble the fajitas or set all the garnishes out and let each person make their own.

Modernist Notes
For a fun garnish I like to use my whipping siphon to make a foam to use as a sauce for the fajitas. There are many different foams that work well but one I really like is a mango-habanero froth. It has the right mixture of heat and sweet without being overpowering. You can make fresh mango juice by pureeing several mangos and straining them but I usually will just buy some at the grocery store.

In a pot combine 2 cups mango juice with some habanero pepper. I'll usually use between ¼ and 1 pepper, depending on how spicy I want it. Bring the mango juice to a simmer then remove from the heat. Strain the mango juice then blend in about 2 grams of xanthan gum. Pour the juice into the whipping siphon then seal and charge it. Dispense it on top of the meat in the fajitas before serving.

CHUCK POT ROAST WITH ROASTED VEGETABLES

Cook: 161°F (71.7°C) for 1 to 2 days • Serves: 4 to 8

Much is made of sous vide's ability to transform cuts of meat, creating new textures and serving meat at temperatures that were not practical in the past. However, sometimes it shines brightest when it's just creating a perfect version of an old dish. That's the case here with a great traditional pot roast. The meat is fall apart tender but still very juicy, unlike the sometimes dried texture of many braised pot roasts.

When I make pot roasts I almost always use a chuck roast. It's a wonderful cut of meat with lots of fat to render leaving a flaky, moist meat behind. There are many different time and temperature combinations you can use for a traditional-style roast. I usually cook it at 185°F (85°C) for 12 hours for a very braise-like texture or 161°F (71.7°C) for 24 to 48 hours, for a firmer, but still flaky texture.

In this recipe I pair it with a medley of roasted vegetables for a lighter take on the typical mashed potatoes and gravy. It's all tossed with a lemon vinaigrette for even more brightness.

Ingredients

For the Pot Roast
2 to 3 pounds chuck roast (900g to 1350g)
2 teaspoons garlic powder
2 teaspoons onion powder
1 teaspoon paprika
1 teaspoon mustard powder
½ teaspoon ancho chile powder or chile powder of your choice
Salt and pepper
4 sprigs thyme
4 sprigs rosemary

For the Roasted Vegetables
10 large carrots
20 multi-colored baby potatoes
1 medium onion, chopped
1 red pepper, chopped
10 garlic cloves, roughly diced
4 tablespoons olive oil
2 tablespoons thyme leaves
Salt and pepper

To Assemble
Olive oil
Lemon

For the Pot Roast

At least 1 to 2 days before serving
Preheat a water bath to 161ºF (71.7ºC).

Cut the chuck roast into 2" (50mm) slabs, if desired. Mix together the spices in a bowl. Lightly salt and pepper the meat then coat with the spices. Place the meat in a sous vide bag with the herbs then seal. Cook the meat for 1 to 2 days.

For the Roasted Vegetables

70 minutes before serving
Preheat an oven to 425ºF (218ºC).

Peel the carrots and cut into ¾" (19mm) chunks. Cut the baby potatoes into chunks as well. Toss all the vegetables together with the olive oil and thyme then salt and pepper them. Place them in a roasting pan or rimmed baking sheet in a single layer. Roast in the oven until starting to brown and the carrots and potatoes have softened and are cooked through, about 30 to 45 minutes. Once cooked, remove from the heat.

To Assemble

Remove the cooked meat from the sous vide bag, reserving the juices, and pat dry. Lightly salt the outside of the meat then quickly sear it until it is just browned.

Place some of the roasted vegetables on a plate, squeeze the lemon over the top then drizzle with the olive oil. Add a portion of the pot roast to the vegetables and spoon some of the sous vide juices over top then serve.

CHUCK ROAST WITH BACON AND KALE

Cook: 131ºF (55ºC) for 36 to 60 hours • Serves: 6 to 12

This recipe showcases how a low temperature and long cooking time can really transform a cut of meat. Compared to the traditional pot roast cooked at a high temperature in the previous recipe, this chuck roast is cooked at 131ºF (55ºC) for 36 to 60 hours, resulting in a meltingly tender meat that tastes similar to prime rib or a rib roast.

In this recipe I pair it with a sauteed kale and bacon side. It adds some salty and smoky notes from the bacon with a little brightness from the lemon.

Ingredients

For the Chuck Roast
2 to 3 pounds chuck roast (900g to 1350g)
1 tablespoon garlic powder
2 teaspoons ground cumin
1 teaspoon dried oregano
Salt and pepper
1 bay leaf

For the Bacon and Kale
7 bacon strips, cut into batons
1 onion, sliced
5 garlic cloves, minced
1 teaspoon red pepper flakes
1 bunch kale, cleaned and chopped
½ cup water
2 tablespoons lemon juice
Salt and pepper

To Assemble
Olive oil
Lemon zest
Fresh oregano, chopped

For the Chuck Roast

At least 36 to 60 hours before serving
Preheat a water bath to 131ºF (55ºC).

Cut the chuck roast into 2" (50mm) slabs, if desired. Mix together the spices in a bowl. Lightly salt and pepper the meat then coat it with the spices. Place the meat in a sous vide bag with the bay leaf then seal. Cook the meat for 36 to 60 hours.

For the Bacon and Kale

70 minutes before serving
Place the bacon in a pan and heat over medium heat until the bacon becomes crispy and the fat is rendered out. Remove the bacon from the pan and set aside to add back in later. Discard all but 2 tablespoons of the rendered fat.

Add the onion to the pan and cook until translucent, 10 to 15 minutes. Add the garlic, red pepper flakes, and kale then saute until the kale starts to wilt slightly. Add the water to the pan then cover it. Cook until the kale is tender, about 10 to 20 minutes, adding more water as needed.

Once tender, stir in the lemon juice and salt and pepper to taste.

To Assemble

Remove the cooked meat from the sous vide bag and pat dry. Lightly salt the outside then quickly sear it until the meat is just browned. Slice the chuck roast into strips.

Place some of the kale on a plate and top with several strips of the chuck roast. Drizzle with the olive oil and sprinkle lemon zest and oregano on top then serve.

Modernist Note

To add some extra texture to the dish I will take some of the uncooked kale and deep dry it in 350°F (176°C) oil. It removes the moisture and results in a tender, crispy kale leaf. I use it as a garnish on top of the steak.

PRIME RIB ROAST WITH HORSERADISH CREAM

Cook: 131°F (55°C) for 5 to 10 hours • Serves: 6 to 12

My family and I always do prime rib for our Christmas dinner and now with sous vide it's incredibly easy and convenient to make. I like to serve it with a tart pear and pomegranate salad as well as a whipped horseradish cream.

I prefer my prime rib medium rare, so I always do it at 131°F (55°C) but if you like it more well done you can go up to 141°F (60.6°C). Because of the high fat content, the rib roasts can benefit from some tenderization and I've found they are ideal after 5 to 10 hours, depending on the size of the meat. I'll usually cut the meat into 2" (50mm) slabs to even out the cooking process, and maximize the browning surface, but you can leave it whole if you prefer.

Ingredients

For the Prime Rib
2 to 3 pounds prime rib (900g to 1350g)
2 teaspoons thyme leaves
1 teaspoon paprika
½ teaspoon ground coriander
Salt and pepper

For the Horseradish Cream
1 cup heavy cream
2 tablespoons prepared horseradish

For the Spicy Candied Walnuts
¼ cup white sugar
¼ teaspoon chipotle chile powder
½ teaspoon ground cinnamon
1 cup shelled walnuts

For the Pear Salad
2 pears, sliced
2 ounces blue cheese (56g)
2 cups arugula
2 cups baby spinach
2 tablespoons rice wine vinegar
¼ cup olive oil
⅓ cup pomegranate seeds
Salt and pepper

For the Prime Rib Roast

At least 5 to 10 hours before serving
Preheat a water bath to 131°F (55°C).

Cut the prime rib into 2" (50mm) slabs, if desired. Mix together the spices in a bowl. Salt and pepper the prime rib then coat with the spices. Place the prime rib in a sous vide bag then seal. Cook the roast for 5 to 10 hours.

For the Horseradish Cream

At least 15 minutes before serving
Place the heavy cream and horseradish in a bowl or the base of a mixer with a whisk attachment. Whisk until stiff peaks form and the mixture resembles whipped cream. The whipped cream will last in the refrigerator for 30 to 60 minutes.

For the Spicy Candied Walnuts

At least 20 to 30 minutes before serving
Pre-heat an oven to 350°F (176°C).

Mix together the sugar, chile powder, and cinnamon. Lightly wet the walnuts with water then toss with the sugar mixture. Bake for 10 to 15 minutes, until the sugar caramelizes and turns brown.

Remove from the heat and let cool. Once cooled, the walnuts can be stored for several days in a sealed container.

For the Pear Salad
10 to 20 minutes before serving
Toss the pear slices, blue cheese, arugula and baby spinach together. Whisk together the vinegar and olive oil then stir in the pomegranate seeds. Dress the salad with the vinaigrette right before serving.

To Assemble
Remove the cooked prime rib from the sous vide bag and pat dry. Lightly salt the outside of the meat then quickly sear it until the meat is just browned. Cut into serving-sized pieces.

Place the pear salad on the plate and top with the vinaigrette and the candied walnuts. Arrange the prime rib around the salad and top with a dollop or two of the whipped horseradish cream then serve.

SHORT RIBS WITH FETA AND BEET SALAD

Cook: 175°F (79.4°C) for 12 to 24 hours • Serves: 6 to 12

Short ribs are a classic "must make" sous vide dish. Due to the high fat content they can be cooked anywhere from 131°F to 185°F (55°C to 85°C) for 12 hours to 3 days and the final dish will greatly depend on the time and temperature you use. The end result will range from a traditional braise-like texture to a chewy steak, or anything in between.

For a melty, steak-like texture, cook the ribs at around 131°F (55°C) for 48 to 72 hours, they are worth the wait. A more traditional, fall-apart texture will occur when cooked at 175°F (79.4°C) for 12 to 24 hours. A good in between texture is achieved at 150°F (65.6°C) for 18 to 36 hours. The longer the short ribs cook, the more tender they become so an 18 hour cook will be firmer than a 36 hour cook at the same temperature.

The short ribs can hold up to something rich and heavy or can be contrasted with something light and bright. In this recipe I opt for a feta and roasted beet salad with preserved lemon and tarragon. The short ribs are also great with the "Rustic Mashed Potatoes" or the "Butter Poached Turnips". Searing with a torch works best because these ribs are so tender they tend to fall apart, but a quick sear in a hot pan can also work well.

Ingredients

For the Short Ribs
2 to 3 pounds short ribs, trimmed (900g to 1350g)
1 teaspoon garlic powder
1 teaspoon ground coriander
½ teaspoon ground cumin
Salt and pepper

For the Feta and Beet Salad
5 beets
Olive oil
Salt and pepper
2 tablespoons lemon juice
2 tablespoons olive oil
½ cup crumbled feta cheese
2 tablespoon diced preserved lemon
1 shallot, minced
2 garlic cloves, minced
2 tablespoons chopped tarragon

To Assemble
Dual-Cooked Creamy Potato Puree, page 198
Olive oil
Lemon zest
Fresh oregano, chopped

For the Short Ribs

At least 12 to 24 hours before serving
Preheat a water bath to 175°F (79.4°C).

Mix together the spices in a bowl. Lightly salt and pepper the meat then coat it with the spices. Place the meat in a sous vide bag and seal. Cook the meat for 12 to 24 hours.

For the Feta and Beet Salad

80 minutes before serving
Preheat an oven to 400°F (200°C)

Peel the beets then set each beet on a square of aluminum foil or parchment paper. Drizzle with olive oil then salt and pepper them. Wrap each beet in the aluminum foil and place on a sheet pan. Bake until the beets are tender and cooked through, about 45 to 60 minutes. Remove from the heat and let cool. Unwrap the beets and dice.

Whisk together the lemon juice and 2 tablespoons of olive oil. Add the beets and the remaining ingredients then toss to combine. Salt and pepper to taste.

To Assemble

Remove the cooked meat from the sous vide bag and pat dry. Lightly salt the outside then quickly sear it until the meat is just browned.

Place a spoonful of the potato puree on the plate and top with a serving of short rib meat. Spoon some of the salad on top of the meat. Drizzle with olive oil and zest some lemon on top then serve.

Modernist Note

Adding xanthan gum is a great way to get the vinaigrette to better coat the beets and the feta cheese. Just blend in 0.15% into the lemon juice and olive oil before tossing with the other ingredients. You may need to double the amount of oil and vinegar for it to blend easily.

BEEF CARNITAS WITH TANGERINE-CHIPOTLE SAUCE

Cook: 156°F (68.8°C) for 18 to 24 hours • Serves: 6 to 12

When I want shredded beef I turn to either brisket or chuck roast due to the extensive marbling. In order to fully break down the fat, you will want to cook it at a higher temperature, usually above 155°F (68.3°C). Brisket and chuck cooked for lower temperatures for several days are great but they have the texture of steak and aren't nearly as shreddable.

My favorite time and temperature combination is probably 156°F (68.8°C) for around 18 to 24 hours, it's shreddable but not too tender. Some other popular combinations are 165°F (73.9) for 18 to 24 hours or 176°F (80°C) for 12 hours.

I turn the shredded beef into flavorful carnitas covered in a sweet and spicy tangerine-chipotle sauce. Then I serve them with corn tortillas and avocado so they are easy to pick up and eat.

Ingredients

For the Carnitas
2 pounds chuck roast (900g)
2 teaspoons garlic powder
1 teaspoon onion powder
1 teaspoon1 ground cumin
1 teaspoon dried oregano
¼ teaspoon ground allspice
¼ teaspoon ground cloves
Salt and pepper

For the Tangerine-Chipotle Sauce
2 tangerines, deseeded and
    diced
½ cup sous vide juices
2-3 chipotle peppers in adobo
    sauce
1 tablespoon oregano leaves
1 tablespoon honey

To Assemble
Corn tortillas
Avocado, cut into slices

For the Carnitas
At least 18 to 24 hours before serving
Preheat a water bath to 156°F (68.3°C).

Mix together the spices in a bowl. Lightly salt and pepper the roast then coat with the spices. Place the roast in a sous vide bag then seal. Cook the roast for at least 18 to 24 hours.

For the Tangerine-Chipotle Sauce
At least 20 minutes before serving
Combine all the ingredients in a pot. Bring to a simmer and let cook for 10 minutes then blend well. The sauce can be made several hours ahead of time, just blend in the sous vide juices when they are ready.

To Assemble
Remove the roast from the sous vide bag. Shred the beef and set aside.

Place a tortilla on a plate and add some of the shredded beef. Top with the tangerine-chipotle sauce and avocados then serve.

Modernist Notes
For a more upscale presentation the tangerine-chipotle sauce can be turned into fluid gel pudding which greatly adds to the mouthfeel of the sauce. When you combine the ingredients for the sauce in the pot blend in 0.6% agar. After it is done simmering pour the sauce into a container so it can set completely. Once set, puree well with an immersion or standing blender. The sauce can still be made several hours ahead of time.

TOP ROUND FRENCH DIP SANDWICHES

Cook: 131°F (55°C) for 1 to 2 days • Serves: 6 to 12

French dip sandwiches are a classic deli food and they are very easy to make at home using sous vide. Once the meat is cooked long enough to be tenderized it is seared and thinly sliced. I like to pile the slices on a hoagie roll with melted swiss cheese but you can serve it however you prefer.

A top round roast is a pretty tough piece of meat but if it is sous vided for a few days it comes out really tender. If I'm eating the beef plain I will usually cook it for 2 to 3 days, but for these sandwiches I want a little more bite so I keep the cooking time to just a day or two.

Ingredients

For the Top Round Roast
2 pounds top round roast (900g)
1 tablespoon garlic powder
2 teaspoons onion powder
1 teaspoon ancho chile powder
   or chile powder of your
   choice
1 teaspoon dried sage
½ teaspoon ground cloves
¼ teaspoon ground cinnamon
¼ teaspoon ground nutmeg
Salt and pepper

To Assemble
Hoagie rolls or small baguettes
Swiss cheese slices
Red onion, sliced
Dill pickles

For the Top Round Roast
At least 1 to 2 days before serving
Preheat a water bath to 131ºF (55ºC).

Mix together the spices in a bowl. Lightly salt and pepper the roast then coat with the spices. Place the roast in a sous vide bag then seal. Cook the roast for 1 to 2 days.

To Assemble
Remove the cooked roast from the sous vide bag, reserving the juice in the bag, and pat dry. Pour the juices into a pan and bring to a simmer. Remove from the heat and strain the scum that forms on the top with a chinois or cheesecloth. Quickly sear the roast until just browned. Remove from the heat and slice the roast as thinly as you can.

Place the cheese on the rolls and toast in an oven with the broiler on or in a toaster oven until the cheese melts and the rolls begin to brown. Remove the rolls from the oven and pile the roast beef on top then add the red onion. Pour the strained juices into ramekins or small bowls for dipping, place a dill pickle on the side, then serve.

EASY CORNED BEEF

Cook: 135ºF (57.2ºC) for 1 to 3 days • Serves: 6 to 12

Corned beef is both a favorite meal and sandwich meat of mine. I've cooked it many different ways and my favorite is 135ºF (57.2ºC) for 2 days. However, when cooked at 146ºF (63.3ºC) it was also very good, a little drier but also tenderer. Either temperature will result in fantastic corned beef. For a faster cooking time that will result in a more traditional texture, you can cook it as high as 180ºF (82.2ºC) for about 10 hours.

One potential issue with corned beef is the saltiness. Many are cured with the expectation they will be boiled, which draws out much of the salt. You can prevent this by soaking the corned beef in water for a few hours either before or after cooking it. The water will draw out the salt from the corned beef.

Ingredients

For the Corned Beef
2-3 pounds cured, uncooked corned beef (900g to 1350g)

For the Corned Beef

At least 1 to 3 days before serving
Preheat a water bath to 135ºF (57.2ºC).

Place the corned beef in a sous vide bag with any included spices then seal. Place in the water bath and cook for around 2 days.

To Assemble

Remove the corned beef from the water bath and pat dry. Quickly sear the corned beef over high heat until the meat is just browned. Remove from the heat and slice into thin strips then serve.

TRI-TIP WITH ROASTED FENNEL AND ORANGE SALAD

Cook: 131°F (55°C) for 10 to 12 hours • Serves: 4 to 8

Tri-tip is a flavorful cut of meat from around the sirloin region. It is usually grilled and cut across the grain to help make it more tender and with sous vide it can benefit from extended cooking times. I like to pair it with a rich, flavorful salad of oranges and roasted fennel.

The longer you cook tri-tip the more tender it will become, so you can choose your time according to what you are trying to accomplish. For a more traditional texture you can cook it for 3 to 4 hours. Eight hours will give you a more tender, but still toothy result and 24 hours will result in super tender meat. I usually prefer somewhere in the 10 to 12 hour range.

Ingredients

For the Tri-Tip

2 pounds tri-tip (900g)
2 teaspoons ground coriander
2 teaspoons onion powder
1 teaspoon ground cumin
½ teaspoon ground cloves
Salt and pepper

*For the Fennel and Orange
Salad*

3 fennel bulbs
3 garlic cloves, chopped
½ cup olive oil
2 oranges
1 lemon
2 shallots, diced
1 cup roughly chopped mixed
    pitted olives
2 tablespoons chopped mint
2 tablespoons chopped parsley

For the Tri-Tip

At least 10 to 12 hours before serving
Preheat a water bath to 131°F (55°C).

Mix together the spices in a bowl. Lightly salt and pepper the tri-tip then coat with the spices. Place the tri-tip in a sous vide bag then seal. Cook for 10 to 12 hours.

For the Fennel and Orange Salad

80 minutes before serving
Preheat an oven to 400°F (204°C).

Remove the fronds from the fennel and set aside for later. Cut the fennel into large chunks. Toss the fennel with the garlic and half of the olive oil, then salt and pepper it. Roast the fennel in the oven for 45 to 60 minutes, until tender and cooked through. Remove the fennel from the oven.

Over a bowl, cut the orange into supremes by slicing off the peel and pith, then cutting out the segments between the membranes. Set the supremes aside and squeeze out any remaining juice from the leftover flesh on the orange.

Zest the lemon and set the zest aside for later. Quarter the lemon and squeeze half of it into the orange juice. Whisk in the remaining ¼ cup of olive oil until it forms a vinaigrette.

Combine the fennel, orange supremes, shallots and olives then toss with the dressing. Mix in half the herbs then sprinkle the other half on top along with the lemon zest. Chop some of the reserved fennel fronds and sprinkle on top.

To Assemble

Remove the tri-tip from the sous vide bag and pat dry. Quickly sear until just browned. Remove from the heat and slice it into 1" (25mm) slabs.

Serve the slices of tri-tip with the fennel and orange salad.

Modernist Notes

To help the sauce cling to the fennel I will usually add xanthan gum to it. Just blend in 0.15% xanthan gum to the orange juice and olive oil before combining the dressing with the vegetables.

MEMPHIS-STYLE BEEF RIBS AND SPICY LIME CORN

Cook: 131ºF (55ºC) for 48 to 60 hours • Serves: 6 to 12

Beef ribs aren't nearly as common as their pork counterparts but when cooked properly they can be really great. In this recipe I pair it with a Memphis-style dry rub for added flavor. I serve it with grilled corn with chipotle-lime salt and feta cheese.

They need a long cooking time to fully tenderize and the temperature used to cook them affects the time as well. The most common temperatures are 131ºF (55ºC) for medium-rare, 141ºF (60.6ºC) for more fall-apart medium ribs, and 156ºF (68.8ºC) for a traditional braise-like rib. The first two require 2 to 3 days, while the hotter cook only takes 1 to 2 days. I prefer the 141ºF (60.5) temperature for 48 to 60 hours, it results in really tender meat that isn't overcooked.

Ingredients

For the Ribs

3-4 pounds beef ribs (1350g to 1800g)

3 teaspoons brown sugar

3 teaspoons paprika

2 teaspoons garlic powder

1 teaspoon freshly ground black pepper

1 teaspoon onion powder

1 teaspoon ground cumin

1 teaspoon dried thyme

1 teaspoon celery seeds

½ teaspoon mustard powder

½ teaspoon chipotle chile powder

Salt and pepper

For the Chipotle-Lime Salt

3 tablespoons kosher salt

1 teaspoon chipotle chile powder

2 limes

To Assemble

Cooked corn on the cob

Feta cheese, crumbled

For the Ribs

At least 48 to 60 hours before serving

Preheat a water bath to 141ºF (60.6ºC).

Mix together the spices in a bowl. Lightly salt and pepper the ribs then coat with half of the spice mixture, reserving the rest for use before searing. Place the ribs in a sous vide bag then seal. Cook the ribs for 48 to 60 hours.

For the Chipotle-Lime Salt

At least 60 minutes before serving

Preheat an oven to 250ºF (120ºC).

Combine the salt and chipotle powder in a bowl. Zest the limes over top and mix together. Place on a roasting sheet and bake until the lime zest has dried out.

The chipotle-lime salt will usually last in a sealed container for several weeks.

To Assemble

Remove the ribs from the sous vide bag, and pat dry. Coat the ribs with the reserved spice mixture then sear the ribs until just browned.

Lightly coat the corn with the chipotle-lime salt and place on the plate with the ribs. Sprinkle the feta cheese on the corn and serve.

THICK CUT PASTRAMI REUBENS

Cook: 145ºF (62.8ºC) for 36 to 48 hours • Serves: 6 to 12

I've always been a fan of pastrami and I really enjoy making my own. The process takes awhile but the actual work required is very small. Making your own also allows you to tweak the spices however you want, resulting in a bunch of fun directions you can take the pastrami.

When cooking pastrami, or any cured brisket like corned beef, the time and temperature combinations you can use are widely varied. For this pastrami I really like 145ºF (62.8ºC) for 36 to 48 hours, it creates the more traditional texture of pastrami while still being nice and moist. For a really moist pastrami you can do 135ºF (57.2ºC) for 2 to 3 days, or for a more traditional texture I recommend 156ºF (68.9º) for 12 to 24 hours.

Ingredients

For the Brine
1 gallon water
1 ½ cups salt
1 cup sugar
8 teaspoons pink salt
1 tablespoon pickling spice
½ cup brown sugar
5 garlic cloves, minced
1 tablespoon coriander seeds
1 tablespoon black peppercorns

For the Pastrami
3-4 pounds short ribs, brisket, or
  other tough cut (1350g to
  1800g)

To Assemble
Rye bread, sliced
Swiss cheese slices
About 1 cup thousand island
  dressing
High quality Dijon mustard
Sauerkraut

For the Brine

At least 3 to 5 days before serving
To make the brine combine all the brine ingredients into a pot and bring to a boil. Reduce to a simmer for 5 minutes then remove from the heat and cool.

For the Pastrami

At least 3 to 5 days before serving
Place the brisket in a non-reactive container large enough to hold it. Cover with the cooled brine. Place in the refrigerator for 2 to 3 days, making sure the meat stays submerged the entire time.

Take your brisket out of the brine and smoke it. There are three normal methods for adding smoke to the pastrami, use whichever method you prefer.

1) Use a smoker or grill with wood chips to smoke the meat for a few hours before sous viding.

2) Grill the short rib meat quickly over on a hot grill to capture some smoke and charcoal flavor.

3) When sealing the meat in the sous vide bag add Liquid Smoke to it.

Once you have added the smoke to your short rib meat preheat your sous vide water bath to 137°F.

Seal the meat in a sous vide bag and place the bag into your water bath. Let it cook for 36 to 48 hours.

To Assemble

Remove the pastrami from the sous vide bag and slice thinly.

Brush one side of the bread slices with olive oil and toast them until browned. Place the cheese on the un-toasted side of the bread and toast in an oven or toaster oven with the broiler on until the cheese melts.

Add the thousand island dressing to half of the slices and the mustard to the other half. Pile the pastrami on the slices with the mustard and top with the sauerkraut. Place the two halves together and serve.

Rogan Josh Spiced Lamb Loin

Cook: 131°F (55°C) for 2 to 4 hours • Serves: 4 to 8

Rogan Josh is a classic lamb dish from Kashmir, India, and one of my favorite Indian dishes. In this recipe I take the spices normally used in it to create a rub for the lamb loin, creating a quick-to-make weekday meal. The herbs in the salad help to add some brightness to counteract the richness and flavor of the Rogan Josh spiced loin.

Lamb loin is already very tender so it just needs to be heated through. I prefer my lamb medium-rare so I tend to cook it at 131°F to 135°F (55°C to 57.2°C) but if you cook it for 3 hours or less you can go a little bit lower for a rare lamb loin.

Ingredients

For the Lamb Loin

2-3 pound lamb loin (900g to 1350g)

1 tablespoon garlic powder

2 teaspoons paprika

1 teaspoon ground coriander

½ teaspoon ground cloves

½ teaspoon ground cinnamon

¼ teaspoon ancho chile powder, or chile powder of your choice

¼ teaspoon cayenne chile powder, or chile powder of your choice

1 bay leaf

Salt and pepper

For the Herb Salad

½ cup chopped mint

¼ cup chopped dill

1 cup arugula

1 cup coarsely chopped frisée lettuce

To Assemble

Lemon

Olive oil

For the Lamb Loin

At least 2 to 4 hours before serving

Preheat a water bath to 131°F (55°C).

Mix together the spices in a bowl. Salt and pepper the lamb and then coat it with the spices. Place the lamb in a sous vide bag with the bay leaf then seal. Cook for 2 to 4 hours.

For the Herb Salad

10 minutes before serving

Toss the mint, dill, arugula and frisee together in a bowl.

To Assemble

Remove the cooked lamb from the sous vide bag and pat dry. Sear over high heat until just browned. Cut into ½" to 1" (13mm to 25mm) slices.

Place a slice of lamb on a plate. Top with the herb salad. Squeeze some fresh lemon juice over the top and drizzle with olive oil then serve.

RACK OF LAMB WITH QUINOA-MINT SALAD

Cook: 131°F (55°C) for 2 to 4 hours • Serves: 4 to 8

Lamb ribs are tender already so they just need to be heated through, usually 2 to 4 hours, depending on the thickness of them. After sous viding I cover them with a sweet honey-lemon glaze before searing them. Then I serve them with a quinoa-mint salad with some cucumber and red onion.

Ingredients

For the Rack of Lamb
2 racks of lamb
2 teaspoons dried oregano
2 teaspoons garlic powder
2 teaspoons smoked paprika
1 teaspoon ground coriander
1 teaspoons ground cumin
Salt and pepper

For the Quinoa-Mint Salad
3 cups cooked quinoa
3 tablespoons chopped mint
2 cups roughly chopped
   watercress
½ cucumber, diced
½ red onion, diced
2 tablespoons lemon juice
¼ cup olive oil
Salt and pepper

For the Honey-Lemon Glaze
3 tablespoons honey
1 tablespoon lemon juice
3 garlic cloves, minced

To Assemble
Fresh oregano, chopped
Smoked Maldon salt
Olive oil

For the Rack of Lamb

At least 2 to 4 hours before serving
Preheat a water bath to 131°F (55°C).

Mix together the spices in a bowl. Salt and pepper the rack of lamb and then coat it with the spices. Place the lamb in a sous vide bag then seal. Cook for 2 to 4 hours.

For the Quinoa-Mint Salad

20 minutes before serving
Combine the quinoa, mint, watercress, cucumber, and red onion in a bowl and toss to combine. Whisk the lemon juice and olive oil together then drizzle over the quinoa mixture. Salt and pepper to taste.

For the Honey-Lemon Glaze

At least 15 minutes before serving
Combine all the ingredients in a bowl and whisk together. The glaze can be made several hours ahead of time.

To Assemble

Remove the lamb from the sous vide bag and pat dry. Brush some glaze on the rack of lamb and either grill or sear under the broiler for 60 seconds. Turn the ribs, brush with glaze, and cook for 60 seconds. Repeat again on both sides then remove from the heat. Slice the rack of lamb into individual ribs.

Place a few spoonfuls of the quinoa salad on a plate. Add several lamb ribs to the top of the salad. Add some fresh oregano, sprinkle with the smoked salt, and drizzle with the olive oil then serve.

Modernist Notes
The vinaigrette for the Quinoa-Mint Salad can be thickened and made more clingy by blending in 0.1% xanthan gum when the lemon juice and olive oil are combined.

PORK

There are two ways to cook pork, to a tender, pork chop-like consistency or to a traditional braise-like texture. The time and temperature you use will depend on your desired texture. Many people like to brine their pork before sous viding it since it helps add even more moisture and flavor to the meat.

Tender, Pork Chop-Like Texture

For a chewier texture similar to traditional pork chops, a lower temperature will be used. Typically pork is cooked anywhere between 136°F to 149°F (57.8°C to 65°C), which ranges from medium rare to medium well. My go-to temperature is 140°F (60°C) because it's a nice mix of tender and moist but most of the pink is now gone.

The time needed to cook the pork will depending on the specific cut and the temperature used. For tender cuts, they just need to be "heated through". The amount of time needed to do this will depend on the temperature and the thickness of the pork. There are specific times in the "Sous Vide Thickness Times" chapter but in general a piece of pork ½" (13mm) thick will be done in 20 minutes, a 1" (25mm) piece will take 50 minutes, a 1.5" (38mm) piece will take 1:45 and a 2" (50mm) piece will take 3 hours.

Tougher cuts will need to be cooked for longer periods of time, up to several days for a cut like pork shoulder. I give specific recommendations in the recipes as well as the "Sous Vide Time and Temperature" chapter.

Fall-Apart, Braise-Like Texture

For a more braise-like texture pork needs to be cooked at higher temperatures. These range from 145°F to 180°F (62.8°C to 82.2°C) and the pork is usually cooked for at least 12 hours and sometimes up to several days. I usually cook my pork somewhere in between, around 156°F to 165°F (68.8°C to 73.9°C) for about 18 to 24 hours. I give more recommendations for specific cuts in the recipes as well as the "Sous Vide Time and Temperature" chapter.

HONEY-CHIPOTLE GLAZED COUNTRY STYLE RIBS

Cook: 140°F (60°C) for 24 hours • Serves: 4 to 8

Country style ribs are very similar to pork shoulder, and are sometimes cut directly from it. They are a rich and fatty cut that holds up well to strong BBQ sauces. I like to serve them glazed in a simple honey-chipotle sauce served alongside corn slathered in a sweet honey butter.

Country style ribs are usually cooked for 8 to 24 hours, depending on how tender you want them, and the temperature ranges from 140°F to 180°F (60°C to 82.2°C). Some common time and temperature combinations are 24 hours at 140°F (60°C) for a tender, meaty rib; 12 hours at 176°F (80°C) results in fall-apart ribs; and 12 hours at 156°F (68.8°C) lands in between the two extremes.

Ingredients

For the Country Style Ribs
2-3 pounds country style ribs (900g to 1350g)
2 teaspoons ground coriander
2 teaspoons smoked paprika
1 teaspoon ground cumin
1 teaspoon mustard powder
1 teaspoon ancho chile powder
Salt and pepper

For the Honey-Chipotle Glaze
1 ½ cups water
2-4 chipotles in adobo sauce
½ cup honey
1 tablespoon molasses
1 tablespoon liquid smoke
1 tablespoon Worcester sauce
1 tablespoons paprika
1 teaspoon mustard powder
2 teaspoons ground coriander
1 teaspoon ground cumin

For the Honey Butter
½ stick butter, softened at room temperature
3 tablespoons honey
1 tablespoon finely chopped parsley
⅛ teaspoon freshly ground black pepper

To Assemble
Fresh parsley, chopped
Orange zest
Corn on the cob, cooked

For the Country Style Ribs

At least 24 hours before serving
Preheat a water bath to 140ºF (60ºC).

Mix together the spices in a bowl. Salt and pepper the country style ribs and then coat them with the spices. Place the pork in a sous vide bag then seal. Cook the pork for 24 hours.

For the Honey-Chipotle Glaze

At least 20 minutes before serving
Blend all of the ingredients together then bring to a boil. Let simmer for 10 minutes while stirring occasionally. Remove from the heat

The honey-chipotle glaze can be stored in the refrigerator for about a week.

For the Honey Butter

At least 20 minutes before serving
To make the butter place all of the ingredients in a bowl and mix and mash thoroughly using a fork. The butter will last in the refrigerator for several days or in the freezer for a month.

To Assemble

Preheat a grill to high heat or the broiler in the oven.

Remove the ribs from the sous vide bag and pat dry. Brush the country style ribs with the honey-chipotle glaze and sear them on the first side for a minute. Brush the glaze on the side facing up and turn the ribs. Repeat several times until it is coated with the glaze, cooking about 30 to 60 seconds per turn. Remove from the heat, brush once more with the glaze, and place on a plate.

Add the corn to the plate, sprinkle with the parsley and orange zest then serve.

Modernist Notes

Once you remove the honey-chipotle glaze from the heat you can blend in 0.2% xanthan gum, about 1 gram. This will thicken the sauce and it will better coat the country style ribs.

CUBAN PORK CHOPS WITH FRIJOLES NEGROS

Cook: 140°F (60°C) for 2 to 3 hours • Serves: 4 to 8

Pork chops are a staple around my house and I almost always cook them sous vide. Using sous vide allows me to cook them at a lower temperature than using traditional methods, resulting in a moist and tender chop. This sauce, a homemade Cuban-style mojo sauce, is one of my favorites. Traditionally it would use sour orange juice but a half lime juice and half orange juice mixture is a good approximation and much easier to find. I serve the pork with frijoles negros, a classic side of black beans over rice.

Pork chops are tender cuts and just have to be heated long enough to heat them through and pasteurize them, about 2 to 3 hours depending on the thickness. They can be cooked at many different temperatures, depending on what your preference is. The normal range is from 136°F to 149°F (57.7°C to 65°C) and ranges from medium rare to medium well. I usually cook mine at 140°F (60°C), it's still very tender but most of the pink is now gone.

Ingredients

For the Pork Chops
Salt and pepper
1-2 pounds pork chops (450g to 900g)
1 tablespoon garlic powder
1 tablespoon ground cumin
2 teaspoons dried oregano
2 teaspoons onion powder

For the Mojo Sauce
3 tablespoons olive oil
8 garlic cloves, minced
⅓ cup orange juice
⅓ cup lime juice
1 teaspoon ground cumin
1 tablespoon chopped oregano
Salt and pepper

For the Frijoles Negros
Olive oil
1 medium onion, diced
1 green pepper, diced
4 garlic cloves, minced
2 cups cooked black beans
1 tablespoon dried oregano
1 teaspoon ground cumin
Salt and pepper

To Assemble
Cooked white rice
Fresh oregano, chopped

For the Pork Chops

At least 2 to 3 hours before serving
Preheat a water bath to 140°F (60°C).

Mix together the spices in a bowl. Salt and pepper the pork and then coat it with the spices. Place the pork in a sous vide bag then seal. Cook the pork for 2 to 3 hours.

For the Mojo Sauce

At least 20 minutes before serving
To prepare the mojo sauce heat the olive oil and garlic in a pan over medium-high heat. Cook until the garlic begins to soften, about 1 minute, then add the orange juice, lime juice and cumin. Bring to a simmer then stir in the oregano and remove from the heat.

For the Frijoles Negros

At least 30 minutes before serving
Heat the oil over medium to medium-high heat. Add the onion and green pepper and cook until soften. Add the garlic and cook for 1 minute. Add the beans, oregano, and cumin and cook for 10 minutes for the flavors to meld. Salt and pepper to taste. Keep warm until ready to serve.

To Assemble

Preheat a grill to high heat or the broiler in the oven.

Take the pork out of the bag and pat dry. Sear them on the grill until grill marks form on the first side, a couple of minutes. Brush the mojo on the side facing up and flip the chops. Repeat several times until they are coated with the mojo, cooking about 30 to 45 seconds per turn. Remove from the heat and place on a plate.

Place a spoonful of white rice on the plate. Top with the black beans. Sprinkle with oregano and serve with any excess mojo sauce on the side.

Modernist Notes

A whipping siphon can easily turn the mojo sauce into a froth for a fancier presentation. Make double the sauce you normally would and set half of it aside to glaze the pork with.

Take the other half of the mojo sauce and blend it very well, then strain it. Add 0.3% xanthan gum to the strained mojo sauce and blend to combine. Pour into a whipping siphon, seal and charge it. Dispense the mojo froth onto the pork when serving.

BOURBON GLAZED TENDERLOIN WITH PEA PESTO

Cook: 140°F (60°C) for 3 to 6 hours • Serves: 4 to 8

This bourbon glaze is probably my most popular recipe and definitely the one people mention to me the most. It's a great combination of sweet, sour, and smoky with nice bourbon background notes. It lightly coats the pork, adding rich flavors without being overpowering.

As the name suggests, pork tenderloin is a very tender cut but it also dries out quickly. This is one reason why sous vide is so ideal, keeping the tenderloin moist throughout the entire cooking process. The meat just needs to be cooked long enough to heat it through and, if you want, pasteurize it. This takes 3 to 4 hours for a normal sized tenderloin, though going a few extra hours won't hurt it. I usually cook my pork tenderloin at 140°F (60°C) to maximize the tenderness. It also gives me a little extra time to sear the outside before it affects the middle.

Ingredients

For the Pork Tenderloin
1-2 pounds pork tenderloin
 (450g to 900g)
1 teaspoon dried sage
1 teaspoon ground allspice
½ teaspoon ginger powder
Salt and pepper

For the Bourbon Glaze
1 cup bourbon whiskey
½ cup brown sugar
½ cup ketchup
2 teaspoons Worcester sauce
1 teaspoon liquid smoke
¼ cup apple juice
1 tablespoon lemon juice
1 teaspoon minced garlic
½ teaspoon cayenne chile
 powder
¼ teaspoon mustard powder
Salt and pepper

For the Pea Pesto
2 cups frozen peas
1 cup packed fresh spinach
½ cup pecans
¼ cup water
2 garlic cloves, roughly
 chopped
8-12 mint leaves
½ cup olive oil
3 tablespoons parmesan cheese
Salt and pepper

To Assemble
Basil leaves
Carrot, cut into batons

For the Pork Tenderloin

At least 3 to 6 hours before serving
Preheat a water bath to 140ºF (60ºC).

Mix together the spices in a bowl. Salt and pepper the pork then coat it with the spices. Place the pork in a sous vide bag then seal. Cook the pork for 3 to 6 hours.

For the Bourbon Glaze

At least 40 minutes before serving
To prepare the glaze mix together all of the ingredients in a pot over medium-high heat and bring to a simmer, stirring occasionally. Cook for about 30 minutes, until it thickens. The glaze can be stored in the refrigerator overnight.

For the Pea Pesto

At least 30 minutes before serving
To make the pesto put the peas, spinach, pecans, water, garlic, and mint into a food processor or blender and process until well mixed. Add the olive oil and process until it is all incorporated. Stir in the parmesan cheese and season to taste. The pea pesto can be made a few hours ahead of serving and the flavors will develop over time.

To Assemble

Preheat a grill to high heat or the broiler in the oven.

Remove the pork from the sous vide bag and pat dry. Brush the tenderloin with the glaze and sear it on the first side for a couple of minutes. Brush the glaze on the side facing up and turn the tenderloin. Repeat several times until it is coated with the glaze, cooking about 30 to 60 seconds per turn. Remove from the heat, brush once more with the glaze, slice into 1" (25mm) rounds.

Place a scoop of the pea puree on the plate. Add a round or two of the pork. Top with some of the bourbon glaze, carrot batons, and the basil then serve.

Modernist Notes

I love the flavor of the bourbon glaze and I like to thicken it up using agar. Make 1.5 times the bourbon glaze the recipe calls for and set one half aside to use as the glaze. To the other half blend in 0.5% agar, about 1.2 grams. Bring to a boil and let simmer for 3 to 5 minutes. Remove from the heat, pour into a container, and let set. Once fully set, puree the gel until smooth.

PULLED PORK WITH PINEAPPLE CHUTNEY

Cook: 156°F (68.8°C) for 18 to 24 hours • Serves: 12 to 20

Pulled pork is usually made using the pork butt, sometimes called the pork shoulder or Boston Butt, and is cooked over low heat, usually in a smoker, for several hours. There are lots of options when making a traditional-style pulled pork with sous vide, it's best to experiment and see which one you prefer. Here's some guidelines to help you out.

For times, the longer you cook it, the more tender the meat becomes and the more it breaks down. At higher temperatures you don't have to cook it as long because the meat breaks down faster. Most pork shoulders are cooked for 18 or more hours, but if the temperature is above 170°F(76.7) or so then you can get away with shorter times.

Smoked pulled pork is traditionally done at around 190°F to 200°F (87.8°C to 93.3°C). With sous vide you can easily cook at lower temperatures but I recommend over 155°F (68.3°C) for traditional pulled pork otherwise the fat doesn't break down much. The higher the temperature, the more fat will be rendered but the dryer the meat will be.

My favorite combination is probably 156°F (68.8°C) for around 18 to 24 hours, it's shreddable but not over-tender. Some other popular combinations are 165°F (73.9) for 18 to 24 hours or 176°F (80°C) for 12 hours.

Ingredients

For the Pulled Pork

4 to 5 pounds pork shoulder
   (1800g to 2250g)

3 teaspoons paprika

2 teaspoons ancho chile powder

2 teaspoons ground coriander

2 teaspoons ground cumin

½ teaspoon freshly ground black
   pepper

5 sprigs thyme

For the Pineapple Chutney

1 pineapple, skinned and diced

2 serrano chiles, minced

2 tablespoons lime juice

¼ cup olive oil

Salt and pepper

¼ cup chopped cilantro

To Assemble

Cucumber, sliced

Carrots, thinly sliced

Cherry tomatoes, quartered

Parsley leaves

For the Pulled Pork

At least 18 to 24 hours before serving

Preheat a water bath to 156ºF (68.8ºC).

If the pork shoulder is too large to fit into a bag, cut it into multiple pieces. Mix the spices together in a bowl then coat the pork with them. Place the pork in a sous vide bag with the thyme then seal. Cook the pork for 18 to 24 hours.

For the Pineapple Chutney

At least 75 minutes before serving

Combine a third of the pineapple and half the serrano chile with all the lime juice and olive oil. Blend until the pineapple is broken down and the mixture is smooth. Salt and pepper to taste. Place the remaining ingredients in a bowl and pour the blended pineapple over the top and mix well. The chutney is better if it sits for at least an hour and can last in the fridge for a few days.

To Assemble

Remove the pork from the sous vide bag and pat dry. Shred the pork with a fork and tongs then lightly salt it. Make a pile of the pulled pork and top with the pineapple chutney then serve.

Modernist Notes

When making the pineapple chutney I usually add 0.15% xanthan gum, about 0.4 grams, during the initial blending step. This helps make the sauce richer and bind together.

St. Louis Ribs with Bourbon BBQ Sauce

Cook: 156°F (68.8°C) for 8 to 12 hours • Serves: 4 to 8

Rich, smoky, and tender... ribs are such a fantastic food! I especially love St. Louis style, with its sticky, sweet sauce that clings to the ribs. This recipe combines my favorite BBQ sauce with excellent sous vide ribs for a delicious dish that people will be talking about for days.

Ribs are traditionally smoked until tender, but that often isn't practical due to time or location constraints. When cooking with sous vide the smoke flavor has to be introduced through other means. Briefly smoking the meat before sous viding it, using liquid smoke or pre-smoked ingredients like paprika, or a final run through a smoker at the end are the most common methods.

There are many different suggestions for how long and what temperature to cook ribs. It can be confusing but the time and temperature combination you want to use depends on how you'd like your final ribs to turn out. The hotter the temperature, the faster they cook and the more they tenderize. The amount of time you cook them for determines how tender they end up. These time and temperature combinations work for most kinds of pork ribs, including St. Louis cut, baby back, back, and spare ribs.

If you prefer traditional-style ribs, then cooking them at 160°F to 167°F (71.1°C to 75°C) for 4 to 10 hours is what you want. These ribs are flaky and falling off the bone. Sous vide them for 4 hours for ribs with a lot of bite to them and for 10 hours for ribs barely hanging on the bone.

For tender ribs that are more pork chop-like you can cook them at 141°F to 149°F (60.6°C to 65°C) for 1 to 2 days. They do not have the texture of traditional ribs but retain a lot more of their moisture.

Cooking the ribs at a temperature in between those two extremes results in firmer, but still flaky, ribs. They don't fall off the bone but they are much closer to traditional ribs. I often cook mine at 156°F (68.8°C) for 8 to 12 hours.

Ingredients

For the Ribs

2 racks St. Louis ribs or baby back ribs

2 teaspoons smoked paprika

2 teaspoons celery salt

2 teaspoons garlic powder

1 teaspoon onion powder

1 teaspoon ancho chile powder

1 teaspoon ground coriander

1 teaspoon ground cumin

½ teaspoon mustard powder

Salt and pepper

For the Bourbon BBQ Sauce

2 cups ketchup

1 cup Bourbon whiskey

½ cup brown sugar

½ cup water

¼ cup balsamic vinegar

3 tablespoons chopped garlic

2 tablespoons ancho chile powder

2 tablespoons liquid smoke

2 tablespoons Worcester sauce

3 teaspoons chipotle chile powder

1 tablespoon molasses

2 tablespoons whole grain mustard

For the Ribs

At least 8 to 12 hours before serving

Preheat a water bath to 156ºF (68.8ºC).

Trim any silver skin or connective tissue from the ribs if you want. Mix the spices together in a bowl. Salt and pepper the ribs then coat with the spice mixture, you may have some spice mixture leftover. Place the ribs into sous vide bags, cutting the racks in half if needed. Seal the bags and then cook for 8 to 12 hours.

For the Bourbon BBQ Sauce

At least 30 minutes before serving

Whisk together all of the ingredients in a pot over medium-high heat and bring to a simmer. Gently simmer for 5 to 10 minutes and then remove from the heat. The sauce will last for several days in the refrigerator.

To Assemble

Preheat a grill to high heat or the broiler in the oven.

Remove the pork from the sous vide bags and pat dry. Brush the ribs with the BBQ sauce and sear them on the first side for a minute. Brush the BBQ sauce on the side facing up and turn the ribs. Repeat several times until it is coated with the glaze, cooking about 30 to 60 seconds per turn. Remove from the heat, brush once more with the glaze, and serve.

PROSCIUTTO-WRAPPED PORK LOIN ROAST

Cook: 140ºF (60ºC) for 3 to 7 hours • Serves: 4 to 8

Pork loin roasts are wonderful to cook. They are full of flavor, are juicy, and are easy to work with. For a decadent meal I like to cook a roast sous vide, wrap it with prosciutto, and quickly sear it under the broiler. Loin roasts are usually very tender so they just need to be heated through, usually 3 to 4 hours works well, but they can go as long as 6 or 7.

I like to serve the prosciutto wrapped pork roast with lemon asparagus. It's a very simple side to fix but it is also very versatile and the acidity of the lemon helps cut the richness from the prosciutto and the roast.

Ingredients

For the Pork Loin Roast
2-3 pounds pork loin roast (900g to 1350g)
Salt and pepper
8 sage leaves
6 sprigs thyme

For the Lemon Asparagus
1 bunch asparagus, tough ends cut off
1 lemon
Salt and pepper
Olive oil

To Assemble
Enough prosciutto to cover the roast, 7 to 10 slices
Fresh parsley, chopped
Fresh oregano, chopped
Lemon zest
Parmesan cheese, for grating

For the Pork Loin Roast

At least 3 to 7 hours before serving
Preheat a water bath to 140ºF (60ºC).

Salt and pepper the pork then place it in a sous vide bag. Add the sage and thyme then seal. Cook the pork for 3 to 7 hours.

For the Lemon Asparagus

35 minutes before serving
Zest the outside of the lemon, reserving it for garnish, then cut the lemon in half.

Bring a pot of salted water to a boil. Add the asparagus and cook until it becomes tender, 5 to 10 minutes depending on the thickness of the asparagus.

Drain the asparagus and place it in a bowl. Salt and pepper the asparagus then squeeze the lemon over the top. Drizzle with olive oil then toss well to combine.

To Assemble

Preheat the broiler in an oven.

Remove the pork from the sous vide bag and pat dry, discarding the herbs. Layer the prosciutto on the pork roast, fully covering it. Cook the prosciutto wrapped roast under the broiler until it begins to brown and sizzle, about 5 minutes. Remove from the heat and slice into 1" (25mm) slabs.

Place a slice of the roast on a plate and add the lemon asparagus. Sprinkle with some oregano, parsley, and lemon zest. Grate some parmesan cheese over the top then serve.

PORK RILLETTES

Cook: 156°F (68.8°C) for 18 to 24 hours • Serves: 12 to 20

Pork rillettes is pork meat simmered in its own fat until it is completely tender and then briefly blended together with the fat. It is great when served on hot, crusty bread or as part of a charcuterie platter and is very similar to a pate.

The most common combination of meat to use is pork shoulder and pork belly, often with some bacon added for flavor. To get a full breakdown of the pork shoulder you want a temperature similar to pulled pork. I prefer 156°F (68.8°C) for 18 to 24 hours.

Once cooked the rillettes can be mashed with a fork, pastry cutter, or food processor, whichever works best for you. I tend to use a food processor because it's faster and helps break up the bacon better. For longer term storage, add a ½" (13mm) layer of pork fat or olive oil on top of the rillettes before refrigerating them, this helps to keep the air out and sometimes they can last several months.

Ingredients

For the Pork Rillettes
1 pound pork shoulder (450g)
⅓ pound bacon, preferably slab
   bacon, cut into cubes
2 teaspoons salt
1 teaspoon black pepper
1 tablespoon thyme leaves
1 tablespoon chopped rosemary
1 tablespoon garlic powder
½ teaspoon mustard seeds
2 bay leaves

To Assemble
2 tablespoons cognac
Salt and pepper

For the Pork Rillettes

At least 24 to 30 hours before serving
Preheat a water bath to 156°F (68.8°C).

Roughly chop the pork shoulder into cubes about 1" (25mm) in size. Combine with the bacon and toss with the spices. Add to sous vide bag with the bay leaves, seal, and place in the water bath for 18 to 24 hours.

To Assemble

Once cooked, remove the pork from the sous vide bag, reserving the fat and juices in the bag. Discard the bay leaves.

Combine the pork and the cognac in a food processor. Add some of the reserved fat and juices then process just until the meat has been chopped slightly and still is chunky. More fat and juices can be added as needed until you have created the texture you want. Salt and pepper to taste, remembering that this will usually be served cold so bolder seasoning is required.

The rillettes can be served warm or cold. If you are serving them cold place the rillettes in small containers, usually glass jars with lids, and refrigerate for several hours, and up to a week, before serving. When serving, let them come up to room temperature first.

SAUSAGE AND GROUND MEATS

The main safety concern to remember with sausages, hamburgers, and other ground meats is that they need to be fully pasteurized. Usually the bacteria only live on the outside of meat which is why medium-rare steak is safe to eat, because the outside is still seared. However, if it's ground, the potentially contaminated outside section of the meat is mixed up with the rest so the whole thing has to be cooked to a pasteurized temperature. With traditional cooking this means cooking ground meats to done or well-done. Using sous vide you can cook the middle to your preferred temperature, pasteurize the meat at lower temperatures than normally available, and prevent overcooking and the bursting of sausages.

As long as the pasteurization is accomplished you can cook them at any temperature you like. You can view all the pasteurization times for the different types of meat in the "Sous Vide Thickness Times" chapter but in general it will take 1 to 2 hours for a 1" (25mm) thick sausage or patty and 2-3 hours for a 1½" (38mm). I usually use temperatures of 135°F to 141°F (57.2°C to 60.6°C) depending on the cut but I give other recommendations for other temperatures in the recipes for a specific cut.

For sausages, be sure to sear them after sous viding them. The sous vide process won't cook the casings and they will be chewy if left un-seared, ruining the sausage. I prefer to grill the sausage, or sometimes pan fry it, those methods seem to brown it most efficiently without bursting the sausage.

When sealing meatballs, hamburgers or other patties use a light vacuum or Ziploc bags since a stronger vacuum can crush and deform them.

BEER BRAT GRINDERS WITH GUINNESS MUSTARD

Cook: 141°F (60.6°C) for 2 to 3 hours • Serves: 6

Beer braised brats are a great summertime BBQ dish. I really like it served with a strongly flavored Guinness mustard on a toasted bun with peppers and onions.

Bratwurst is made from veal, beef, or pork and is great when cooked to 141°F (60.6°C), though you can go a little lower if you prefer. Because the sausage is made up of ground meats, you will want to hold it at temperature long enough to pasteurize the middle of it, usually 2 to 3 hours.

Because the beer is sealed in the bags with the sausage, if you don't have a chambered vacuum sealer I recommend just using Ziploc bags to hold the brats. I prefer to finish the brats by grilling them, but you can sear them any way you want. If you don't grill them, you can roast or pan fry the peppers and onions as well.

Most Guinness mustard recipes just add a few tablespoons of Guinness to store bought mustard, which works fine in a pinch, but this recipe creates the mustard from scratch, filling it full of great Guinness flavor. It needs to be started a day ahead of time and the longer it sits the better it will taste. It will last for several weeks in the refrigerator.

Ingredients

For the Bratwurst
6 links bratwurst
5 ounces beer, preferably a lager

For the Guinness Mustard
¼ cup yellow mustard seeds
¼ cup brown mustard seeds
½ cup malt vinegar
1 cup Guinness
2 tablespoons brown sugar
½ teaspoon ground allspice
¼ teaspoon ginger powder
¼ teaspoon garlic powder
1 teaspoon salt
½ teaspoon black pepper

For the Grilled Onions and Peppers
2 onions
1 red pepper
1 orange pepper
1 poblano pepper
Salt and pepper

To Assemble
6 grinder or hot dog buns
Olive oil

For the Bratwurst

At least 2 to 3 hours before serving
Preheat the water bath to 141ºF (60.6ºC).

Place the bratwurst into the sous vide bag and add the beer. Seal the bag then place in the water bath and cook for 2 to 3 hours.

For the Guinness Mustard

At least 12 hours before serving
Combine the mustard seeds, malt vinegar, and Guinness in a bowl. Cover with plastic wrap and let sit for several hours or preferably overnight.

The next day, add the soaked mustard seeds and their liquid to a blender or food processor. Add the remaining ingredients and process until it is the consistency you desire. The mustard can be refrigerated for several weeks.

For the Grilled Onions and Peppers

40 minutes before serving
Peel the onions and then cut into slices about ½" to ¾" (13mm to 19mm) thick, trying to keep the slices together. You can also thread the onion slices onto a shish-kabob skewer.

Cut the sides off of the peppers, leaving them whole. Salt and pepper the onions and peppers and then drizzle with the canola oil.

Heat a grill to high heat. Add the onions and peppers and cook until they just begin to brown and are cooked through. Remove them from the heat. Once they have cooled enough to handle slice the peppers into ½" (13mm) strips and cut the onions in half.

To Assemble

Remove the bratwurst from their bag and pat them dry. Sear the brats on the grill over high heat, about 1 or 2 minutes per side.

Brush the inside of the buns with oil and then grill briefly until they just start to brown. Remove from the heat then smear some Guinness mustard on the buns, add a bratwurst, and top with the peppers and onions then serve.

Modernist Notes

Adding 0.3 grams of xanthan gum to the Guinness Mustard before blending it helps it hold together better and keep its shape when plating.

ITALIAN SAUSAGE WITH ACORN SQUASH PUREE

Cook: 140°F (60°C) for 2 to 3 hours • Serves: 4 to 8

I really like rich Italian sausage paired with a sweet and spicy maple-acorn squash puree. I first had a roasted acorn squash similar to this at my friend Sean Rielly's house. He's known for his Carolina-style smoked pork shoulders but I really enjoyed the maple and miso-glazed acorn squash he served on the side. I've added some heat with the chipotle powder and turned it into a light puree by blending it with some milk.

The sausage is first sous vided long enough to pasteurize it, typically 2 to 3 hours. It can be cooked at many different temperatures, usually ranging from 136°F to 149°F (57.8°C to 65°C), depending on what your preference is. I usually cook mine at 140°F (60°C), it's still very moist but almost all of the pink is gone. It also gives me a little longer to sear the outside to ensure the casing is no longer chewy.

Ingredients

For the Italian Sausage
8 Sausage links

For the Acorn Squash Puree
3 tablespoons maple syrup
1 tablespoon miso paste
2 tablespoons olive oil
1 teaspoon chipotle chile
     powder
1 acorn squash
Salt and pepper
½ cup milk

To Assemble
Maple syrup
Oregano, chopped
Thyme leaves

For the Italian Sausage

At least 2 to 3 hours before serving
Preheat a water bath to 140ºF (60ºC).

Place the Italian sausage in a sous vide bag then seal. Cook the sausage for 2 to 3 hours.

For the Acorn Squash Puree

At least 60 minutes before serving
Preheat an oven to 400ºF (204ºC). Cover a roasting pan with aluminum foil.

In a large bowl whisk together the maple syrup, miso paste, olive oil, and chipotle powder. Peel, deseed, and chop the acorn squash then toss with the maple syrup mixture. Salt and pepper the squash then place on the roasting pan and cook until tender 35 to 45 minutes.

Once tender, remove the squash from the heat and place in a blender. Add the milk then blend together until a smooth puree forms. Salt and pepper to taste. For a more refined presentation you can run the puree through a chinois or strainer.

To Assemble

Take the sausage out of the sous vide bag and pat dry. Briefly sear them until just browned.

Place a large spoonful of the acorn squash puree on a plate. Top the puree with a sausage link or two. Drizzle some maple syrup around the sides and sprinkle the whole dish with the oregano and thyme.

BACON, PINEAPPLE, AND POBLANO CHEESEBURGER

Cook: 135°F (57.2°C) for 2 to 3 hours • Serves: 4

Hamburgers are one of the few beef preparations that I usually eat cooked past medium-rare because it's the only way to ensure the safety of the food. I do love a good medium-rare burger though and there are more high-quality burger places that take enough care with their beef for it to be safe. Using sous vide allows you to cook the hamburgers long enough to pasteurize them at any temperature you prefer, resulting in moist, tender burgers that are just as safe as traditionally cooked ones.

The temperature you will want to use for your burgers is all up to your personal preference. Some people go as low as possible, using 130°F (54.4°C) as their base temperature. I prefer a slightly more done burger and lean towards 135°F to 139°F (57.2°C to 59.4°C). For a more traditional doneness 141°F to 145°F (60.6°C to 62.8°C) is common. If you are using high quality meat that you've ground yourself and feel safe eating non-pasteurized many people swear by a rare burger at 125°F to 129°F (51.6°C to 53.8°C), just make sure to use safe beef and cook it for less than 2 hours to keep it out of the danger zone.

You can pair your burgers with any toppings that you prefer but I like this take on an Hawaiian-style burger. Combining the beef with smokey bacon, sweet pineapple, and slightly spicy poblano puree. I give you my recipe for making hamburger patties but you can always buy pre-made patties from a high-quality butcher because the sous vide process will pasteurize them.

Ingredients

For the Hamburger Patties
1 pound ground beef (450g)
2 teaspoons ground cumin
2 teaspoons ground coriander
1 teaspoon paprika
1 teaspoon ancho chile powder
Salt and pepper

For the Poblano Puree
2 poblano peppers, deseeded
    and roughly chopped
½ onion, roughly chopped
3 garlic cloves, roughly
    chopped
2 tablespoons olive oil
Salt and pepper
Water

To Assemble
4 hamburger buns
Canola oil
4 pineapple rings
4 slices cheddar cheese
8 cooked bacon strips

For the Hamburger Patties

At least 2 to 3 hours before serving
Preheat a water bath to 135°F (57.2°C).

Place all the ingredients for the hamburgers into a large bowl. Using your hands mix them together gently until combined. Form the meat into 4 patties of equal size. Place into the sous vide bag in a single layer. Gently seal the bag, being careful not to crush the patties. Place the sous vide bag in the water bath and cook for at least 2 to 3 hours.

For the Poblano Puree

At least 40 minutes before serving
Preheat an oven to 400°F (200°C).

Toss the peppers, onion, and garlic with the olive oil then salt and pepper them. Place on a roasting sheet and cook until just starting to blacken, about 15 to 25 minutes. Remove from the heat.

Puree the roasted vegetables with a blender or food processor until smooth, adding water if needed.

To Assemble

Lightly brush the inside of the buns with canola oil. Place the buns oil-side down on whatever you are using to sear the hamburgers and cook until just toasted, 1 to 3 minutes. Remove from the heat and smear the inside of the top of the bun with the poblano puree.

Sear the pineapple rings with whatever you are using to sear the hamburgers and cook until just browning, 4 to 5 minutes.

Remove the cooked burgers from the sous vide bag and pat dry. Lightly salt the outside then quickly sear it until the meat is just browned. Remove from the heat.

Place the cheese on the patties, you can place them under the broiler or toaster to quickly melt the cheese if needed. Add 2 strips of bacon to each patty then top with a pineapple ring.

Place a bun on the plate, add the burger with the toppings then serve.

SPAGHETTI AND MEATBALLS

Cook: 135ºF (57.2ºC) for 2 to 3 hours • Serves: 4 to 6

Using sous vide to cook meatballs makes it really easy to have a tender inside with a crunch, crispy outside. Cooking them at 135ºF (57.2ºC) leaves the inside moist and medium-rare, though some people prefer it without as much pink so they use 141ºF (60.6ºC). These meatballs need to be cooked just long enough to pasteurize the multiple types of meat in them, 1 to 3 hours depending on the size of the meatballs.

The multiple types of meat in these meatballs add a lot of flavor and depth but you can go with 100% ground beef if you prefer. I prefer a fattier ground beef mix since the fat really adds flavor, if you go with a 90% lean mix they will often turn out a little dry. I deep fry my meatballs to ensure a super-crisp crust but pan frying them works as well. I often make extra meatballs because once they are sous vided you can chill the bags in an ice bath and then store them in the refrigerator for a few days or freeze them for up to 6 months.

Ingredients

For the Meatballs
⅓ pound ground beef (150g)
⅓ pound ground pork (150g)
⅓ pound ground veal (150g)
4 garlic cloves, minced
1 large egg
¼ cup grated parmesan cheese
1 slice of bread, diced
Pepper

For the Marinara Sauce
2 tablespoons olive oil
4 garlic cloves, minced
½ yellow onion, diced
1 red pepper, diced
2 tablespoons tomato paste
7 roma tomatoes, diced
2 tablespoons balsamic vinegar

To Assemble
Canola or vegetable oil, for frying
12 ounces cooked spaghetti, or pasta of your choice (340g)
Parmesan cheese
Fresh basil, chopped
Fresh oregano, chopped

For the Meatballs

At least 2 to 3 hours before serving
Preheat a water bath to 135ºF (57.2ºC).

Place all the ingredients for the meatballs into a large bowl. Using your hands mix them together gently until combined. Form the meat into 1.5" (38mm) balls and place into the sous vide bag. Gently seal the bag, being careful not to crush the meatballs. Place the sous vide bag in the water bath and cook for 2 to 3 hours.

For the Marinara Sauce

At least 40 minutes before serving
Add the olive oil to a pot and heat over medium to medium-high heat. Cook the onion until it begins to soften and turn translucent. Add the garlic and red pepper and cook for 2 to 3 minutes. Add the tomato paste and cook while stirring for 2 minutes. Add the roma tomatoes and their juices, along with the balsamic vinegar and let simmer for several minutes until it thickens and the flavors come together.

To Assemble

Heat several inches (50mm to 100mm) of oil in a big pot to 375ºF (190ºC). Place a wire rack over a baking sheet.

Take the meatballs out of the bag and pat dry. Gently add the meatballs to the oil, working in batches if needed. Let the meatballs cook until the outside is browned and crispy. Remove the meatballs from the oil and set on a wire rack to drain.

Place the cooked spaghetti in individual bowls and top with a spoonful or two of the marinara sauce. Add a meatball or two to each bowl, grate the parmesan cheese on top, and sprinkle the herbs over everything.

CHICKEN SAUSAGE WITH CAPRESE SALAD

Cook: 141°F (60.6°C) for 2 to 4 hours • Serves: 4

Caprese salad is a tasty combination of mozzarella cheese, basil, and fresh tomatoes. I often serve it with chicken sausage to help turn it into a light meal. I also top it with some good balsamic vinegar to add brightness to the dish. I usually just prepare the caprese salad separately but for a more refined presentation I like to slice the ingredients, including the sausage, and stack them into individual servings of salad "towers".

I usually cook my chicken sausage at 141°F (60.6°C) for 2 to 4 hours, ensuring that they are pasteurized and safe to eat. You can go as as low as 136°F (57.8°C) or as high as 147°F (63.9°C) depending on your preferences. Make sure you sear the sausage at the end otherwise the casing can be chewy.

Ingredients

For the Chicken Sausage
8 chicken sausage links

For the Caprese Salad
3 tomatoes
10 ounces (280g) fresh
    mozzarella cheese
1 cup chopped basil leaves
3 tablespoons balsamic vinegar
¼ cup olive oil
Salt and pepper

For the Chicken Sausage

At least 2 to 4 hours before serving
Preheat a water bath to 141°F (60.6°C).

Place the chicken sausage in a single layer in a bag. Seal the bag then cook the chicken sausage for 2 to 4 hours.

For the Caprese Salad

30 minutes before serving
Remove the stems then dice the tomatoes. Dice the mozzarella cheese and combine with the tomatoes. Add the basil leaves, balsamic vinegar, and olive oil then toss to combine. Salt and pepper to taste.

To Assemble

Remove the chicken sausage from the bag, pat dry and sear until the casing has browned slightly.

Place a scoop of the caprese salad on a plate and top with two chicken sausage links then serve.

CHICKEN, TURKEY, AND POULTRY

Chicken, turkey, and other types of poultry work really well with sous vide cooking, especially white meat. It consistently turns out tender and moist. Dark meat can be cooked to a tender, meaty texture or to a shreddable state.

When determining how long and what temperature to cook poultry at there are a few divisions. The first is if it is a bird usually cooked until it is well-done, like chicken and turkey, or one eaten rare or medium-rare like duck or goose. The other division is whether you are cooking white meat or dark meat. It's usually better to cook the types of meat separately as they are ideally cooked at different temperatures.

CHICKEN, TURKEY, AND OTHER "WELL-DONE" POULTRY

When cooking chicken or other birds usually cooked to a "well-done" temperature you want to make sure you cook it long enough to pasteurize it. The times to pasteurize depend on the thickness and the temperature and are listed in the "Sous Vide Thickness Times". Chicken and turkey are also often brined before cooking, though it's not required with sous vide cooking since most of the moisture stays in anyway.

White Meat
I prefer my chicken and turkey breasts cooked at 141ºF (60.6ºC) for 2 to 4 hours. They are safe as low as 136ºF (57.8ºC) but then they are a little too raw-tasting for me. Some people like them as high as 147ºF (63.9ºC) but I find them a little too dry for my taste. I usually don't sear the chicken after sous viding it, it's hard to get any browning without over cooking it. I'll usually just eat it straight from the bag but you can grill or sear it if you prefer that style.

You can view all the pasteurization times in the "Sous Vide Thickness Times" chapter but here are some for 141ºF (60.6ºC), my favorite white meat temperature. A thickness of ½" (13mm) takes 40 minutes, 1" (25mm) takes 1:10 and 1.5" (38mm) takes 2 hours. Those are the minimum times needed to make the chicken safe, but the texture is still good for up to 4 hours or so.

Dark Meat

Dark meat, such as chicken thighs and turkey legs, is usually cooked to either be tender or shreddable. For tender dark meat the temperature used is normally 141°F up to 156°F (60.6°C to 68.9°C) and I personally like 148°F (64.4°C) the best. They just don't need to be tenderized too much, if at all, so the time range is typically 2 to 5 hours, depending on how tender you want the meat.

For shreddable dark meat, the range goes much higher but is often between 160°F to 170°F (71.1°C to 76.7°C). I usually split the difference and use 165°F (73.9°C). They are cooked longer as well to allow for more breakdown, usually for 8 to 12 hours.

DUCK, GOOSE, AND OTHER "MEDIUM-RARE" POULTRY

If you are cooking a bird that you normally would eat at a temperature besides well-done you don't necessarily have to pasteurize it. If you would traditionally feel comfortable eating it at a lower temperature, then you just need to heat it through to the temperature you prefer. Of course, with sous vide you can still pasteurize it at any temperature above 130°F (54.4°C) and that's usually what I do to be on the safe side.

For tender cuts of duck and goose, usually the breast, I normally cook them just enough to heat them through and pasteurize them at a medium-rare temperature. This normally takes 2 to 3 hours for temperatures from 129°F to 135°F (53.8°C to 57.2°C). I tend to use 131°F (55°C) when I cook it.

For tougher cuts like legs and thighs there are more options depending on if you want it shreddable or tender. Shreddable meat is usually cooked at 167°F (75°C) for at least 8 hours and up to 24 hours or for 144°F (62°C) for 18 to 24 for a less fall-apart texture. If you want it to be more tender and not shreddable I recommend dropping the temperature down to 135°F to 141°F (57.2°C to 60.6°C) and cooking it for 5 to 12 hours. Tougher cuts are also often lightly cured in a flavored salt cure for up to 12 hours before cooking them to introduce additional flavors.

CHICKEN PARMIGIANA

Cook: 141°F (60.6°C) for 2 to 4 hours • Serves: 4 to 8

Chicken Parmigiana is one of my favorite dishes and the one I get when go to an Italian restaurant for the first time. I've had the gamut of chicken, from thin and tough to thick and juicy and everything in between. This recipe is pretty much foolproof and results in some of the most tender Chicken Parmigiana I've had.

You can either use full-sized chicken breasts or cut them in half, depending on how thick you like your Chicken Parmigiana, since the breasts are cooked with sous vide they are perfect either way. I stick to 141°F (60.6°C) when cooking the chicken, it keeps them moist while still allowing you a decent amount of time to fry them afterward the sous vide process is done.

Ingredients

For the Chicken
4 chicken breasts
Salt and pepper
½ teaspoon garlic powder
4 sprigs thyme
4 sprigs rosemary

For the Marinara Sauce
2 tablespoons olive oil
4 garlic cloves, minced
½ yellow onion, diced
1 red pepper, diced
2 tablespoons tomato paste
7 roma tomatoes, diced
2 tablespoons balsamic vinegar

For the Coating
¾ cup flour
2 teaspoons salt
1 teaspoon black pepper
2 eggs
¾ cup dried Italian bread
   crumbs
¼ cup grated parmesan cheese
2 tablespoons chopped parsley

To Assemble
½ cup chopped basil
8-10 ¼" slices of fresh mozzarella
   (6mm), or 1 cup shredded
4 tablespoons grated parmesan
   cheese
Fresh oregano, chopped

For the Chicken
At least 3 to 5 hours before serving
Preheat a water bath to 141°F (60.6°C).

Salt and pepper the chicken then sprinkle with the garlic powder. Place in a sous vide bag with the thyme and rosemary and seal. Cook the chicken for 2 to 4 hours.

For the Marinara Sauce
At least 30 minutes before serving
Add the olive oil to a pot and heat over medium to medium-high heat. Cook the onion until it begins to soften and turn translucent. Add the garlic and red pepper and cook for 2 to 3 minutes. Add the tomato paste and cook while stirring for 2 minutes. Add the roma tomatoes and their juices, along with the balsamic vinegar and let simmer for several minutes until it thickens and the flavors come together. The sauce can be made up to several hours ahead of time.

For the Coating
30 minutes before serving, once the chicken is cooked
Set up three stations for the coating. Combine the flour, salt, and pepper on a plate. Beat the eggs into a wide mouth bowl. Combine the bread crumbs, parmesan cheese, and parsley on another plate.

Preheat a pan to medium-high heat.

Remove the chicken from the sous vide bag and pat dry. Dredge the chicken in the flour, then the egg, then the bread crumb mixture.

Add about ½" (13mm) of oil to the pan and heat to about 350°F to 375°F (176°C - 190°C). Sear the dredged chicken breasts until the crust becomes golden brown, flip and repeat on the other side. Remove from the heat and set on a sheet pan.

To Assemble

Preheat the broiler on the oven.

Top each chicken breast with the basil and cover with the mozzarella and parmesan cheeses. Broil in the oven until the cheese is browned and bubbly. Remove from the oven and place the chicken on a plate, add some pasta and top with the marinara sauce. Sprinkle the oregano over everything and serve.

FRIED BUTTERMILK CHICKEN

Cook: 141°F (60.6°C) for 2 to 4 hours • Serves: 4

Chicken that is coated is notoriously difficult to cook properly. It's hard to time the browning of the coating and cooking of the chicken to happen all at the same time. Using sous vide to pre-cook the chicken allows you to focus on the browning of the coating without worrying about the chicken itself.

You can make this recipe with either white or dark meat but it's best to cook the white and dark meat separately if you are using both. If you are using dark meat, see the recipe for Chicken Thighs With Poblano-Cheddar Polenta for time and temperatures.

Ingredients

For the Chicken
4 chicken breasts
4 lemon slices
4 sage leaves
Salt and pepper

For the Fried Chicken
3 cups flour
2 tablespoons garlic powder
2 tablespoons paprika
1 teaspoon chipotle or cayenne
  chile powder
3 cups buttermilk
Canola oil for frying

For the Chicken

At least 3 to 5 hours before serving
Preheat a water bath to 141°F (60.6°C).

Salt and pepper the chicken then place in a bag with a sage leaf and a lemon slice per breast. Seal the bag then cook the chicken for 2 to 4 hours.

For the Fried Chicken

60 minutes before serving, once the chicken is cooked
Set up the batter stations and frying oil.

Combine the flour, garlic powder, paprika, and chipotle powder into a shallow dish and mix thoroughly. Pour the buttermilk into a separate shallow dish. Fill a deep pot with canola oil to a depth of around 3" (76mm) and heat to 365°F to 375°F (185°C to 190°C), or use a deep-fryer if you have one. Be sure the oil fills the pot less than halfway since it will expand when the chicken breasts are added.

Remove the chicken from the sous vide bag and pat dry. Working with one at a time, take a breast and dredge it in the flour mixture, then dip it in the buttermilk, and finally dredge it in the flour one more time. Set aside on a plate and repeat for all the chicken breasts.

Add the chicken breasts slowly, one at a time, into the hot oil and cook until the coating is browned and very crunchy. Remove from the oil, sprinkle with salt and pepper, and drain on a wire rack. Once all the chicken is fried it is ready to serve.

CHICKEN WINGS

Cook 150ºF (65.6ºC) for 2 to 5 hours • Makes: 20 to 30 wings

There's many different ways to cook chicken wings but the best methods tend to involve double cooking them. Using sous vide for the first cook makes it very convenient and it easily tenderizes the chicken, leaving the frying process to just crisp the skin. This means the crisping can then be done at a hotter temperature, resulting in a more crispier wing.

This recipe calls for the wings to be cooked at 150ºF (65.6ºC) for 2 to 5 hours but anything between 148ºF to 156ºF (64.4ºC to 68.8ºC) will result in very tender chicken. For dryer, but even more tender, wings you can cook them at 160ºF to 170ºF (71ºC to 76.7ºC) for 4 to 12 hours. After the sous vide process is done you can also chill the wings in an ice bath and store them in the refrigerator or freezer and then fry them just before you want to eat them.

Ingredients

For the Chicken Wings
3 pounds chicken wings (1,350g)
Salt and pepper
Peanut or canola oil

For the Buffalo Sauce
¼ cup butter
¼ cup hot sauce, preferably
    Frank's

To Assemble
Blue cheese, crumbled
Cucumber, cut into sticks
Carrots, cut into sticks
Basil leaves

For the Chicken Wings

At least 2 to 5 hours before serving
Preheat the water bath to 150ºF (65.6ºC).

If using whole wings, cut them into drummettes and wing flats, discarding the tips. Salt and pepper the chicken pieces. Seal them in a sous vide bag and place into the water bath. Cook for 2 to 5 hours. Remove from the sous vide bag, pat dry, and let rest at least an hour.

They can also be stored in the refrigerator or frozen at this point. It is best to deep fry them just before serving.

Heat the oil to 400ºF (204ºC). Set up a drying station with a metal rack set over a sheet pan.

Add the chicken in batches, being sure not to overcrowd the pan. Cook just until the skin is golden brown and crispy, turning if needed. Remove from the heat and set on the metal rack.

For the Buffalo Sauce

At least 30 minutes before serving
Melt the butter in a pot over medium heat then whisk or blend in the hot sauce. It will last in the refrigerator for several days.

To Assemble

Toss the wings with the Buffalo sauce then place in a bowl next to the cucumber and carrots. Top with the blue cheese crumbles and basil leaves then serve.

SHREDDED CHICKEN THIGH ENCHILADAS

Cook: 165°F (73.9°C) for 8 to 12 hours • Serves: 4 to 6

This recipe takes sous vide cooked chicken and combines it with a tomatillo-based verde sauce for excellent enchiladas. The chicken thighs hold up well to the other flavorful components of the enchiladas. These enchiladas are also convenient to prepare because each step can be done ahead of time.

For shredded chicken thighs, they are normally cooked anywhere between 160°F to 170°F (71.1°C to 76.7°C) for 8 to 12 hours. I usually split the difference and use 165°F (73.9°C). Either boneless or bone-in chicken thighs can be used. If there is skin it won't crisp up during the sous vide process but it can be removed and crisped in the oven if desired.

Ingredients

For the Chicken

4 chicken thighs

2 teaspoons garlic powder

2 teaspoons onion powder

2 teaspoons dried oregano

¼ teaspoon chipotle chile
    powder, or chile powder of
    your choice

Salt and pepper

For the Salsa Verde

4 garlic cloves, halved

½ onion, roughly chopped

2 poblano peppers, deseeded
    and destemmed

1 jalapeno pepper, deseeded and
    destemmed

10 tomatillos, destemmed,
    dehusked, and rinsed

1 tablespoon honey

¼ cup coarsely chopped cilantro

To Assemble

12 small corn tortillas

1 12-ounce can black beans

1 cup cooked corn kernels

½ cup shredded mild cheddar
    cheese

1½ cups shredded Monterey
    Jack cheese

2 cups diced tomatoes

Sour cream

For the Chicken

At least 9 to 13 hours hours before serving
Preheat a water bath to 165°F (73.9°C).

Mix the spices together in a small bowl. Salt and pepper
the chicken then sprinkle with the spices. Place in a sous
vide bag and seal. Cook the chicken for 8 to 12 hours.

For the Salsa Verde

At least 40 minutes before serving
Preheat the broiler on your oven.

Place the garlic, onion, poblanos, jalapeno, and
tomatillos on a roasting sheet with raised sides. Salt and
pepper them and drizzle with oil. Cook them until they
begin to soften and brown, 10 to 15 minutes. Remove
the pan from the oven. Scrape the roasted veggies and
their juices into a food processor or blender. Add the
honey and cilantro then process to the consistency you
prefer. Salt and pepper to taste. The salsa verde will last
for several hours or for a few days in the refrigerator

To Assemble

Preheat an oven to 450°F (232°C).

Remove the chicken from the sous vide bag and shred.
Cover the bottom of a baking dish with some of the salsa
verde.

Lay out the tortillas and top each one with the chicken,
beans, corn, and some cheddar cheese. Roll up the
tortillas and place in the baking dish side by side. Top
with the remaining salsa verde and the Monterey Jack
cheese. Place in the oven and bake until they are bubbly
and the cheese is melted, about 10 to 15 minutes.
Remove from the heat, top with the diced tomatoes and
sour cream, then serve.

CHICKEN THIGHS WITH CHILE-CHEDDAR POLENTA

Cook: 148ºF (64.4ºC) for 2 to 5 hours • Serves: 4

Chicken thighs are my favorite part of the chicken to cook. I usually just grill them because they are so forgiving and I love the char the grill adds but sometimes I'm looking for a hands-off meal and I'll turn to my sous vide machine.

When looking for tender chicken thighs, versus shredded thighs, they are usually cooked anywhere from 141ºF up to 156ºF (60.6ºC to 68.8ºC) but I've found them most enjoyable at 148ºF (64.4ºC). I'll usually cook them for 2 to 5 hours, depending on how tender I'd like them and what my plans for the night are.

Ingredients

For the Chicken
4 chicken thighs
Salt and pepper
1 teaspoon garlic powder
1 teaspoon ground coriander
4 sprigs thyme

For the Poblano-Cheddar Polenta
2 tablespoons butter
1 poblano pepper, diced
1 cup milk
2 cups chicken stock
Water as per the directions on
   the polenta package
1 ⅓ cups quick cooking polenta
1 ½ cups shredded sharp white
   cheddar
2 tablespoons chopped cilantro
Salt and pepper

To Assemble
Fresh oregano, chopped
Olive oil

For the Chicken

At least 2 to 5 hours before serving
Preheat a water bath to 148ºF (64.4ºC).

Salt and pepper the chicken thighs then sprinkle with the garlic powder and coriander. Place in a sous vide bag with the thyme and seal. Cook the chicken for 2 to 5 hours.

For the Poblano-Cheddar Polenta

45 minutes before serving
Heat a pot over medium-high heat. Add the butter and melt. Add the poblano pepper and cook for a few minutes until it softens.

Add the milk, chicken stock, and enough water to bring the volume of liquid to the amount called for by the directions on the polenta package. Bring the liquid to a boil and then whisk in the polenta and cook, stirring, until it thickens. Stir in the cheddar cheese and cook until it melts. Remove from the heat and stir in the cilantro then season to taste.

To Assemble

Remove the chicken from the sous vide bag and pat dry. Quickly sear the chicken thighs until just browned.

Place a spoonful of the polenta on a plate and set the chicken thigh in the middle. Sprinkle the fresh oregano on top, drizzle with the olive oil, then serve.

TURKEY BREAST WITH CRANBERRY CHUTNEY

Cook: 141°F (60.6°C) for 2 to 4 hours • Serves: 4 to 8

Turkey is a classic Thanksgiving food but sometimes you don't want to wait until the holiday to enjoy it. This is a great meal anytime and pairs the turkey with a sweet and sour cranberry chutney. The chutney can even be made ahead of time to be used for a quick weeknight meal.

I cook my turkey breasts at 141°F (60.6°C) for 2 to 4 hours but anywhere between 136°F (57.8°C) and 147°F (63.9°C) is common. I'll often skip the searing step after sous viding the turkey to maximize the tenderness of the meat.

Ingredients

For the Turkey Breasts
2 pounds turkey breasts (900g),
   cut into portions
Salt and pepper
1 lemon, sliced
8 sage leaves

For the Cranberry Chutney
12 ounces cranberries (340g)
1 cup orange juice
½ cup water
⅓ cup brown sugar
⅓ white sugar
1 dried ancho pepper
1 tablespoon peeled and grated
   fresh ginger
¼ cup triple sec or Grand
   Marnier
2 teaspoons ground cinnamon
1 teaspoon ground cloves

To Assemble
Sage leaves, chopped
Orange zest

For the Turkey Breasts

At least 2 to 4 hours before serving
Preheat a water bath to 141°F (60.6°C).

Salt and pepper the turkey then place in a sous vide bag. Evenly distribute the lemon slices and sage leaves among the turkey. Seal the bag and cook the turkey for 2 to 4 hours.

For the Cranberry Chutney

At least 45 minutes before serving
Combine the cranberries, orange juice, water, brown sugar, white sugar, ancho pepper, and ginger in a pot. Bring to a simmer and let cook until the cranberries have released their juices, about 10 to 15 minutes. Remove the pot from the heat and discard the ancho pepper.

Add the triple sec, cinnamon, and cloves then blend well. You want the chutney to bind together but still have chunks of cranberry in it.

The cranberry chutney will last for several days in the refrigerator and can be served cold or reheated.

To Assemble

Remove the turkey from the bag and pat dry. Lightly sear the turkey if desired. Place the turkey on the plate and top with the cranberry chutney. Sprinkle the sage leaves and orange zest over the top then serve.

Modernist Notes

I will often add 0.4% xanthan gum, about 1.6 grams, to the chutney when I add the triple sec. It helps to thicken the chutney and hold it all together.

SHREDDED DUCK LEGS WITH SESAME NOODLES

Cook: 167°F (75°C) for 16 to 24 hours • Serves: 4

My wife always orders cold sesame noodles from our local Chinese restaurant so I decided to try and make my own. I found this version to be the most flavorful and the one that I could easily find all the ingredients for at my local supermarket. It's topped with shredded duck legs because they can hold up to the strong flavors of the noodles. You can either eat this dish hot or cold, it's great either way. You can add more or less chile-garlic paste depending on how spicy you want it.

There are a few options when you want to shred duck legs. Many people recommend 167°F (75°C) for at least 8 hours and up to 24 hours. This time and temperature combination also works well for duck confit. Cooking them at 144°F (62.2°C) for 18 to 24 hours is also highly recommended for a less fall-apart texture.

Duck legs can also be lightly cured first to add flavor, which is something I do for this recipe. Just spice the duck legs, cover them with salt and sugar, then let them sit for up to 12 hours.

Ingredients

For the Duck Legs
4 duck legs, about 3 pounds (1350g)
4 cups salt
½ cup sugar
3 tablespoons ground coriander
4 garlic cloves, minced
2 tablespoons orange zest
1 tablespoon ground cloves
1 teaspoon black pepper, coarsely ground
1 bay leaf, crushed

For the Sesame Noodles
12 ounces Chinese egg noodles or soba noodles, (340g)
3 tablespoons sesame oil, preferably dark
3 tablespoons soy sauce
2 tablespoons rice wine vinegar
2 tablespoons sesame paste or tahini
2 tablespoons peanut butter, preferably smooth
2 tablespoons brown sugar
1 tablespoon chile-garlic paste, such as sambal
2 garlic cloves, minced
2 scallions, thinly sliced
1 1" (25mm) piece of ginger, peeled and minced

To Assemble
1 cucumber, julienned
1 carrot, peeled and julienned or grated
1 cup bean sprouts
Fresh cilantro, chopped
Peanuts, roughly chopped
Sesame seeds, preferably toasted

For the Duck Legs
At least 24 to 36 hours before serving
Mix together the salt and sugar in a bowl. In a separate bowl mix together the remaining spices then coat the dug legs with them. Place the duck legs in a plastic bag or non-reactive container and pack the salt and sugar cure evenly around them. Refrigerate for 8 to 12 hours.

Preheat a water bath to 167°F (75°C).

Wash the cure off of the duck legs then place into a sous vide bag and seal. Cook the duck for 16 to 24 hours.

Once cooked, remove the duck from the sous vide bag and pat dry. Sear the duck legs in a hot pan until crispy. Remove the meat from the bones and shred.

For the Sesame Noodles
40 minutes before serving
Bring a pot of water to a boil and then add the noodles. Cook until tender but still slightly firm. Drain the noodles.

Blend together the sesame oil, soy sauce, rice wine vinegar, sesame paste, peanut butter, and brown sugar. Stir in the chile-garlic paste, garlic, scallions, sesame seeds, and ginger. Toss the noodles with the sauce. If serving cold you can let them cool and then refrigerate them at this point.

To Assemble
Place a pile of noodles on a plate or in a bowl. Top with the cucumber, carrots, and sprouts. Add the peanuts then the shredded duck. Sprinkle with the cilantro and sesame seeds, then serve.

Modernist Notes
I usually add 0.15% xanthan gum when I blend together the oil, soy sauce and rice wine vinegar for the noodle sauce. This helps with the mouthfeel of the sauce and it clings to the noodles better.

DUCK BREAST WITH PORT REDUCTION

Cook: 131ºF (55ºC) for 2 to 3 hours • Serves: 4 to 6

Duck has such a strong flavor and it holds up well to bold flavors. I like to combine a duck breast with garlic mushrooms and a port reduction.

Duck is usually sous vided enough to heat it through and pasteurize it at a medium-rare temperature. This normally takes 2 to 3 hours for temperatures from 129ºF to 135ºF (53.8ºC to 57.2ºC). I tend to use 131ºF (55ºC) when I cook it.

Ingredients

For the Duck Breast
2 duck breasts
8 sprigs thyme
Salt and pepper

For the Port Reduction
8 shallots, coarsely chopped
Olive oil
Salt and pepper
3 cups port

For the Garlic Mushrooms
16 ounces mushrooms, cleaned
    and cut to size (450g)
3 tablespoons butter
4 garlic cloves, minced
½ teaspoon fresh thyme leaves
Salt and pepper

To Assemble
Thyme leaves

For the Duck Breast

At least 2 to 3 hours before serving
Preheat a water bath to 131ºF (55ºC).

Salt and pepper the duck breasts then place into a sous vide bag. Add the thyme to the bag and seal. Cook the duck for 2 to 3 hours.

For the Port Reduction

50 minutes before serving
Preheat an oven to 450ºF (232ºC).

Toss the shallots with the olive oil then salt and pepper them. Place them on a sheet pan and cook until they start to brown, 15 to 25 minutes.

Once browned, scrape the shallots into a pot and cover with the port. Cook over medium to medium-high heat until the port is reduced by half, 10 to 20 minutes. Some alcohol will burn off so be sure not to have open flame above the port. Remove from the heat.

For the Garlic Mushrooms

25 minutes before serving
Heat a pan over medium heat.

Add the butter to the pan and let it melt. Add the garlic and let it cook for about 1 minute. Add the mushrooms and thyme and cook until the mushrooms begin to brown, about 5 minutes. Stir the mushrooms and continue cooking until they are tender.

To Assemble

Remove the duck from the sous vide bag and pat dry. Sear the duck in a hot pan with the fat side down until the fat has begun to render and turn crispy. Quickly sear the non-fat side then remove from the heat. Slice the duck breast into ¾" (19mm) slices.

Place some of the mushrooms on a plate and place the slices of duck breast on top. Drizzle the duck with the port reduction, sprinkle with thyme leaves, then serve.

Modernist Notes

For a modernist take I will use a port pudding instead of the port reduction. I also like the fresh taste of un-boiled port so I will only simmer half of it. You also only need 2 cups of port because none is lost through the reduction process.

Blend 1 cup of port with the 2.4 grams of agar (about 0.5% of the total liquid). Add the roasted shallots to the port and agar mixture then bring to a boil. Let simmer for 3 to 5 minutes then blend in a final cup of port. Remove from the heat, pour into a container, and let set.

Once fully set, puree the gel until smooth. If it is too thick you can add some fresh port to it.

EGGS

A whole book could be written on the nuances of sous vide eggs but I've tried to distill the information enough for you to get started enjoying eggs today. Eggs contain three main parts: the yolk, the tight white contained in the membrane, and the loose white outside the membrane. All three parts cook differently, at different temperatures, and at different speeds. This is why there is so much variability to cooking eggs.

Eggs are typically cooked directly in their shells but they can also be removed and cooked in sous vide bags, mason jars, or plastic wrap. The eggs will take on the shape of the container they are in, leading to some fun preparations such as "egg flowers" that use plastic wrap to create fun flower-like shapes.

EGG TEMPERATURES

Even a degree of difference can change the texture of eggs but there is a range that you can use to determine how the eggs will turn out. For a great look at egg temperatures I recommend either the Chef Steps online calculator or the Serious Eats Guide to Sous Vide-Style Eggs, both of which are linked up from: MCMEasy.com/SVEggs.

"Raw" Pasteurized Eggs
From 130°F to 135°F (54.4°C to 57.2°C) the egg will remain "raw" and if it is held at this temperature for at least 75 to 90 minutes it will be fully pasteurized and safe to eat. It can then safely be used in place of raw eggs in preparations such as mayonnaise, cookie dough, or salad dressings.

Soft Boiled and Poached Eggs
The soft boiled or poached range is about 140°F to 145°F (60°C to 62.8°C) and the eggs are cooked for 45 to 60 minutes. For a firmer white without affecting the texture of the yolk the egg can be briefly boiled for 2 to 3 minutes either before or after the sous vide process. This will also help with removing the shell from the eggs.

Eggs cooked at this temperature can be chilled and refrigerator until you need to use them or held at 130°F (54.4°C) without changing the texture.

For a cleaner presentation of poached or soft boiled eggs you can gently crack them into a small bowl and then use a slotted spoon to remove the egg. This will leave the runny loose white behind. The eggs can also be briefly poached in boiling water once they have been removed from the shell for a more traditional poached look.

Semi Hard and Hard Boiled Eggs

At 150°F (65.6°C) the yolk begins to firm up until it becomes crumbly around 165°F (73.9°C). Hard boiled eggs start in the middle of this range, though I still prefer to use the traditional boil in a pot method for them.

SOFT BOILED EGG ON CHEDDAR HASH BROWNS

Cook: 145°F (62.8°C) for 45 minutes • Serves: 4

Soft boiled eggs contain a great combination of firm whites with runny yolks. I especially like them over crispy hash browns covered with melted cheddar cheese. The pre-boil step was first suggested by J. Kenji López-Alt from Serious Eats and it is a great way to maintain the traditional firmer egg white texture while still taking advantage of the benefits of the sous vide process. I like to cook them at 145°F (62.8°C) but you can go a few degrees higher or lower depending on the consistency you prefer for egg yolks.

Ingredients

For the Eggs
4 Eggs

For the Cheddar Hash Browns
4 red potatoes
4 strips bacon, cut into batons
Cheddar cheese, grated
Salt and pepper

To Assemble
Ground paprika

For the Eggs

50 to 60 minutes before serving
Preheat a water bath to 145°F (62.8°C). Bring a pot of water to a boil. Prepare a ice bath with ½ ice and ½ water.

Gently place the eggs in the boiling water and cook for 3 minutes. Remove from the water and place in the ice bath for 1 to 2 minutes then transfer to the water bath. Let the eggs cook for 45 minutes. Once cooked, remove from the water bath.

For the Cheddar Hash Browns

At least 30 to 40 minutes before serving
Clean the potatoes then grate using a cheese grater.

Heat the bacon in a pan over medium heat until the fat has rendered and the bacon is crispy, 15 to 20 minutes. Remove and discard all but about 1 tablespoon of the bacon fat.

Add the grated potatoes to the pan and mix well with the bacon. Salt and pepper to taste. Spread into a thin layer, about ½" to 1" (13mm to 25 mm) thick, pressing down on the potatoes. Let sit until the bottom begins to brown, 5 to 10 minutes.

Turn the heat to medium-high then flip the hash browns. It is ok if the hash browns break apart some during the flipping process, just be sure all the pieces have been flipped at the end. Let cook until the bottom is crispy and browned. Flip the hash browns a final time and top with the grated cheese. Cover the pan and let the cheese melt, then remove from the heat.

To Assemble

Place the hash browns on a plate then crack a soft boiled egg on top. Sprinkle with the paprika then serve.

FRENCH-STYLE SCRAMBLED EGGS

Cook: 165°F (73.9°C) for 15 to 20 minutes • Serves: 2 to 4

French style scrambled eggs are a creamy, almost custard like style of scrambled egg, a lot different than the sometimes rubbery American style ones. With sous vide they are easy to make and come out super creamy.

Just whisk together some eggs with salt, pepper, and cheese then pour into a Ziploc bag (or lightly seal in a vacuum bag). Cook them at 165°F (73.9°C) until they firm up, massaging them every 5 to 10 minutes. They should be done in 15 to 20 minutes. You can vary the herbs, spices, and garnishes you use to take the eggs in several different directions.

Ingredients

For the Eggs
4 Eggs
2 tablespoons unsalted butter
2 tablespoons heavy cream
2 tablespoons parmesan cheese
Salt and pepper

To Assemble
3 pieces of cooked bacon, cut
    into lardons
Basil leaves, cut into strips
Parmesan cheese, for grating

For the Eggs

At least 15 to 20 minutes before serving
Preheat a water bath to 165ºF (73.9ºC).

Beat together the eggs, cream, salt and pepper until mixed well. Grate a few tablespoons of the cheese into the scrambled egg mixture then pour the mixture into a Ziploc bag or sous vide bag, add the butter, and seal.

Every 5 to 10 minutes, remove the sous vide bag from the water and lightly massage the eggs to break them up. Once they are fully cooked, about 15 to 20 minutes, remove them from the heat.

To Assemble

Pour the scrambled eggs into bowls, top with the bacon and basil then grate some parmesan cheese on top.

13 MINUTE EGG ON WILTED SPINACH SALAD

Cook: 167ºF (75ºC) for 13 minutes • Serves: 4

The 13 minute egg is one of the most popular ways to cook eggs because it's easy, fast, and the results are really great. I first heard of the 13 minute eggs from *Ideas in Food* but many other chefs use this technique as well. The timing in this recipe is critical because of the high heat, it's one of the rare sous vide recipes where you are not trying to bring the food up to the temperature of the water bath. The high temperature cooks the whites of the egg much more than the yolks, leaving a runny yolk with a firmer white.

Ingredients

For the Eggs
4 Eggs

For the Wilted Spinach Salad
8 cups baby spinach
4 strips bacon, cut into batons
2 shallots, diced
4 garlic cloves, minced
3 tablespoons lemon juice

To Assemble
Basil, minced
Parmesan cheese for grating
Lemon quarters

For the Eggs
15 to 20 minutes before serving
Preheat a water bath to 167ºF (75ºC).

Gently place the eggs in the water bath and let cook for 13 minutes. Once cooked, remove from the water bath and set aside.

For the Wilted Spinach Salad
At least 30 to 40 minutes before serving
Place the spinach in a bowl and set aside.

Heat the bacon over medium heat until the fat has rendered and the bacon is crispy, 15 to 20 minutes. Remove and discard all but about 1 tablespoon of the bacon fat. Add the shallots and garlic, cook until the shallots turn translucent, 3 to 5 minutes. Stir in the lemon juice then pour the mixture over the spinach and toss well to combine. Salt and pepper to taste.

To Assemble
Place some spinach in a bowl, leaving an indentation at the top to hold the egg. Crack a 13 minute egg over the top of the spinach, sprinkle with the basil, then grate the parmesan cheese on top. Squeeze some lemon juice over the dish then serve.

CHOCOLATE CHIP COOKIE DOUGH BALLS

Cook: 135ºF (57.2ºC) for 75 minutes • Serves: 25 to 40 servings

I love eating raw cookie dough, maybe even more than baked cookies! Of course, there's always the nagging issue of eating the raw eggs in it. Luckily we can use sous vide to fully pasteurize the eggs, rendering them completely safe to eat. The white will solidify slightly, but once you mix up the dough it will blend in perfectly. I've provided a cookie dough recipe for you to follow, but if you have a favorite of your own feel free to use that instead.

Ingredients

For the Pasteurized Egg
1 large egg, still in the shell

For the Cookie Dough
⅔ cup butter, slightly softened
½ cup white sugar
½ cup brown sugar
1 teaspoon vanilla extract
1 teaspoon salt
1 pasteurized egg
1½ cups flour
5 ounces chocolate chips (150g)

For the Pasteurized Egg

At least 2 hours before serving
Pre-heat a water bath to 135ºF (57.2ºC).

Place the egg in the water bath and cook for 75 minutes. Remove and let cool.

For the Cookie Dough

At least 15 minutes before serving
Combine the butter, white sugar, brown sugar, vanilla, salt, and pasteurized egg and mix well to combine, preferably with a hand mixer or standing mixer. Stir in the flour until it is completely combined. Add the chocolate chips and fold them into the dough

To Assemble

Roll the dough into small balls and serve in a bowl or on a plate. You can also serve them as a topping on ice cream or brownies. They will last in the refrigerator for several days.

FISH AND SHELLFISH

Fish and shellfish are two of the most subjective and variable items to cook, whether using traditional methods or sous vide. Some people love tender, rare fish, others want it hard and flaky, and people have preferences through that spectrum. Some people also can get fresh fish from a few miles away, others only have access to imported grocery store-quality fish. All these factors play into how you want to cook your fish.

FISH TIME AND TEMPERATURES

In general, fish is much more time sensitive than steak. You can cook fish to a set temperature, or set it at a higher temperature and cook until the core temperature reaches the point you'd like. The doneness ranges from raw sushi to lightly heated mi-cuit up through flaky, fully cooked fish. The time and temperature you use will depend on the preparation you are after, your own personal preference, and the quality of seafood you are using.

Almost all fish, and most shellfish, just need to be heated through and extra cooking will just start to turn them to mush. There are specific times in the "Sous Vide Thickness Times" chapter but in general fish is cooked through in 20 minutes when it is ½" thick (13mm) and 50 minutes when it is 1" (25mm) thick. Be sure to use sashimi or sushi grade fish unless you are cooking it above 131°F (55°C) for an extended time and not serving it to immunodeficient people. Most sous vide fish is not pasteurized, just like most traditionally cooked fish.

For raw or just-cooked fish the temperatures range from a low of about 104°F (40°C) up to about 110°F (43.3°C). Above that temperature the fish begins to take on a meaty, slightly cooked texture that becomes more pronounced as the temperature increases up to about 120°F (48.9°C). From there the fish begins to become more and more flaky until topping out around 141°F (60.6°C).

In this chapter I've given several time and temperatures for specific fish and in this introduction I explain the differences between the various temperatures and their effect on fish. You should try to use the ones that will make the fish most similar to what you or your guests prefer. If you don't like just-cooked fish then bump the temperature of the "Halibut with Honey Roasted Beets" up to 135°F (57.2°C) instead of the recommended 114°F (45.6°C).

PREPPING FISH FOR SOUS VIDE

Many types of fish benefit from a quick brine in a 5% salt solution. This helps firm the flesh as well as pull out the albumin for a cleaner finished dish. The fish can also be lightly coated in salt, wrapped in plastic wrap, and refrigerated for 4 to 8 hours to achieve the same benefits through the light curing processes.

Be careful when vacuum sealing fish because stronger vacuums can crush the fish and change the texture of the meat. I usually use Ziploc bags when I'm cooking fish to ensure the sealing doesn't affect the texture.

Always portion the fish before cooking it. Sous vided fish is typically very delicate and can be hard to handle. Cutting it into portions ahead of time and minimizing post-sous vide handling helps the fish hold together.

If you are cooking fish with skin it is usually best to remove the skin and cook it separately. It can be pan fried, baked at 300°F (148°C), or even cooked on a sheet of aluminum foil sprayed with Pam and placed in the oven or toaster oven.

FINISHING SOUS VIDE FISH

Many types of fish do not require a post-sous vide sear, though it does help make them more appealing. I often only sear one side to keep the middle the correct temperature. When searing, a very quick sear is all that is needed to lightly brown the fish. I usually use a torch to sear one side of the fish or a cast iron or other heavy skillet with some oil that is just starting to smoke.

Fish is almost always best cooked right before eating and doesn't hold well. There are exceptions to this rule, especially if you are serving the fish cold, but in general it's ideal to serve it hot out of the bag or after the sear. For warm dishes, I'll put the plates in a low oven to heat them up and help the temperature of the fish stay high through the serving process.

SHRIMP COCKTAIL WITH CHIPOTLE SAUCE

Cook: 132°F (55.6°C) for 15 to 35 minutes • Serves: 4 to 8 as an appetizer

Not all sous vide cooking has to be fancy and this super-easy shrimp cocktail is a great case in point. You simply sous vide cleaned shrimp until they are just cooked through, then chill them in an ice bath. I like to serve them with a spicy chipotle cocktail sauce, but you can use your favorite cocktail sauce or dip.

I prefer my shrimp cooked at 132°F (55.6°C) which is very similar to traditionally cooked shrimp. Many people prefer it rarer and cook it at 122°F (50°C), just make sure you use high-quality shrimp because the temperature isn't hot enough to kill any bacteria. Depending on their size, 15 to 35 minutes is usually enough time to heat the shrimp through.

Ingredients

For the Shrimp
1 pound shrimp (450g)
Salt and pepper

For the Chipotle Cocktail Sauce
2 small tomatoes
3 garlic cloves
1 chipotle pepper in adobo
   sauce, less or more to taste
1 tablespoon honey
1 tablespoon lime juice
¼ cup tomato paste
¼ cup cilantro
Salt and pepper

For the Shrimp

At least 60 minutes before serving
Preheat a water bath to 132°F (55.6°C).

Salt and pepper the shrimp, place in a sous vide bag in a single layer then seal. Cook the shrimp for 15 to 35 minutes.

Prepare an ice-bath with ½ water and ½ ice. Once cooked, remove the sous vide bag from the water bath and place in the ice bath. Let cool until chilled then refrigerate until serving.

For the Chipotle Cocktail Sauce

At least 20 minutes before serving

Combine all of the ingredients for the cocktail sauce in a blender or food processor. Process until it is mixed well and the consistency you prefer. Taste and adjust the flavors to your preferences. If you want it thicker you can also add more tomato paste. The cocktail sauce can be refrigerated for several days.

To Assemble

Fill a bowl or serving glass with ice. Remove the shrimp from the sous vide bag and place several of them in the bowl. Serve with the cocktail sauce on the side for dipping.

Modernist Notes

For a fun presentation a dehydrator can be used to make cocktail sauce leather that is draped over individual shrimp. I first saw this done by the Seattle Food Geek and it's a great twist on a normal party food.

When the cocktail sauce is blended, add in 0.1% xanthan gum. Spread the cocktail sauce out in a thin layer on a solid dehydrator rack, or on parchment paper. Dehydrate for 2 to 4 hours until it has dried but is still pliable. If you don't have a dehydrator you can do this in an oven set to low with the door ajar.

Once dried, cut the cocktail sauce into strips about ¾" wide by 2" long (19mm by 50mm). Drape a strip over each shrimp before serving.

SALMON WITH APPLE AND JALAPENOS

Cook: 122°F (50°C) for 30 to 60 minutes • Serves: 4 to 8

Salmon is one of the most transformative foods you can cook sous vide. The time and temperature you use will greatly change the texture of the final dish. For rare and mi-cuit salmon, the temperature should stay below 110°F to 115°F (43.3°C to 46.1°C). At 120°F (48.9°C) it will begin to become flakey, which tops out at around 140°F (60°C) with a more traditional texture. If I can find high quality salmon I prefer it cooked at 122°F (50°C) until heated through, 30 to 60 minutes.

I usually brine the salmon in a 5% salt solution for 10 minutes. It firms up the flesh and reduces the amount of albumin in the finished dish.

Ingredients

For the Salmon
2 cups water
3.5 tablespoons salt
2 cups cold water
1-2 pounds salmon (450g to
    900g)
Salt and pepper

For the Jalapeno Vinaigrette
1 jalapeno, minced
½ shallot, minced
6 tablespoons olive oil
3 tablespoons lemon juice
1 teaspoon yellow mustard
Salt and pepper

To Assemble
Granny Smith apple
Jalapeno, sliced
Lemon confit (see page 194),
    diced
Fresh parsley, chopped

For the Salmon

At least 65 to 95 minutes before serving
Preheat a water bath to 122°F (50°C).

Combine 2 cups of water with the salt and heat until the salt is dissolved. Add the 2 cups of cold water and let the water cool to room temperature.

Remove the skin from the salmon. Cut it into 1" by 3" pieces (25mm by 75mm). Place the salmon into the salted water and let sit for 10 minutes. Remove the salmon and lightly pepper it then place in a sous vide bag and seal. Cook the salmon for 30 to 60 minutes, until heated through.

For the Jalapeno Vinaigrette

At least 20 minutes before serving
Combine all the ingredients and blend together until fully emulsified. The vinaigrette can be made several hours ahead of time and refrigerator, then whisked together before serving.

To Assemble

Cut the apple into ¼" (7mm) cubes. Remove the salmon from the sous vide bag and pat dry. Place a section of fish on a plate then top with some diced apples and a jalapeno slice. Add some lemon confit and parsley to the top then drizzle with some of the jalapeno vinaigrette.

Modernist Notes

Before serving I like to smoke the salmon using a smoking gun or other smoker. After removing the salmon from the bag and patting it dry set it on a plate. Place a bowl or other container over the salmon and run the tube from the smoking gun under it. Fill the container with smoke and let sit for 1-2 minutes. Remove the salmon and continue plating.

I also will blend in 0.15% xanthan gum to the vinaigrette so it better coats the salmon and vegetables.

MI-CUIT SALMON

Cook: 104ºF (40ºC) for 45 to 60 minutes • Serves: 4 to 8

Mi-cuit salmon translates to "half cooked" and it is a tender, barely cooked version of salmon that is easy to do with sous vide. Mi-cuit looks at a small part of the salmon temperature range, usually from 104ºF to 115ºF (40ºC to 46.1ºC). The salmon is first brined in a 10% salt solution, usually with some sugar added, for about an hour. Then the salmon is cooked for 45 to 60 minutes, enough to heat through and tenderize it slightly. The salmon is then cooled completely and served cold or at room temperature.

I like to serve the salmon like traditional lox, with cucumber, red onion, capers and dill. Instead of cream cheese I use a maple creme fraiche for added flavor.

Ingredients

For the Salmon
1½ cups water
¼ cup salt
¼ cup white sugar
1½ cups cold water
1 pound salmon, skin and
    bones removed (450g)
2 tablespoons olive oil

For the Maple Creme Fraiche
2 cups creme fraiche
¼ cup maple syrup

To Assemble
Cucumber, thinly sliced
Red onion, thinly sliced
Capers
Fresh dill, minced

For the Salmon

At least 8 hours before serving

Combine 1½ cups of water with the salt sugar in a pot and heat until the sugar and salt are dissolved. Remove the brine from the heat, add the 1½ cups of cold water and let the brine cool to room temperature. Place in the refrigerator until it is cold.

Place the salmon in the brine and let soak for 45 to 60 minutes.

Preheat a water bath to 104ºF (40ºC).

Remove the salmon from the brine and place in a sous vide bag with the olive oil. Seal the bag and then cook for 45 to 60 minutes.

Prepare an ice-bath with ½ water and ½ ice.

Once cooked, remove the sous vide bag from the water bath and place in the ice bath. Let cool until chilled then refrigerate for 4 to 6 hours.

For the Maple Creme Fraiche
At least 20 minutes before serving
Add the maple syrup and creme fraiche in a bowl and whisk to combine. The creme fraiche will last in the refrigerator for several hours or over night.

To Assemble
Slice the cooled salmon into serving portions. Place a portion on a plate and add a small dollop of the maple creme fraiche to the top. Place some cucumber, red onion, and capers around the salmon. Sprinkle with some dill then serve.

Modernist Notes
For a more modernist presentation I will create a thick foam from the creme fraiche. Once the creme fraiche is combined with the maple syrup add it to a whipping siphon. Seal and charge the siphon and then dispense a dollop of foam on top of the salmon.

HALIBUT WITH HONEY-ROASTED BEETS

Cook: 114°F (45.6°C) for 25 to 40 minutes • Serves: 4 to 8

These beets were a huge hit at a recent family dinner. They are easy to prepare but turn out really sweet and flavorful. They complement the delicate halibut without overpowering its subtle flavors. The juice from red beets can stain everything from your cutting board to your hands so don't peel them over a nice cutting board!

For this recipe I cook the halibut to 114°F (45.6°C). At that low of a temperature it takes on a wonderful meaty texture but no longer tastes raw.

Ingredients

For the Halibut
1-2 pounds halibut, cut into
   portions and skin removed
   (450g to 900g)
Salt and pepper
1 tablespoon chopped oregano
1 tablespoon olive oil
1 tablespoon lemon zest

For the Honey-Roasted Beets
8 beets
Olive oil
Honey
Salt and pepper

For the Dill Butter
½ stick butter, softened at room
   temperature
3 tablespoons minced dill
⅛ teaspoon black pepper

For the Halibut

At least 35 to 50 minutes before serving
Preheat a water bath to 114ºF (45.6ºC).

Salt and pepper the halibut then place in a sous vide bag with the oregano, olive oil, and lemon zest. Seal the bag and cook for 25 to 40 minutes, just until heated through.

For the Honey-Roasted Beets

At least 70 minutes before serving
Preheat an oven to 400ºF (200ºC).

Peel the beets then set each beet on a square of aluminum foil or parchment paper. Drizzle with honey and olive oil then salt and pepper them. Wrap each beet in the aluminum foil and place on a sheet pan. Bake until the beets are tender and cooked through, about 45 to 60 minutes. Remove from the heat, unwrap the beets, and thinly slice.

For the Dill Butter

At least 20 minutes before serving
To make the butter place all of the ingredients in a bowl and mix and mash thoroughly using a fork. The butter can be refrigerated for several days or stored in the freezer for up to a month.

To Assemble

Remove the fish from the bag and pat dry. Briefly sear the fish on one side until just browned.

Lay out a ring of beets on a plate. Place the halibut, seared side up, in the middle then top with a dollop of dill butter.

SEA BASS WITH MICROGREENS AND MUSTARD OIL

Cook: 135°F (57.2°C) for 25 to 40 minutes • Serves: 4 to 8

Sea bass is a light and flavorful fish and I try not to overpower its taste when I serve it. The recipe pairs it with a pungent mustard oil that really shines with a basil, radish, and tomato salad with microgreens. If you can't find microgreens, any spring lettuce mix can act as a substitute.

I prefer my sea bass cooked at 135°F (57.2°C) until heated through, usually 25 to 40 minutes.

Ingredients

For the Sea Bass
1-2 pounds sea bass, cut into
   portions and skin removed
   (450g to 900g)
Salt and pepper
1 teaspoon garlic powder
1 tablespoon butter

For the Mustard Oil
2 tablespoons yellow mustard
   seeds
2 tablespoons brown mustard
   seeds
2 cups olive oil

To Assemble
Microgreens
Basil leaves
Pink radish, thinly sliced
Cherry tomatoes, halved
Lemon, quartered

For the Sea Bass

At least 25 to 40 minutes before serving
Preheat a water bath to 135ºF (57.2ºC).

Salt and pepper the sea bass and sprinkle with the garlic powder. Place in a sous vide bag with the butter then seal. Cook the fish until heated through, about 25 to 40 minutes.

For the Mustard Oil

At least 12 hours before serving
Combine the mustard seeds and olive oil in a pot and set over low heat. Bring to a sizzle then remove from the heat and let cool to room temperature. Pour into a non-reactive container, cover and refrigerate overnight. Strain the oil to remove the seeds. The oil will keep in the refrigerator for several days.

To Assemble

Remove the fish from the bag and pat dry. Briefly sear the fish if desired.

Place the fish in the middle of a plate. Set some radish slices and tomato halves around the fish. Drizzle some of the mustard oil around the fish. Add some microgreens and basil to the top of the fish. Squeeze the lemon over the top and serve.

Modernist Notes

The mustard oil can be turned into a foam for a playful take on this dish. Once the mustard oil has been prepared place it in a pot over medium heat. Add 5% mono and diglyceride (glycerin) flakes, about 12 grams, and stir until they have melted. Remove the pot from the heat and carefully pour into a heat resistant whipping siphon. If you prefer, you can let the oil cool to room temperature before pouring.

Seal and charge the whipping siphon then refrigerate it for several hours. Once cold, the oil will be ready to dispense but it will last in the refrigerator for several days.

MONKFISH IN DASHI WITH SNOW PEAS

Cook: 114°F (45.6°C) for 15 to 35 minutes • Serves: 4 to 8

I first had a variation of this recipe at Serpico in Philadelphia and it was amazing. I've tried to recreate it at home ever since. This version combines sweet and flavorful monkfish medallions with a light dashi garnished with snow peas, radishes, and cucumbers. I cook the monkfish at 114°F (45.6°C) so it is lightly cooked but still not flaky. The dashi should be chilled so plan ahead for the time that takes. The fish will cool down once it's in the dashi, resulting in a fun cool and warm sensation as you eat it with the cold dashi.

Ingredients

For the Monkfish

1-2 pounds monkfish (450g to 900g)

Salt and pepper

1 lemon

1 tablespoon butter

For the Dashi

3 4" (100mm) pieces of kelp or kombu

2 quarts water

2 cups bonito flakes or katsuobushi

To Assemble

Snow peas, julienned

Pink radish, thinly sliced

Cucumber, diced

Mint leaves, minced

Mirin

Sesame Oil

Lemon wedges

For the Monkfish

At least 35 to 55 minutes before serving

Preheat a water bath to 114°F (45.6°C).

Clean the monkfish and remove all membranes and connective tissue. Cut into 1" (25mm) medallions. Lightly salt and pepper the medallions then zest the lemon over the top. Place the monkfish in a sous vide bag with the butter then seal. Cook for 15 to 35 minutes, until heated through.

For the Dashi

At least 4 hours before serving

Remove some of the powdery coating from the kombu by gently wiping it with a damp cloth or paper towel. Add the kombu to a pot and cover with the water. Soak for 45 minutes.

Slowly heat the water to 160°F (71.1°C) over medium heat, this should take about 10 minutes. Remove the kombu from the pot and discard.

Turn the heat up to high and bring to a boil. Add the bonito flakes and remove from the heat. Let steep for 5 minutes. Strain the liquid to remove the bonito and any floating particles. Let the dashi cool and then place in the refrigerator to fully chill.

The dashi can be stored in the refrigerator for a week.

To Assemble

Remove the fish from the bag and pat dry. Briefly sear the medallions on one side.

Place the fish in the middle of a shallow bowl with the seared side up. Set some snow peas, radish slices and cucumber around the fish. Sprinkle some mint leaves on top of the fish. Pour the dashi around the fish. Drizzle some mirin and sesame oil in the dashi, squeeze a lemon wedge over the fish then serve.

RED SNAPPER TOSTADAS WITH MANGO SALSA

Cook: 132°F (55.6°C) for 20 to 40 minutes • Serves: 4 to 8

The combination of flaky fish and crunchy fried tostada is always so enjoyable to me. I like to pair it with a mango, tomato, and cucumber salsa to add more flavor and some additional crispness. It also has jalapeno in it to add some low-level heat to the dish.

For this dish I prefer my fish to be flaky so I cook it at a slightly higher temperature than usual, at 132°F (55.6°C), until just heated through. I usually don't sear the fish after cooking it but you can if you'd like it to be crispier.

Ingredients

For the Snapper
1-2 pounds red snapper filets (450g to 900g)
1 teaspoon garlic powder
½ teaspoon ground cumin
½ teaspoon ground coriander
Salt and pepper

For the Mango Salsa
1 mango, diced
1 tomato, diced
1 jalapeno chile, diced
½ cucumber, diced
¼ red onion, diced
3 tablespoons lime juice
2 tablespoons olive oil
2 tablespoons chopped basil
2 tablespoons chopped oregano
2 tablespoons honey
Salt and pepper

For the Tostadas
8 flour tortillas
Canola oil

To Assemble
Fresh oregano, chopped

For the Snapper

At least 20 to 40 minutes before serving
Preheat a water bath to 132°F (55.6°C).

Mix together the spices in a bowl. Salt and pepper the snapper then sprinkle with the spices. Place in a sous vide bag and seal. Cook until heated through, 20 to 40 minutes.

For the Mango Salsa

At least 20 minutes before serving
Combine all of the ingredients in a bowl and mix well. The salsa can be made a few hours before eating and stored in the refrigerator, the extra time will help the flavors to meld together.

For the Tostadas

At least 30 minutes before serving
Take a pan large enough to fit one of the tortillas and heat it over medium to medium-high heat with about ½" of oil in it. One at a time place a tortilla in the pan and cook until it turns a golden brown. Remove it from the heat and set on a paper towel or wire rack. Repeat for all of the tortillas.

To Assemble

Remove the fish from the bag, pat dry, and lightly flake with a fork.

Place a tostada on a plate and top with a scoop of the salsa. Add some of the fish then sprinkle with the oregano and serve.

SESAME CRUSTED TUNA WITH AVOCADO SALAD

Cook: 110°F (43.3°C) for 20 to 60 minutes • Serves: 4 to 8

I love a nice seared piece of tuna that is rare on the inside, but cooking it at a very low temperature with sous vide ensures that it is evenly cooked throughout. It also softens the fish slightly, making it even more delicious. You aren't trying to cook the tuna much so stick to a low temperature, I usually do 110°F (43.3°C) until it is just heated through.

Ingredients

For the Tuna
2 large tuna steaks
Salt and pepper
¼ cup olive oil

For the Avocado Salad
3 tablespoons peanut oil
1 tablespoons sesame oil
2 tablespoons lime juice
1 tablespoons rice vinegar
2 tablespoons soy sauce
1 tablespoon fish sauce
2 tablespoons grated fresh
    ginger
1 shallot, minced
½ serrano chile, minced
1 avocado, diced
1 cucumber, cut into half
    moons
2 carrots, peeled and juilenned
¼ cup peanuts, chopped
1 scallion, thinly sliced

To Assemble
Canola oil
¼ cup black sesame seeds
¼ cup white sesame seeds

For the Tuna

At least 30 to 70 minutes before serving
Preheat a water bath to 110ºF (43.3ºC).

Salt and pepper the tuna then place in a sous vide bag. Add the olive oil then seal. Cook until heated through, 20 to 60 minutes.

For the Avocado Salad

At least 10 minutes before serving
Whisk together the peanut oil, sesame oil, lime juice, vinegar, soy sauce and fish sauce. Whisk in the ginger, shallot, and serrano chile. Toss the remaining ingredients with the dressing.

To Assemble

Heat the canola oil in a pan over medium to medium-high heat.

Combine the sesame seeds in a bowl. Remove the tuna from the bag, pat dry, and coat with the sesame seeds. Sear on the top and bottom until the sesame seeds become fragrant and begin to toast. Remove from the heat and slice into ½" strips (13mm).

Place several slices of the tuna on a plate. Add the avocado salad to the side then serve.

Modernist Notes

A good way to make this dish fancier is to make an avocado mousse. Remove the flesh from 2 avocados and blend them with half of a serrano pepper and 1 cup of heavy cream. Strain the mixture into a whipping siphon, seal and charge it. It will last in the refrigerator for a day or two. The mousse can be dispensed on top of the tuna steaks when serving.

SCALLOPS WITH ORANGE AND CHILE STRIPS

Cook: 125ºF (51.6ºC) for 30 to 45 minutes • Serves: 4 to 8

Scallops have such a delicate flavor and they can be easily overwhelmed so I like to keep the flavors simple when I cook with them. This recipe uses some dried orange peel and ancho pepper to add bursts of flavor and texture without overshadowing the scallops themselves. The orange and chile strips should be sliced very thinly, it's better to err on the side of too thin than too thick. If you don't have the time to dehydrate them the flavors will still work well.

Using sous vide to cook scallops ensures that they will be perfectly cooked. My go-to temperature for scallops is 125ºF (51.6ºC) but recipes range from 120ºF to 140ºF (48.9ºC to 60ºC), depending on how you like your scallops done. They are only cooked for 30 to 45 minutes, just enough to heat them through. Then the scallops are quickly pan fried to give them a light crust, usually 30 to 60 seconds per side.

Ingredients

For the Scallops
16 large scallops
Salt and pepper
1 teaspoon smoked paprika
½ teaspoon ground cumin
3 tablespoons olive oil

For the Dried Garnishes
1 orange
1 dried ancho pepper

To Assemble
3 tablespoons butter

For the Scallops

At least 40 to 55 minutes before serving
Preheat a water bath to 125ºF (51.6ºC).

Salt and pepper the scallops then dust with the paprika and cumin. Place in a sous vide bag with the olive oil and seal. Cook until heated through, 30 to 45 minutes.

For the Dried Garnishes

At least 2 or 3 hours before serving
Take the orange peel off in strips using a vegetable peeler. Cut the strips into batons about an inch and a half long (38mm) and as thin as possible. Cut the ancho pepper into similarly sized strips.

Dehydrate the orange and chile pepper strips until they become crispy, about 2 hours in a dehydrator or 3 hours in an oven on low.

To Assemble

Remove the scallops from the bag and pat dry.

Melt the butter in a pan over medium to medium-high heat. Once the foaming subsides add the scallops and sear briefly for 30 to 60 seconds on each side. Remove from the heat.

Place the scallops on a plate and top with some of the dried orange peel and chile strips then serve.

CALAMARI WITH ASIAN-FLAVORED VEGETABLES

Cook: 138ºF (58.9ºC) for 2 to 4 hours • Serves: 4 to 8

I really like the toothy texture of squid but it's hard to find it served as anything but the breaded and fried calamari. This dish combines the unfried squid rings with rich Asian-flavored mixed vegetables for a flavorful dish.

There is a wide range of time and temperature combinations that are used with squid, both in traditional and sous vide cooking. For a really toothy squid that will be pan fried after cooking many people do a short 45 to 60 minute cook at 113ºF to 120ºF (45ºC to 48.9ºC). For a more tender version 138ºF (58.9ºC) for 2 to 4 hours works well. For an even more tender squid a short 1 to 2 hour cook at a high temperature like 180ºF (82.2ºC) is good. You can either sear the squid after sous viding it or serve it plain, sometimes the searing can toughen up the outside so it depends on the dish you are creating.

Ingredients

For the Squid
14 ounces squid, cleaned
   (400g)
Salt and pepper

For the Asian Vegetables
2 tablespoons sesame oil
½ onion, halved and sliced
3 cups sugar-snap peas, cleaned
1 orange or yellow bell pepper,
   cut into strips
1 red bell pepper, cut into
   strips
¼ cup water chestnuts, diced
4 garlic cloves, minced
2 teaspoons grated ginger
3 tablespoons soy sauce
6 tablespoons oyster sauce
5 tablespoons rice wine
   vinegar
1 tablespoon sriracha sauce
½ cup chicken stock
2 tablespoons cornstarch
4 tablespoons cold water

To Assemble
Sesame oil
Sesame seeds
Basil leaves, chopped

For the Squid
At least 2 to 4 hours before serving
Preheat a water bath to 138ºF (58.9ºC).

Rinse the squid under cold running water and cut into rings or thin strips. Season the squid with salt and pepper and seal in the sous vide bag. Add to the water bath and cook for 2 to 4 hours, until it becomes tender.

For the Asian Vegetables
20 minutes before serving
In a pan over medium heat add the oil and warm. Add the onion and cook until it turns translucent, about 5 minutes. Add the peas, peppers, ginger, water chestnuts, and garlic and cook for 3 more minutes. Add the soy sauce, oyster sauce, vinegar, sriracha, and stock and simmer for 2 minutes.

In a separate bowl whisk the cornstarch and cold water together. Add this to the pan with the vegetables and sauce while stirring quickly. Bring to a boil, let thicken slightly then remove from the heat.

To Assemble
Remove the squid from the sous vide bag and pat dry. Briefly sear the squid if desired. Place a spoonful of the Asian vegetables on a plate. Add several of the squid rings. Drizzle with the sesame oil and sprinkle with the sesame seeds and basil then serve.

COD CHOWDER WITH SOURDOUGH CROUTONS

Cook: 122°F (50°C) for 15 to 30 minutes • Serves: 4 to 8

During winter I always start to crave seafood chowder because it is so warm and comforting. I especially like it in a sourdough bread bowl but they can be hard to find so I'll often use sourdough croutons. I like the cod cooked to 122°F (50°C) so it is starting to become flaky but it is still very tender.

Ingredients

For the Cod
1-2 pounds cod, cut into
    portions (450g to 900g)
2 teaspoons garlic powder
1 teaspoon paprika
1 teaspoon liquid smoke
Salt and pepper

For the Chowder
4 strips bacon, diced
1 red potato, diced
1 yellow onion, diced
1 carrot, peeled and diced
2 garlic cloves, coarsely
    chopped
2 tablespoons flour
1 teaspoon yellow mustard
½ teaspoon Worcester
    sauce
1 cup milk
3 cups fish stock

For the Sourdough Croutons
Sourdough bread
Olive oil
Salt and pepper

To Assemble
Fresh parsley, chopped
Lemon zest
Olive oil

For the Cod

At least 15 to 30 minutes before serving

Preheat a water bath to 122°F (50°C).

Salt and pepper the cod then sprinkle with the spices. Brush the liquid smoke on it. Place in the sous vide bag and seal. Cook until heated through, usually 15 to 30 minutes.

For the Chowder

At least 60 minutes before serving

Add the bacon to a pot and cook over medium heat until the fat is rendered and it begins to crisp up. Remove the bacon and set aside, discarding all but 1 tablespoon of bacon fat. Add the potato, onion, carrot, and garlic to the pot and cook until the potato begins to turn tender. Add the flour, mustard, and Worcester sauce and mix well. Slowly whisk in the milk and half of the fish stock. Bring to a simmer and continue whisking in fish stock until it is the consistency you prefer.

For the Sourdough Croutons

At least 20 minutes before serving

Cut the sourdough bread into croutons 1" wide (25mm) and ½" tall (13mm). Lightly toss them with the olive oil then salt and pepper them. Bake at 400°F (200°C) until just browned on all sides. Remove from the heat.

To Assemble

Remove the fish from the bag and pat dry. Fill a shallow bowl or deep plate with chowder. Set a portion of the cod in the middle of it. Sprinkle with parsley and lemon zest. Drizzle with the olive oil then serve.

FRUITS AND VEGETABLES

Vegetables are almost always cooked above 180°F (82.2°C), the minimum temperature needed to break them down. There are variations in the temperature used among vegetables but I've found 183°F (83.9°C) usually works best though some people prefer 185°F (85°C) or even 190°F (87.8°C). The higher the temperature and the longer the vegetables are cooked, the more tender they become. Most vegetables take between 25 and 90 minutes, though I try to give more specific recommendations for each recipe.

Fruit and vegetables can tend to release more gas than meat and fish so be sure to check on your bags to make sure they aren't floating. I will also usually leave extra space at the tops of the bags where the gas can accumulate above the surface of the water without pulling the vegetables out.

Due to the wide variety of fruits and vegetables, even within a certain type, the cooking times are estimates and can change greatly based on the specific variety and ripeness of the one you are cooking. For example, a late-season, ripe Bosc pear will cook much faster than an early-season, less ripe Bartlett pear. As you become more comfortable sous viding fruits and vegetables you will be able to better tweak the times for the specific produce you are using.

ASPARAGUS WITH DIJON MUSTARD VINAIGRETTE

Cook: 183°F (83.9°C) for 10 to 30 minutes • Serves: 2 to 4 as a side

Asparagus cooked sous vide is similar to blanched asparagus but ends up with a stronger flavor and slightly firmer texture. Because asparagus is so tender to start with you only need a short cooking time, usually 10 to 30 minutes, depending on the thickness of the asparagus. For thicker asparagus it can be helpful to peel off the tougher outer layer and they might need a little longer in the water bath.

Asparagus and Dijon mustard pair really well so I make a simple Dijon vinaigrette to dress the finished asparagus with. It adds tangy base flavors while not overpowering the asparagus itself.

Ingredients

For the Asparagus
1 bunch asparagus
Salt and pepper

For the Dijon Vinaigrette
1 tablespoon white wine vinegar
1 tablespoon lemon juice
1½ tablespoons Dijon mustard
¼ cup olive oil
2 tablespoons chopped tarragon
Salt and pepper

To Assemble
Tarragon leaves, chopped

For the Asparagus

At least 10 to 30 minutes before serving
Preheat the water bath to 183°F (83.9°C).

Place the asparagus in a sous vide bag, trying to keep the thickness of the bag less than 1" (25mm) for even cooking. Salt and pepper the asparagus then seal the bag. Place in the water bath and cook for 10 to 30 minutes.

Once the asparagus is tender remove it from the bag.

For the Dijon Vinaigrette

At least 20 minutes before serving
Combine all the ingredients and whisk or blend together. The vinaigrette can be made several hours ahead of time and re-whisked just before serving.

To Assemble

Place the asparagus on a plate and drizzle the Dijon mustard vinaigrette over the top. Sprinkle the tarragon on top and serve.

Modernist Notes

I almost always thicken the vinaigrette by blending in 0.2% to 0.3% xanthan gum. It really clings to the asparagus a lot better with the addition of the xanthan gum.

BROCCOLI WITH PARMESAN AND LEMON

Cook: 183ºF (83.9ºC) for 30 to 60 minutes • Serves: 4 to 6 as a side

Broccoli is one of the foods that can be more conveniently cooked by using sous vide but it isn't transformed by the process the way some other foods are. It typically cooks for about 30 minutes, though sometimes it needs to go longer based on how thick or tough the pieces are.

This recipe is nice and light, combining tender broccoli with salty parmesan cheese and bright lemon juice.

Ingredients

For the Broccoli
1 head of broccoli
2 tablespoons butter
Salt and pepper

To Assemble
Parmesan cheese
Fresh basil, chopped
1 lemon

For the Broccoli

At least 30 to 60 minutes before serving
Preheat the water bath to 183ºF (83.9ºC).

Cut the broccoli into large pieces and place into the sous vide bag with the butter, trying to keep the thickness of the bag less than 1" (25mm) for even cooking. Salt and pepper the broccoli and then seal the bag. Place the bag in the water bath and cook for 30 to 60 minutes, until the broccoli is tender.

To Assemble

Remove the broccoli from the bag and place on a plate. Shave off thin strips of the parmesan cheese and place them on top of the broccoli. Sprinkle with some basil then squeeze the lemon over the top and serve.

Modernist Notes

To add more brightness to the dish I often make a lemon-infused olive oil. Peel two lemons, being careful to leave the pith behind. Combine the lemon peel with a sprig of rosemary and 2 cups olive oil.

If you have a whipping siphon add the oil, lemon peel, and rosemary to the siphon then seal and charge it. Let it sit for 2 minutes then vent the siphon and strain the olive oil. Let the oil sit for 5 minutes before serving.

If you don't have a whipping siphon, heat the olive oil over medium heat just until the lemon or rosemary begins to sizzle then remove from the heat and let sit for 15 minutes. Strain the olive oil.

When assembling the dish drizzle the lemon infused olive oil on the broccoli.

Sweet and Spicy Glazed Carrots

Cook: 183°F (83.9°C) for 45 to 60 minutes • Serves: 4 as a side

Using sous vide to glaze carrots is a simple process that results in a great side dish. You simply peel some carrots and cut them into the size you want. Then pick the seasonings and toss the carrots with them. Add it all to a sous vide bag with some butter and cook them for 45 to 60 minutes at 183°F (83.3°C) or higher and you're all set. You can also briefly cook carrots and their juices in a pan after sous viding them to reduce the sauce for a richer dish. This recipe also works well for other root vegetables such as turnips, radishes, and parsnips.

Ingredients

For the Sweet and Spicy Carrots

4 large carrots, peeled and
　　chopped into ½" (13mm)
　　pieces or 8 smaller carrots,
　　peeled

1 tablespoon butter or olive oil

1 teaspoon white vinegar

1 tablespoon honey

1 teaspoon sweet paprika

½ teaspoon chile powder

½ teaspoon salt

To Assemble

4 tablespoons chopped parsley

For the Sweet and Spicy Carrots

At least 45 to 60 minutes before serving

Preheat the water bath to 183ºF (83.9ºC).

Combine all ingredients into a sous vide bag, trying to keep the thickness of the bag less than 1" (25mm) for even cooking, and seal. Place in the water bath and cook for 45 to 60 minutes.

To Assemble

Once the carrots are tender remove them from the bag and place directly on the plate. Top with the parsley and sprinkle some coarse salt over the top.

BUTTER-POACHED BEET SALAD WITH PECANS

Cook: 183°F (83.9°C) for 60 to 90 minutes • Serves: 4 to 8 as a side

Sous vide is great at tenderizing beets without turning them mushy. This salad uses the bitter frisee and sweet Mandarin oranges to complement the beets with a blue cheese crumble for added depth of flavor. Beets are usually tender after 60 to 90 minutes, depending on how thick they are cut.

Ingredients

For the Beets
8 beets
1 orange
Salt and pepper
2 tablespoons honey
2 tablespoons butter

To Assemble
Mandarin oranges
Frisee lettuce
Blue cheese, crumbled
Pecans
Tarragon leaves
Olive oil
Salt and pepper

For the Beets

At least 60 to 90 minutes before serving
Preheat the water bath to 183°F (83.9°C).

Peel the beets and cut them into bite-sized chunks then place them in a sous vide bag, trying to keep the thickness of the bag less than 1" (25mm) for even cooking. Zest the orange into the sous vide bag then salt and pepper the beets. Add the honey and butter and seal. Cook the beets for around 60 to 90 minutes. Once tender, remove the beets from the sous vide bag.

To Assemble

Place some frisee on a plate and add Mandarin oranges and cooked beets to it. Top with some blue cheese, pecans and tarragon. Drizzle with olive oil then salt and pepper the salad.

CORN ON THE COB WITH BASIL

Cook: 183ºF (83.9ºC) for 15 to 25 minutes • Serves: 4 to 8 as a side

Sweet summer corn is one of my favorite treats and I love it grilled, boiled or roasted. After I tried sous viding corn I've got a new favorite method (well...maybe besides grilling). Because sweet corn only needs a little heat to break down the outer layers of the kernels the cook time is pretty short, only about 15 to 25 minutes, though you can go up to 45 for starchier, less sweet, corn. I cook the corn with butter and then finish it off with fresh basil and lime zest to complement the natural sugars of the corn.

Ingredients

For the Corn on the Cob
4 ears of corn
Salt and pepper
4 tablespoons butter

To Assemble
Fresh basil, finely chopped
Lime zest

For the Corn on the Cob

At least 15 to 25 minutes before serving
Preheat the water bath to 183ºF (83.9ºC).

Remove the husks from the corn and discard. Place the corn cobs into the sous vide bag in a single layer along with the salt, pepper, and butter. Seal the bag and cook them for around 15 to 25 minutes. Once tender, remove the corn from the sous vide bag.

To Assemble

Sprinkle the corn with the basil and lime zest. Drizzle with the butter from the bag then serve.

ORANGE-SAFFRON FENNEL CONFIT

Cook: 183°F (83.9°C) for 30 to 60 minutes • Serves: 4 to 8 as a side

Fennel cooked sous vide becomes very tender and retains the majority of its flavor. The length of time you cook it for depends on how tender you want it. At 30 minutes it's just beginning to tenderize, after 60 minutes it retains a little bite, and after 90 minutes it is completely tender. Cooking the fennel with a large dose of olive oil confits the fennel, resulting in a tender, juicy fennel. The excess olive oil can be used on other dishes or in vinaigrettes and will last in the refrigerator for several days.

Ingredients

For the Orange-Saffron Fennel
3 fennel bulbs
3 garlic cloves, minced
1 teaspoon saffron
1 orange
Salt and pepper
¾ cup olive oil

For the Orange-Saffron Fennel

At least 30 to 60 minutes before serving
Preheat the water bath to 183°F (83.9°C).

Trim the fennel bulbs, cut them in half, then place them in a sous vide bag in a single layer. Add the garlic and saffron to the bag. Zest the orange into the sous vide bag then salt and pepper the fennel. Add the olive oil and seal. Cook the fennel for 60 minutes. Once tender, remove the fennel from the sous vide bag then serve.

POACHED CHERRY TOMATOES

Cook: 131°F (55°C) for 30 minutes • Serves: 4 to 8 as a side

Using sous vide to lightly poach tomatoes results in a tender and moist side dish. The tomatoes are just heated through, not broken down, so cooking them at almost any low temperature works well. I usually serve them with steaks so I cook them at 131°F (55°C) because I toss them in with the steaks at the end of their cooking time.

Ingredients

For the Cherry Tomatoes

2 pints cherry tomatoes

4 tablespoons good olive oil

1 tablespoon chopped rosemary
  leaves

1 tablespoon thyme leaves

Salt and pepper

For the Cherry Tomatoes

At least 30 minutes before serving

Preheat a water bath to 131°F (55°C).

Put the cherry tomatoes, olive oil, rosemary and thyme in a sous vide bag and mix together well, trying to keep the thickness of the bag less than 1" (25mm) for even cooking. Salt and pepper the tomatoes then seal the bag. Cook the tomatoes for 30 minutes.

Once cooked, remove the tomatoes from the sous vide bag, place in a bowl and serve as a side.

PRESERVED LEMON CONFIT

Cook: 183°F (83.9°C) for 60 minutes • Makes: 16 large pieces of lemon confit

Lemon confit, or preserved lemon, is a popular ingredient in Moroccan cuisines and is great when you are looking to add a little brightness to a dish. It is traditionally made by packing lemons in salt for several months, but using a sous vide machine speeds up the process to about an hour. The base flavors aren't quite as complex as the traditional method but it's a great substitute when you don't want to wait a few months for preserved lemons.

When you want to use the lemon, cut away the pulp and the pith and discard. Rinse the remaining lemon peel under water to remove the excess salt then cut it into pieces.

Ingredients

For the Lemons
4 lemons, cut into quarters
2 cups kosher salt
½ cup white sugar

For the Lemons

At least 60 minutes before serving
Preheat a water bath to 183°F (83.9°C).

Place the lemon quarters and salt in a sous vide bag and massage the salt into the lemons, ensuring that all the lemons are covered. Seal the bag and then cook for 60 minutes. Remove the bag from the water bath and empty all the contents into a glass jar.

The lemons will last in the refrigerator for several months.

BUTTERNUT SQUASH SALAD

Cook: 183°F (83.9°C) for 45 to 60 minutes • Serves: 4 as a side

Butternut squash is a fun winter squash that can be taken in a variety of ways. It's often served as soups or purees but I also like to serve it in a chunky salad. I combine the squash with walnuts, goat cheese, sage and a drizzle of maple syrup for a savory and sweet salad.

Depending on the ripeness and age of the squash it will usually need to be cooked for 45 to 60 minutes. There is a wide variety of winter squash but most of them benefit from sous vide and are cooked in a similar way. Depending on the type you are cooking the squash will tenderize after 25 to 60 minutes.

Ingredients

For the Butternut Squash Salad
1 butternut squash
6 sage leaves, diced
1 teaspoon ground cinnamon
1 teaspoon ground cloves
2 tablespoons butter
Salt and pepper

To Assemble
½ cup roughly chopped walnuts
½ cup goat cheese
Maple syrup

For the Butternut Squash Salad

At least 60 to 75 minutes before serving
Preheat the water bath to 183°F (83.9°C).

Peel the squash then cut it in half and remove the seeds. Dice the squash into chunks about ½" to ¾" (13mm to 19mm) in size.

Put the squash in a sous vide bag in a single layer. Add the sage, cinnamon, cloves, and butter then salt and pepper the squash. Seal the bag and place it in the water bath and cook for 45 to 60 minutes.

To Assemble

Once the squash is tender remove it from the bag and spoon it onto plates. Top the squash with the walnuts and goat cheese then drizzle with the maple syrup.

BUTTER POACHED TURNIPS

Cook: 183ºF (83.9ºC) for 45 to 60 minutes • Serves: 4 to 8 as a side

I'm a big fan of roasted turnips and I love the sweetness the caramelization adds but sometimes the turnips can get tough. Using sous vide always results in really moist and tender turnips that pack a lot of flavor. I usually cook them for 45 to 60 minutes, though you can do a little shorter or longer if you prefer them more or less tender.

I like to keep the turnips simple to showcase their natural flavors so I cook them with butter and thyme to add richness and some base flavors.

Ingredients

For the Turnips
8 turnips, peeled and quartered
2 tablespoons fresh thyme leaves
2 tablespoons butter or olive oil
Salt and pepper

For the Turnips

At least 45 to 60 minutes before serving
Preheat the water bath to 183ºF (83.9ºC).

Put the turnips, thyme, and butter in a sous vide bag in a single layer and mix together well. Salt and pepper the turnips then seal the bag. Cook the turnips for 45 to 60 minutes.

Once cooked, remove the turnips from the sous vide bag, place in a bowl and serve as a side.

DUAL-COOKED CREAMY POTATO PUREE

Cook: 160°F (71.1°C) for 30 minutes • Serves: 4 to 8 as a side

Chefs have been trying to perfect mashed potatoes for as long as there have been potatoes. Everyone has their own technique and their own version of the ideal mashed potatoes. These potatoes are based on Heston Blumenthal's recipe and result in rich, buttery, and smooth potatoes. I do cut the butter in half, the original recipe uses an entire block of butter, but you can use more if you like the ultra-buttery taste.

Cooking the potatoes at 160°F (71.1°C) helps pre-cook the starch molecules and locks them in place. It only takes 30 minutes of cooking to lock the starch, after which the potatoes are cooled. They are then boiled to fully cook them.

Ingredients

For the Potatoes
2 pounds potatoes, coarsely
  diced (900g)
2 cups water

To Assemble
9 tablespoons butter, cubed
½ cup whole milk or heavy
  cream, at room temperature
Salt and pepper

For the Potatoes

At least 90 minutes before serving
Preheat the water bath to 160°F (71.1°C).

Place the potatoes and water in a sous vide bag. Seal the bag and place in the water bath for 30 minutes.

Remove the potatoes from the sous vide bag, drain them and rinse under cold water. Add the cooled potatoes to a pot and cover with water. Bring to a boil and then simmer for 20 to 30 minutes, until very tender. Drain the potatoes.

To Assemble

Place the butter in a bowl and pass the potatoes through a ricer or fine sieve over top of the butter. Stir well to combine. Add the milk or cream and stir to combine. Salt and pepper to taste. The mixture can be reheated over gentle heat before serving.

RUSTIC ROASTED GARLIC MASHED POTATOES

Cook: 183°F (83.9°C) for 40 to 60 minutes • Serves: 4 to 8 as a side

Even with fancy technology, sometimes you want a rustic feeling to your food. In contrast to the smooth puree from the Dual-Cooked Creamy Potato Puree, these mashed potatoes are hearty, chunky, and full of bold flavors.

The entire cooking process for the potatoes is done in the sous vide machine, speeding up the process and relying on the higher temperatures to fully tenderize the potatoes.

Ingredients

For the Potatoes
2 pounds potatoes, coarsely
    diced (900g)
½ teaspoon freshly ground black
    pepper
1 tablespoon fresh thyme leaves
1 ½ teaspoons salt
2 tablespoons butter

For the Roasted Garlic
1 head garlic
Olive oil
Salt and pepper
1 sprig thyme

To Assemble
Roasted garlic, from above
4 tablespoons butter
½ cup whole milk or heavy
    cream
3 tablespoons chopped basil
2 tablespoon chopped parsley
Salt and pepper

For the Potatoes

At least 60 to 80 minutes before serving
Preheat the water bath to 183ºF (83.9ºC).

Place the potatoes in a sous vide bag, trying to keep the thickness of the bag less than 1" (25mm) for even cooking, and add the remaining ingredients. Seal the bag and place in the water bath for 40 to 60 minutes, until they are very tender.

For the Roasted Garlic

At least 75 minutes before serving
Preheat an oven to 400ºF (204ºC).

Cut off the top of the garlic, drizzle with olive oil and season with salt and pepper. Place it in tin foil with the thyme and wrap it up. Bake until the garlic is soft, about 60 minutes. Remove from the heat and let cool.

Remove the garlic from the tin foil and discard the thyme. Squeeze the garlic out of the cloves into a bowl. Mash up well with a fork.

To Assemble

Remove the potatoes from the sous vide bag and place in a large bowl. Add the roasted garlic, butter, milk, basil and parsley then mash with a potato masher or large fork. Do not over mash or the potatoes will take on a tacky texture. Salt and pepper to taste and serve.

CHIPOTLE SWEET POTATO SALAD

Cook: 183°F (83.9°C) for 45 to 90 minutes • Serves: 4 to 8 as a side

This sweet potato salad is a fun twist on the ubiquitous potato salad served at picnics everywhere. The sweet potatoes are cooked with a flavorful spice mixture and then combined with corn and black beans before being topped with a spicy chipotle vinaigrette.

Sweet potatoes normally take about 30 to 60 minutes to tenderize, depending on how tender you want them and the size of the pieces. For this recipe we cut them all into cubes so the cooking time usually evens out to 45 minutes.

Ingredients

For the Sweet Potatoes
4 sweet potatoes
4 tablespoons butter
2 teaspoons ground coriander
1 teaspoon ground cumin
1 teaspoon ancho chile powder
1 teaspoon kosher salt
1 teaspoon ground cloves
½ teaspoon black pepper

For the Vinaigrette
1 chipotle chile from a can of
    chipotles in adobo
1 garlic clove, finely minced
2 tablespoons ketchup
6 tablespoons lime juice
1 tablespoon honey
½ cup olive oil
Salt and pepper

To Assemble
2 tablespoons olive oil
3 shallots, diced
2 cups corn kernels, cooked
2 cups canned black beans,
    rinsed and drained
½ cup chopped cilantro

For the Sweet Potatoes

At least 75 to 120 minutes before serving
Preheat the water bath to 183°F (83.9°C).

Peel the sweet potatoes and cut into ¾" to 1" (19mm to 25mm) chunks. Add them to the sous vide bag in a single layer along with the butter and the spices then seal. Cook for 45 minutes until the potatoes are soft.

For the Vinaigrette

At least 20 minutes before serving
Put the chipotle, garlic and ketchup into a blender and process until smooth. Add the lime juice, honey, salt and pepper, and process again. Slowly add the olive oil while processing until it is incorporated. The vinaigrette can be refrigerated for several hours and re-whisked before serving.

To Assemble

Heat the olive oil in a pan over medium heat. Add the shallots and heat for 5 minutes. Add the corn and beans and heat through. Remove from the heat.

Remove the sweet potatoes from the sous vide bag and place in a serving bowl. Add the shallots, corn, beans, and cilantro and toss to combine. Spoon the dressing over the salad and toss once more before serving.

SPICED CABBAGE WITH APPLES

Cook: 183°F (83.9°C) for 60 minutes • Serves: 4 to 8 as a side

Cabbage benefits from a low temperature cook and is usually boiled or steamed. Using sous vide allows the flavors to concentrate in the bag as well as freeing you up from having to pay attention to a pot of water. The cabbage usually takes around 60 minutes to tenderize, depending on the kind you are using and whether it is whole or cut into strips.

For this recipe, I combine the cabbage with a flavorful mix of spices as well as some sliced apples. The apples provide some sweetness while the spices round out the flavors. This dish goes great with corned beef or a pork loin roast.

Ingredients

For the Cabbage
1 head of green cabbage
1 apple
1 tablespoon caraway seeds
1 tablespoon fresh thyme leaves
1 tablespoon ground coriander
1 teaspoon ginger powder
Salt and pepper

For the Cabbage

At least 75 minutes before serving
Preheat the water bath to 183°F (83.9°C).

Remove the outer leaves from the cabbage then cut it in half. Remove the core and then slice the cabbage into ½" (13mm) strips. Cut the apple in half then remove the stem and core. Slice the apple into thin strips.

Combine all ingredients in a sous vide bag, trying to keep the thickness of the bag less than 1" (25mm) for even cooking. Seal the bag and place in the water bath. Cook the cabbage for about 60 minutes, until the cabbage is tender.

Once the cabbage is tender, remove it from the bag, salt and pepper to taste, then serve.

Modernist Notes

For a more modernist take on this side dish I will add ¼ cup water to the cabbage then blend it into a smooth puree. Blending in 0.2% xanthan gum will also help hold it together. You can use the puree as a sauce or topping for most cuts of pork.

BOURBON-MAPLE APPLE CHUTNEY

Cook: 185°F (85°C) for 90 to 120 minutes • Serves: 8

This apple chutney is a very flavorful topping that works great on pork or fish. Sometimes I'll even use it as a savory topping on desserts. The apples are cooked in a bourbon, maple syrup, chipotle and thyme mixture. After a brief puree they are ready to go. For a thicker chutney, or if the apples release too many juices, they can be briefly simmered before pureeing them to reduce the juices down. You can leave the skin on or peel them for a more refined presentation.

Depending on your final use of the apples, they can be cooked for anywhere between 1 to 3 hours. For this recipe I do 1½ to 2 hours at 185°F (85°C) so they still have some bite to them.

Ingredients

For the Apple Chutney

2 Braeburn or other baking
  apple, diced
3 tablespoons bourbon
2 tablespoons maple syrup
1 tablespoon thyme leaves
1 tablespoon lemon juice
1 tablespoon melted butter
½ teaspoon chipotle chile
  powder
Salt and pepper

For the Apple Chutney

At least 2 to 2.5 hours before serving
Preheat the water bath to 185°F (85°C).

Place the apples in a sous vide bag, trying to keep the thickness of the bag less than 1" (25mm) for even cooking. Whisk together the remaining ingredients then pour over the apples. Seal the sous vide bag and cook for 90 to 120 minutes.

Once cooked, briefly blend the apple mixture to combine it into a thick puree then serve.

Modernist Notes

The addition of 0.1% to 0.2% xanthan gum helps hold the chutney together and thicken it. Just blend it in during the final pureeing stage.

VANILLA PEARS WITH ROSEMARY CARAMEL

Cook: 185°F (85°C) for 45 to 60 minutes • Serves: 8

I first heard of vanilla-poached pears from SVKitchen, who allowed me to include it in my previous book. Since then I've tweaked it and taken it in a few different directions and this is one of my favorites. It tops the pears with rosemary caramel and walnuts.

The amount of time the pears will take to cook is usually 45 to 60 minutes, depending on the type of pear and how soft you want it. Very ripe pears can be done in as little as 30 minutes and less-ripe, larger pears can take up to 90 minutes.

Ingredients

For the Caramel Sauce
1.5 cups heavy cream
¼ cup rosemary leaves
1 cup sugar
2 tablespoons water

For the Pears
2 tablespoons butter, softened
3 tablespoons sugar
2 teaspoons vanilla paste
½ teaspoon ground cinnamon
½ teaspoon ground allspice
¼ teaspoon ground cloves
4 pears
1 lemon, quartered

To Assemble
Walnuts
Rosemary leaves, finely chopped

For the Caramel Sauce

At least 60 minutes before serving
Combine the heavy cream and rosemary in a pot and bring to a simmer. Remove from the heat and let steep for 15 minutes. Blend the heavy cream and rosemary together then strain the cream.

Mix the sugar and water together in a pot, it should resemble wet sand. Heat the sugar over medium heat without stirring until it melts and bubbles. Once it starts to brown, stir it gently until it turns a nice amber color. If clumps form cook for longer until they melt, almost all clumps should eventually melt out.

Once the sugar is a nice amber color, about 10 to 20 minutes total cooking time, pour in the rosemary cream while stirring, being sure not to burn yourself on the hot steam that is released. Mix well to fully incorporate the cream into the sugar then cook for 2 minutes.

Remove from the heat and let the caramel sauce cool. The caramel sauce will last in the refrigerator for several days.

For the Pears

At least 45 to 60 minutes before serving
Preheat the water bath to 185°F (85°C).

Combine the butter, sugar, vanilla paste and spices.

Peel the pears, squeezing some lemon juice over then to prevent browning. Cut the pears in half length-wise and remove the stem and core.

Place the pears in a sous vide bag in a single layer, using multiple bags if needed. Add the butter mixture to the bag and seal. Cook the pears for 45 to 60 minutes.

Once the pears are tender, remove them from the sous vide bag.

To Assemble

Thinly slice the pears and lay out on a plate. Cover with the warm juices from the bag. Drizzle the rosemary caramel sauce over the pears then top with some walnuts. Add a sprinkling of the finely chopped rosemary leaves then serve.

INFUSIONS

Infusions have been used in cooking for a very long time. Some have been around forever, like limoncello and falernum. Others have come into vogue more recently, like flavored vinegars and oils. Traditionally, they are made by soaking herbs and spices in liquids for long amounts of time, sometimes up to several months. This process can be compressed into a matter of hours by using sous vide during the infusion process.

You can create the infusions using any combination of spices, herbs, fruits, or vegetables. Infusions are typically made with vinegar, alcohol, or oil, though almost any liquid works well. You can make the infusions in plastic bags, mason jars, or even in the glass bottle the liquid came in.

The amount and type of flavor extracted depends on both the temperature it is cooked at and the length of time it is cooked. Most temperatures range from 131°F to 160°F (55°C to 71.1°C) with times usually in the 1 to 2 hour range, though the flavor from some ingredients is best extracted at times and temperatures outside those ranges. I've provided several of my favorites but feel free to experiment to determine what you like best.

The infusions will last for a long time, but if you are using any ingredients that might spoil, like fruits or vegetables, or contain pathogens, like garlic, it is best to store them in the refrigerator. I store most of mine in the refrigerator just to be safe, plus I enjoy most of them cold anyway.

Feel free to adjust the amount of the infusions made in this chapter, they can easily be scaled up or down to your needs.

CHERRY-INFUSED RYE OLD FASHIONED

Cook: 160°F (71.1°C) for 1 to 2 hours • Makes: 375ml rye

An Old Fashioned is a simple but tasty cocktail that works wonderfully to show off the flavor of infusions. It is simply some sugar, bitters, a splash of club soda, and whiskey. Infusing the whiskey with different flavors dramatically changes the flavor profile of the end drink.

This cherry-infused rye is great because of the fruity cherry notes that come through in the final drink but I love to experiment with different flavors. I've had great success infusing bourbon and rye with orange peel, dried chillies, peaches, and basil.

Ingredients

For the Cherry-Infused Rye
2 cups cherries
375ml rye, (1.6 cups)

For the Old Fashioned
1 teaspoon brown sugar
2-3 dashes Bittermans Xocolatl
    Mole Bitters or Angostura
    bitters
Club soda
2 ounces Cherry-Infused Rye,
    from above

For the Cherry-Infused Rye

At least 3 hours before serving
Preheat a water bath to 160°F (71.1°C).

Smash the cherries with the edge of a knife or a rolling pin. Combine the cherries and rye in a sous vide bag or mason jar then seal and place in the water bath. Heat the infusion for 1 to 2 hours.

Prepare an ice bath with ½ ice and ½ water. Remove the bag or mason jar from the water bath and place in the ice bath for 15 to 20 minutes. Strain the rye if desired and store in a sealed container. The cherries can be reserved for a garnish or boozy snack.

For the Old Fashioned

Place the brown sugar at the bottom of an Old-Fashioned glass. Add the bitters and a small splash of club soda. Stir the mixture to dissolve the sugar. Add an ice cube or two and top with the cherry-infused rye. Stir briefly and then serve.

CREAMSICLE WITH ORANGE-VANILLA VODKA

Cook: 140ºF (60ºC) for 1 to 2 hours • Makes: 375ml vodka

This is a sweet and light drink that is perfect after a nice barbecue or on a summer night. The orange-vanilla vodka is combined with fresh orange juice and some half and half to replicate the childhood favorite of a creamsicle. You can adjust the amount of orange juice and half and half for a stronger or weaker drink, whatever you prefer.

Even though this drink is already pretty sweet many people like the addition of some whip cream on it to really push it over the top. The orange-vanilla vodka can be made ahead of time and stored in the liquor cabinet or refrigerator for several weeks.

Ingredients

For the Orange-Vanilla Vodka
2 oranges
1 vanilla bean
375ml vodka, (1.6 cups)

For the Creamsicle
2 ounces orange-vanilla vodka,
 from above
1.5 ounces orange juice
1.5 ounces half and half
1 orange slice

For the Orange-Vanilla Vodka

At least 3 hours before serving
Preheat a water bath to 140°F (60°C).

Lightly scrub the outside of the oranges then remove the zest with a vegetable peeler. Make sure little to no pith came off as well, using a paring knife to remove any. The orange pieces can be reserved for garnishing the drink. Split the vanilla bean in half.

Combine all the ingredients in a sous vide bag or mason jar then seal and place in the water bath. Heat the infusion for 1 to 2 hours.

Prepare an ice bath with ½ ice and ½ water. Remove the bag or mason jar from the water bath and place in the ice bath for 15 to 20 minutes. Strain the vodka and store in a sealed container.

For the Creamsicle

Fill a cocktail shaker with ice. Add the orange-vanilla vodka, orange juice, and half and half to the shaker. Shake vigorously for 15 seconds, until everything is combined well. Strain into a martini glass and garnish with an orange slice.

Modernist Notes

For a really playful presentation I like to make a creamy orange foam to top the drink. Place 1.5 cups orange juice in a pot and add 3.5 grams of gelatin, or about 2 gelatin sheets. Let the gelatin bloom for 5 to 10 minutes.

Once bloomed, heat the pot over medium heat while stirring until the gelatin dissolves. Remove from the heat and stir in ¼ cup of half and half. Pour the mixture into a whipping siphon, seal and charge it fully. Place the siphon in the refrigerator for at least an hour or two to let the gelatin set completely. The foam can be stored in the refrigerator for several days. Dispense the foam on top of the creamsicle when serving.

CHILE-TOMATO INFUSED VODKA BLOODY MARY

Cook: 140°F (60°C) for 1 to 2 hours • Makes: 375ml vodka

The Bloody Mary is a classic brunch drink and it is fun to take it in different directions. This recipe uses guajillo and chipotle chiles to infuse the vodka with smokey and spicy flavors that complement most Bloody Mary mixes. This vodka is very spicy, for a more mellow, sipping style infusion I stick to using only 1 guajillo chile instead.

Ingredients

For the Chile-Tomato Vodka
2 dried guajillo chiles
1 dried chipotle chiles
½ cup sun-dried tomatoes
375ml vodka, (1.6 cups)

For the Bloody Mary
4 ounces Bloody Mary mix
1 ounce Chile-Tomato Vodka,
    from above
½ celery stick
Sun-dried tomatoes, thinly
    sliced
Guajillo chiles, thinly sliced

For the Chile-Tomato Vodka

At least 3 hours before serving
Preheat a water bath to 140ºF (60ºC).

Combine the chiles, tomatoes, and vodka in a sous vide bag or mason jar then seal and place in the water bath. Heat the infusion for 1 to 2 hours.

Prepare an ice bath with ½ ice and ½ water. Remove the bag or mason jar from the water bath and place in the ice bath for 15 to 20 minutes. Strain the vodka if desired and store in a sealed container.

For the Bloody Mary

Combine the Bloody Mary mix and the infused vodka in a glass and stir to combine. Add the celery, sun-dried tomato, and chile strips as garnish, then serve.

RASPBERRY INFUSED VINAIGRETTE

Cook: 140°F (60°C) for 1 to 2 hours • Makes: 375ml vinegar

Infused vinegars are a great way to add subtle flavors to vinaigrettes and sauces but they are often much more expensive than their plain counterparts. Making your own at home is quick and easy, and much less expensive. Every year I get pounds of fresh raspberries from the bushes in my yard and making raspberry infused vinegar is a great way to preserve them. I like to use the raspberry vinegar to make a vinaigrette that I'll serve on spinach salad or even use as a sauce on white fish like cod or bass.

Ingredients

For the Raspberry Vinegar
½ pint raspberries
375ml champagne or white wine
  vinegar, (1.6 cups)

For the Raspberry Vinaigrette
3 tablespoons raspberry vinegar,
  from above
1 tablespoon orange juice
1 tablespoon honey
1 shallot, diced
5 tablespoons olive oil
Salt and pepper

For the Raspberry Vinegar

At least 3 hours before serving
Preheat a water bath to 140°F (60°C).

Combine the raspberries and vinegar in a sous vide bag or mason jar then seal and place in the water bath. Heat the infusion for 1 to 2 hours.

Prepare an ice bath with ½ ice and ½ water. Remove the bag or mason jar from the water bath and place in the ice bath for 15 to 20 minutes. Strain the vinegar and store in a sealed container.

For the Raspberry Vinaigrette

Whisk together the infused vinegar, orange juice, and honey. Stir in the shallots and let sit for 10 minutes. Slowly whisk in the olive oil until fully emulsified. Salt and pepper to taste.

Modernist Notes

Blending in 0.15% xanthan gum and 0.6% lecithin will help strengthen the vinaigrette and prevent it from separating.

Tarragon, Lemon, and Shallot Vinaigrette

Cook: 135°F (57.2°C) for 1 to 2 hours • Makes: 375ml vinegar

Shallot, lemon, and tarragon are classic pairings for many dishes. I like to infuse their flavors into a vinegar and then make a sauce to use over fish. The sauce is light and bright, adding many base layers of flavor to the fish.

Ingredients

For the Infused Vinegar
1 lemon
½ cup tarragon leaves
1 shallot, minced
375ml champagne or white wine
   vinegar, (1.6 cups)

For the Tarragon Vinaigrette
3 tablespoons infused vinegar,
   from above
1 tablespoon honey
5 tablespoons olive oil
Salt and pepper

For the Infused Vinegar

At least 3 hours before serving
Preheat a water bath to 135ºF (57.2ºC).

Lightly scrub the outside of the lemon then remove the zest with a vegetable peeler. Make sure little to no pith came off as well, using a paring knife to remove any. Combine the lemon peel, tarragon, shallot, and vinegar in a sous vide bag or mason jar then seal and place in the water bath. Heat the infusion for 1 to 2 hours.

Prepare an ice bath with ½ ice and ½ water. Remove the bag or mason jar from the water bath and place in the ice bath for 15 to 20 minutes. Strain the vinegar and store in a sealed container.

For the Tarragon Vinaigrette

Whisk together the infused vinegar and honey. Slowly whisk in the olive oil until fully emulsified. Salt and pepper to taste. Serve over warm, white fish.

Modernist Notes

I like to thicken this vinaigrette by blending in 0.15% xanthan gum. It also helps the vinaigrette cling to food when you use it.

ROSEMARY AND SAGE INFUSED OIL

Cook: 131°F (55°C) for 1 to 2 hours • Makes: 2 cups infused oil

When infusing oils there are two main considerations, the taste of the oil and the taste of the flavoring. If you only want the flavoring to stand out, you should use a neutral oil like canola or grapeseed oil which do not bring their own flavors to the infusion. If you want a specific flavor, you can turn to other oils that have distinct characteristics, such as olive oil, walnut oil, or sesame oil.

For this recipe I want to focus on the subtle flavors of the rosemary and sage so I call for a neutral oil. The infusion process is very easy, simply combine the oil and herbs, heat in a sous vide machine for several hours, then cool and store. The time and temperature used will depend on the flavoring agents used but typically ranges from 131°F to 176°F (55°C to 80°C) for 1 to 5 hours. The more herbs and other flavoring agents used the stronger the end infusion will be.

I often use this infused oil to finish fish dishes or to add extra herb notes to vinaigrettes and other sauces.

Ingredients

For the Rosemary and Sage Oil

2 cups canola, grapeseed, or other neutral oil

4 large sprigs rosemary

15 sage leaves

For the Rosemary and Sage Oil

At least 3 hours before serving

Preheat a water bath to 131°F (55°C).

Combine the oil, rosemary, and sage in a sous vide bag or mason jar then seal. Infuse in the water bath for 1 to 2 hours.

Prepare an ice bath with ½ ice and ½ water. Remove the bag or mason jar from the water bath and place in the ice bath for 15 to 20 minutes. Strain the oil and store in a sealed container. It will last for a week or two in the refrigerator.

Modernist Notes

With a whipping siphon you can easily turn this infused oil into a foam. Place the strained oil in a pot and place on medium heat. Add 5% glycerin flakes, about 22 grams, and stir until they have melted. Remove the pot from the heat and carefully pour into a heat resistant whipping siphon. If you prefer, you can let the oil cool to room temperature before pouring.

Seal and charge the whipping siphon then refrigerate it for several hours. Once cold, the oil will be ready to dispense but it will last in the refrigerator for several days.

CHILE PEPPER INFUSED OIL

Cook: 158°F (70°C) for 4 to 5 hours • Makes: 2 cups infused oil

This oil is strongly flavored and picks up the spice and smoke from the chile peppers. You can use any chile peppers you like but I prefer a combination of ancho, guajillo and chipotle. The ancho brings a lot of fruitiness, the chipotle adds heat, and the guajillo complements the smokiness of the other peppers.

I love to use this oil as a flavoring finishing oil for ribs, brisket or pulled pork. It's also great in a smoky vinaigrette to serve over fish or in fish tacos.

Ingredients

For the Chile Pepper Oil

2 cups canola, grapeseed, or
    other neutral oil
2 ancho peppers
2 guajillo peppers
1 chipotle pepper

For the Chile Pepper Oil

At least 5 hours before serving

Preheat a water bath to 158°F (70°C).

Combine the oil and peppers in a sous vide bag or mason jar and seal. Infuse in the water bath for 4 to 5 hours.

Prepare an ice bath with ½ ice and ½ water. Remove the bag or mason jar from the water bath and place in the ice bath for 15 to 20 minutes. Strain the oil and store in a sealed container. It will last for a week or two in the refrigerator.

SWEET AND SOUR

Many different sweet and sour foods including yogurt, cheeses, and custards are made by holding an ingredient at a specific temperature for a long amount of time. Sous vide is ideally suited for this method of cooking and can be used to easily turn out many great dishes.

Most of these dishes are cooked in mason jars or ceramic ramekins. Be sure to use the correct water level when cooking with these vessels, especially if they are open. I will usually place the empty containers in my sous vide bath then fill the bath to the specified height to prevent overflowing. A wire rack can also be used to raise the level of the containers if needed.

SOUS VIDE YOGURT

Cook: 110°F (43.3°C) for 5 hours • Makes: 4 cups yogurt

To make yogurt you heat milk or cream to above 180°F (82.2°C), cool it down and mix with a starter culture, then let it incubate at 100°F to 120°F (37.8°C to 48.9°C) for several hours. Using a sous vide machine allows you to easily maintain the temperatures you are looking for.

Sous vide yogurt is typically made in glass mason jars with the lids either off or not fully tightened. The starter bacteria will give off gasses as they create the yogurt so a sealed container can leak or explode. The yogurt is also usually made in the container you will store or serve it from because moving it to a new one can affect the consistency of the yogurt. You can use the sous vide machine to reach both temperatures but I typically just heat the milk on the stove because it's much quicker than raising and lowering the temperature of the whole water bath.

I call for half and half, which results in a very thick yogurt. If you prefer a thinner one you can substitute whole or 2% milk. To get the incubation going you need to add a ½ cup of yogurt that contains live and active cultures. Yogurt that contains this type of culture will be labelled on the package. The length of the incubation time adds tanginess to the yogurt and can range from 3 hours to 24 hours.

Ingredients

For the Yogurt

4 cups half and half or milk

½ cup plain yogurt with live and
   active cultures

For the Yogurt

At least 8 hours before serving

Fill a water bath to about an inch (25mm) below the height of the mason jars you are using and preheat the water to 110°F (43.3°C).

Heat the half and half in a pot to at least 180°F (82.2°C). Remove it from the heat and let it cool to at least 120°F (48.9°C) then whisk in the yogurt with the live and active cultures. Pour the mixture into the mason jars and seal each with plastic wrap. Place the jars into the water bath and let incubate for 5 hours.

After 5 hours remove the jars from the water bath and refrigerate until chilled. Once the yogurt is cold, seal with the mason jar lids. It will last in the refrigerator for 1 to 2 weeks.

Modernist Notes

For a really interesting take on a yogurt dish you can use a whipping siphon to make a carbonated yogurt foam. Add the yogurt to a whipping siphon and fully charge with CO_2. Let sit for a few hours and then dispense over fresh berries.

SOUS VIDE CREME FRAICHE

Cook: 95ºF (35ºC) for 8 to 10 hours • Makes: 4 cups creme fraiche

Creme fraiche is a "soured cream" that is tangy but not as sour as typical American sour cream. It is made with cream and a culture, usually derived from buttermilk or yogurt, that is cultured at room temperature over 24 hours. Using sous vide to culture the creme fraiche speeds up the process to only 8 to 10 hours and maintains complete control over the temperature. Creme fraiche is often served as a topping on fresh fruit or pies and as a great way to enrich soups and pan sauces.

Be sure you do not use ultra-pasteurized cream, it doesn't work nearly as good as raw or regular pasteurized cream does.

Ingredients

For the Creme Fraiche

2 cups heavy cream or whipping cream, not ultra-pasteurized

3 tablespoons cultured buttermilk

For the Creme Fraiche

At least 10 to 12 hours before serving

Fill a water bath to about an inch (25mm) below the height of the mason jars you are using and preheat the water to 95ºF (35ºC).

Whisk together the heavy cream and buttermilk. Pour the mixture into a mason jar and seal with the lid. Place into the water bath and let cook for 8 to 10 hours.

Remove the jar from the water bath, chill in an ice bath and then refrigerate. It will last for 1 to 2 weeks in the refrigerator.

LEMON CURD

Cook: 165°F (73.9°C) for 45 to 60 minutes • Makes: 1 pint

Lemon curd is a sweet and sour, jam-like condiment that is great on pastries and tarts and can even be worked into savory dishes. Using sous vide to make it takes a lot of the guess work out of the process and makes it a very hands-off dish. This recipe makes a thick curd, for a thinner one just reduce the gelatin by about 50%.

Ingredients

For the Lemon Curd

3 large eggs

½ cup sugar

¼ cup fresh squeezed lemon juice

2 tablespoons lemon zest

4 tablespoons butter, melted

1½ teaspoons gelatin (7.2g)

For the Lemon Curd

At least 4 hours before serving

Preheat a water bath to 165°F (73.9°C).

Place all of the ingredients into a sous vide bag, seal, and place in the water bath. Cook for 45 to 60 minutes.

Once cooked, remove from the water bath, pour into a blender and process until fully emulsified. Let cool, or chill in an ice bath, and then pour into a container to set and refrigerate until ready to use. It will last 1 to 2 weeks in the refrigerator. For a pudding-like consistency you can blend the set curds.

Cinnamon-Vanilla Creme Brulee

Cook: 190°F (87.8°C) for 60 to 90 minutes • Makes: 4 creme brulees

Most people think creme brulee is a real fancy dish but it's actually very simple to make. Using a sous vide machine makes it even easier. This is a classic creme brulee and you can take it in a variety of directions depending on the flavors you want.

To get the ramekins at the proper height it is helpful to put a bowl or strainer upside down in the water bath and place a plate or sheet pan on top of it where the ramekins can sit. If you have a lid for your water bath make sure you use it, it will keep the air hot as well as eliminate evaporation, otherwise be sure to maintain the water level throughout the cooking process.

The best depth for the creme brulee is usually less than an inch (25mm) deep, otherwise the inside might not cook all the way through. For deeper creme brulees you may need to increase the cooking time to offset the depth. If your ramekins are touching each other in the water bath it can help to rotate them half way through the cooking process to ensure they cook evenly.

Ingredients

For the Creme Brulee
2 cups heavy or whipping cream
1 vanilla bean
1 cinnamon stick
4 egg yolks
Pinch of salt
⅓ cup white sugar

To Assemble
Sugar
Mint leaves

For the Creme Brulee

At least 4 to 5 hours before serving

Place an upside down strainer or bowl in your water bath. Top with a sheet pan or plate. Set the ramekins on it and fill the water bath two-thirds of the way up the ramekin. Preheat the water bath to 190°F (87.8°C).

Pour the heavy cream into a pot. Split the vanilla bean and scrape out the seeds, add the seeds and the bean to the cream. Add the cinnamon stick. Bring just to a simmer, stirring regularly. Turn off the heat and let it infuse for 10 minutes. Strain the cream.

Whisk together the egg yolks in another bowl then slowly whisk in the salt and sugar, the mixture should turn glossy and thicken slightly. Slowly whisk in the infused cream. Evenly divide among the ramekins, cover each ramekin with plastic wrap and use a rubber band to hold it in place. Place the ramekins in the sous vide bath with the water level coming two thirds of the way up the side. Cook for 60 to 90 minutes, depending on how thick you prefer your creme brulee.

Once cooked, remove from the water bath and let cool for 15 to 20 minutes. Place in the refrigerator and chill until cold, or preferably overnight.

To Assemble

Spread a thin layer of sugar a few grains thick on the top of the creme brulee and quickly torch until the sugar melts and begins to brown. Add a few mint leaves then serve.

WHITE CHOCOLATE CREME BRULEE

Cook: 190°F (87.8°C) for 60 to 90 minutes • Makes: 4 creme brulees

This creme brulee recipe builds off of the previous recipe and uses white chocolate to turn it into a more decadent dish. I usually serve it with some raspberries on top because they complement each other so well but you can also make a raspberry syrup or use other berries.

You can make other flavored creme brulees using similar adjustments to the flavorings. Using extracts or essential oils is an easy way to change the flavors, as are many other strongly flavored spices.

For more tips on making creme brulee in a sous vide machine please see the introduction to the previous recipe.

Ingredients

For the Creme Brulee
2 cups heavy or whipping cream
6 ounces white chocolate,
    roughly chopped (170g)
4 egg yolks
Pinch of salt
⅓ cup white sugar

To Assemble
Sugar
Raspberries

For the Creme Brulee

At least 4 to 5 hours before serving

Place an upside down strainer or bowl in your water bath. Top with a sheet pan or plate. Set the ramekins on it and fill the water bath two-thirds of the way up the ramekin. Preheat the water bath to 190°F (87.8°C).

Pour the heavy cream into a pot and bring just to a simmer. Slowly add the white chocolate and whisk until combined. Remove from the heat.

Whisk together the egg yolks in another bowl then slowly whisk in the salt and sugar, the mixture should turn glossy and thicken slightly. Slowly whisk in the cream. Evenly divide among the ramekins then cover each ramekin with plastic wrap and use a rubber band to hold in place. Place the ramekins in the sous vide bath with the water level coming two-thirds of the way up the side. Cook for 60 to 90 minutes, depending on how thick you prefer your creme brulee.

Once cooked, remove from the water bath and let cool for 15 to 20 minutes. Place in the refrigerator and chill until cold, or preferably overnight.

To Assemble

Spread a thin layer of sugar on the top of the creme brulee and quickly torch until the sugar melts and begins to brown. Add a raspberries to the top then serve.

DULCE DE LECHE

Cook: 185°F (85°C) for 10 to 15 hours • Makes: 1 pint

Dulce de leche is a caramel-like sauce made from sweetened milk that is very popular in South America. It's very easy to make at home, especially using a sous vide machine. At its most basic you place a can of sweetened condensed milk in a water bath set to 185°F (85°C) and cook it for 10 to 15 hours.

For this recipe I like to add a little vanilla paste and salt but even with just the condensed milk it is fantastic. I'll often serve it on fresh fruits and berries, or as a drizzle for brownies or cake. I make it in ½ pint mason jars because of their great size and their even cooking.

Ingredients

For the Dulce de Leche
2 14-ounce jars sweetened
   condensed milk (800g)
½ teaspoon vanilla paste or
   extract
1 teaspoon salt

For the Dulce de Leche

At least 12 to 17 hours before serving
Preheat a water bath to 185°F (85°C).

Whisk together the sweetened condensed milk, vanilla paste, and salt then pour into ½ pint mason jars and seal with the lids. Place into the water bath and let cook for 10 to 15 hours, until the milk has browned and thickened.

Remove the jars from the water bath, let cool, then refrigerate. They will last for several months in the refrigerator.

SECTION FOUR

REFERENCES

Sous Vide Time and Temperature

You can also get this time and temperature information on your mobile phone if you have an iPhone, iPad or an Android.

Just search for "Sous Vide" and look for the guide by "Primolicious".

One of the most interesting aspects of sous vide cooking is how much the time and temperature used can change the texture of the food. Many people experiment with different cooking times and temperatures to tweak dishes various ways.

The numbers below are merely beginning recommendations and are a good place to start. Feel free to increase or lower the temperature several degrees or play around with the cooking time as you see fit as long as you stay in the safe-zone.

BEEF - ROASTS AND TOUGH CUTS

Bottom Round Roast
Medium Rare   131°F for 2 to 3 Days (55.0°C)
Medium   140°F for 2 to 3 Days (60.0°C)
Well-Traditional 160°F for 1 to 2 Days (71.1°C)

Brisket
Medium Rare   131°F for 2 to 3 Days (55.0°C)
Medium   140°F for 2 to 3 Days (60.0°C)
Well-Traditional 160°F for 1 to 2 Days (71.1°C)

Cheek
Medium Rare   131°F for 2 to 3 Days (55.0°C)
Medium   149°F for 2 to 3 Days (65.0°C)
Well-Traditional 160°F for 1 to 2 Days (71.1°C)

Chuck Roast
Medium Rare   131°F for 36 to 60 Hours (55.0°C)
Flaky and Tender 161°F for 1 to 2 Days (71.6°C)
Well-Traditional 176°F for 12 to 24 Hours (80°C)

Pot Roast
Medium Rare   131°F for 2 to 3 Days (55.0°C)
Medium   140°F for 2 to 3 Days (60.0°C)
Well-Traditional 160°F for 1 to 2 Days (71.1°C)

Prime Rib Roast
Medium Rare   131°F for 5 to 10 Hours (55°C)
Medium   140°F for 5 to 10 Hours (60°C)

Rib Eye Roast
Medium Rare   131°F for 5 to 10 Hours (55°C)
Medium   140°F for 5 to 10 Hours (60°C)

Ribs
Medium Rare   131°F for 48 to 60 Hours (55.0°C)
Flaky and Tender 141°F for 2 to 3 Days (60.5°C)
Well-Traditional 156°F for 1 to 2 Days (68.8°C)

Shank
Medium Rare   131°F for 2 to 3 Days (55.0°C)
Medium   140°F for 2 to 3 Days (60.0°C)
Well-Traditional 160°F for 1 to 2 Days (71.1°C)

Short Ribs
Medium Rare   131°F for 2 to 3 Days (55.0°C)
Flaky and Tender 150°F for 18 to 36 Hours (65.5°C)
Well-Traditional 175°F for 12 to 24 Hours (79.4°C)

Sirloin Roast
Medium Rare   131°F for 5 to 10 Hours (55.0°C)
Medium   140°F for 5 to 10 Hours (60.0°C)

Stew Meat
Medium Rare   131°F for 4 to 8 Hours (55.0°C)
Medium   140°F for 4 to 8 Hours (60.0°C)

Sweetbreads
Medium   140°F for 30 to 45 Min (60°C)
Pre-Roasting   152°F for 60 Min (66.7°C)

Tenderloin Roast
Medium Rare   131°F for 3 to 6 Hours (55.0°C)
Medium   140°F for 3 to 6 Hours (60.0°C)

Tongue
Low and Slow   140°F for 48 Hours (60.0°C)
High and Fast 158°F for 24 Hours (70.0°C)

Top Loin Strip Roast
Medium Rare   131°F for 4 to 8 Hours (55.0°C)
Medium   140°F for 4 to 8 Hours (60.0°C)

Top Round Roast
Medium Rare   131°F for 1 to 3 Days (55.0°C)
Medium   140°F for 1 to 3 Days (60.0°C)
Well-Traditional 160°F for 1 to 2 Days (71.1°C)

Tri-Tip Roast
Medium Rare   131°F for 5 to 10 Hours (55°C)
Medium   140°F for 5 to 10 Hours (60°C)

BEEF - STEAK AND TENDER CUTS

Blade Steak
Medium Rare   131°F for 4 to 10 Hours (55.0°C)
Medium   140°F for 4 to 10 Hours (60.0°C)

Bottom Round Steak
Medium Rare   131°F for 1 to 3 Days (55.0°C)
Medium   140°F for 1 to 3 Days (60.0°C)

Chuck Steak
Medium Rare   131°F for 36 to 60 Hours (55.0°C)
Medium   140°F for 36 to 60 Hours (60.0°C)

Eye Round Steak
Medium Rare   131°F for 1 to 2 Days (55.0°C)
Medium   140°F for 1 to 2 Days (60.0°C)

Flank Steak
Medium Rare   131°F for 2 to 12 Hours (55.0°C)
Medium Rare and Tender   131°F for 1 to 2 Days (55.0°C)
Medium   140°F for 2 to 12 Hours (60.0°C)
Medium and Tender   140°F for 1 to 2 Days (60.0°C)

Flat Iron Steak
Medium Rare   131°F for 4 to 24 Hours (55.0°C)
Medium   140°F for 4 to 24 Hours (60.0°C)

Hamburger
Medium Rare   131°F for 2 to 4 Hours (55.0°C)
Medium   140°F for 2 to 4 Hours (60.0°C)

Hanger Steak
Medium Rare   131°F for 2 to 3 Hours (55.0°C)
Medium   140°F for 2 to 3 Hours (60.0°C)

Porterhouse Steak
Medium Rare   131°F for 2 to 3 Hours (55.0°C)
Medium   140°F for 2 to 3 Hours (60.0°C)

Rib Steak
Medium Rare   131°F for 2 to 8 Hours (55.0°C)
Medium   140°F for 2 to 8 Hours (60.0°C)

Ribeye Steak
Medium Rare   131°F for 2 to 6 Hours (55.0°C)
Medium   140°F for 2 to 6 Hours (60.0°C)

Sausage
Medium Rare   131°F for 2 to 3 Hours (55.0°C)
Medium   140°F for 90 to 120 Min (60°C)

Shoulder Steak
Medium Rare   131°F for 4 to 10 Hours (55.0°C)
Medium   140°F for 4 to 10 Hours (60.0°C)

Sirloin Steak
Medium Rare   131°F for 2 to 10 Hours (55.0°C)
Medium   140°F for 2 to 10 Hours (60.0°C)

Skirt Steak
Medium Rare   135°F for 1 to 3 Hours (57.2°C)
Medium Rare and Tender   131°F for 12 to 24 Hours (55.0°C)
Medium   140°F for 1 to 3 Hours (60.0°C)

T-Bone Steak
Medium Rare   131°F for 2 to 3 Hours (55.0°C)
Medium   140°F for 2 to 3 Hours (60.0°C)

Tenderloin Steak
Medium Rare   131°F for 2 to 3 Hours (55.0°C)
Medium   140°F for 2 to 3 Hours (60.0°C)

Top Loin Strip Steak
Medium Rare   131°F for 2 to 3 Hours (55.0°C)
Medium   140°F for 2 to 3 Hours (60.0°C)

Top Round Steak
Medium Rare   131°F for 1 to 2 Days (55.0°C)
Medium   140°F for 1 to 2 Days (60.0°C)

Tri-Tip Steak
Medium Rare   131°F for 2 to 24 Hours (55.0°C)
Medium   140°F for 2 to 24 Hours (60.0°C)

CHICKEN AND EGGS

Breast

Rare	136°F for 1 to 4 Hours (57.8°C)
Medium / Typical	140°F - 147°F for 1 to 4 Hours (63.9°C)
More Dry	140°F - 147°F for 4 to 12 Hours (63.9°C)

Drumstick

Rare	140°F for 90 to 120 Min (60.0°C)
Ideal	148°F - 156°F for 2 to 5 Hours (64.4°C)
For Shredding	160°F - 170°F for 8 to 12 Hours (71.1°C)

Eggs

Over Easy	140°F - 145°F for 45 to 60 Min (60°C)
Poached	142°F for 45 to 60 Min (61.1°C)
13 Minute	167°F for 13 Min (75°C)
Hard Boiled	155°F for 45 to 60 Min (68.3°C)
Pasteurized	135°F for 75 Min (57.2°C)

Leg

Rare	140°F for 90 to 120 Min (60.0°C)
Ideal	148°F - 156°F for 2 to 5 Hours (64.4°C)
For Shredding	160°F - 170°F for 8 to 12 Hours (71.1°C)

Sausage

White Meat	140°F for 1 to 2 Hours (63.9°C)
Mixed Meat	140°F for 90 to 120 Min (60.0°C)

Thigh

Rare	140°F for 90 to 120 Min (60.0°C)
Ideal	148°F - 156°F for 2 to 5 Hours (64.4°C)
For Shredding	160°F - 170°F for 8 to 12 Hours (71.1°C)

Whole Chicken

Rare	140°F for 4 to 6 Hours (60.0°C)
Typical	148°F for 4 to 6 Hours (64.4°C)
Larger	148°F for 6 to 8 Hours (64.4°C)
Butterflied	148°F for 2 to 4 Hours (64.4°C)

DUCK

Breast

Medium Rare	131°F for 2 to 4 Hours (55.0°C)
Medium	140°F for 2 to 4 Hours (60.0°C)

Drumstick

Medium Rare	131°F for 3 to 6 Hours (55.0°C)
Well	176°F for 8 to 10 Hours (80.0°C)
Confit	167°F for 10 to 20 Hours (75.0°C)

Foie Gras

Foie Gras	134°F for 35 to 55 Min (56.7°C)

Leg

Medium Rare	131°F for 3 to 6 Hours (55.0°C)
Well	176°F for 8 to 10 Hours (80.0°C)
Duck Confit	167°F for 10 to 20 Hours (75.0°C)

Sausage

Breast Meat	131°F for 1 to 2 Hours (55.0°C)
Mixed Meat	131°F for 2 to 3 Hours (55.0°C)

Thigh

Medium Rare	131°F for 3 to 6 Hours (55.0°C)
Well	176°F for 8 to 10 Hours (80.0°C)
Confit	167°F for 10 to 20 Hours (75.0°C)

Whole Duck

Medium Rare	131°F for 3 to 6 Hours (55.0°C)
Medium	140°F for 3 to 6 Hours (60.0°C)
Confit	167°F for 10 to 20 Hours (75.0°C)

FISH AND SHELLFISH

Arctic Char
"Sushi", Rare	104°F for 10 to 30 Min (40.0°C)
"Sushi", Medium Rare	122°F for 10 to 30 Min (50.0°C)
Medium Rare	132°F for 10 to 30 Min (55.6°C)
Medium	140°F for 10 to 30 Min (60.0°C)

Bass
"Sushi", Rare	104°F for 10 to 30 Min (40.0°C)
"Sushi", Medium Rare	122°F for 10 to 30 Min (50.0°C)
Medium Rare	132°F for 10 to 30 Min (55.6°C)
Medium	140°F for 10 to 30 Min (60.0°C)

Black Sea Bass
"Sushi", Rare	104°F for 10 to 30 Min (40.0°C)
"Sushi", Medium Rare	122°F for 10 to 30 Min (50.0°C)
Medium Rare	132°F for 10 to 30 Min (55.6°C)
Medium	140°F for 10 to 30 Min (60.0°C)

Bluefish
"Sushi", Medium Rare	122°F for 10 to 30 Min (50.0°C)
Medium Rare	132°F for 10 to 30 Min (55.6°C)
Medium	140°F for 10 to 30 Min (60.0°C)

Carp
"Sushi", Medium Rare	122°F for 10 to 30 Min (50.0°C)
Medium Rare	132°F for 10 to 30 Min (55.6°C)
Medium	140°F for 10 to 30 Min (60.0°C)

Catfish
"Sushi", Medium Rare	122°F for 10 to 30 Min (50.0°C)
Medium Rare	132°F for 10 to 30 Min (55.6°C)
Medium	140°F for 10 to 30 Min (60.0°C)

Cod
Rare	104°F for 10 to 30 Min (40.0°C)
"Sushi", Medium Rare	129°F for 10 to 30 Min (53.9°C)
Medium Rare	132°F for 10 to 30 Min (55.6°C)

Flounder
"Sushi", Medium Rare	122°F for 10 to 30 Min (50.0°C)
Medium Rare	132°F for 10 to 30 Min (55.6°C)
Medium	140°F for 10 to 30 Min (60.0°C)

Grouper
"Sushi", Rare	104°F for 10 to 30 Min (40.0°C)
"Sushi", Medium Rare	122°F for 10 to 30 Min (50.0°C)
Medium Rare	132°F for 10 to 30 Min (55.6°C)
Medium	140°F for 10 to 30 Min (60.0°C)

Haddock
"Sushi", Medium Rare	122°F for 10 to 30 Min (50.0°C)
Medium Rare	132°F for 10 to 30 Min (55.6°C)
Medium	140°F for 10 to 30 Min (60.0°C)

Hake
"Sushi", Rare	104°F for 10 to 30 Min (40.0°C)
"Sushi", Medium Rare	122°F for 10 to 30 Min (50.0°C)
Medium Rare	132°F for 10 to 30 Min (55.6°C)
Medium	140°F for 10 to 30 Min (60.0°C)

Halibut
"Sushi", Rare	104°F for 10 to 30 Min (40.0°C)
"Sushi", Medium Rare	129°F for 10 to 30 Min (53.9°C)
Medium Rare	132°F for 10 to 30 Min (55.6°C)
Medium	140°F for 10 to 30 Min (60.0°C)

King Crab Tail
King Crab Tail	140°F for 30 to 45 Min (60.0°C)

Lobster
Medium Rare	126°F for 15 to 40 Min (52.2°C)
Medium	140°F for 15 to 40 Min (60.0°C)

Mackerel
"Sushi", Rare	109°F for 10 to 30 Min (42.8°C)
"Sushi", Medium Rare	122°F for 10 to 30 Min (50.0°C)
Medium Rare	132°F for 10 to 30 Min (55.6°C)

Mahi Mahi

"Sushi", Medium Rare	122°F for 10 to 30 Min (50.0°C)
Medium Rare	132°F for 10 to 30 Min (55.6°C)
Medium	140°F for 10 to 30 Min (60.0°C)

Marlin

"Sushi", Rare	104°F for 10 to 30 Min (40.0°C)
"Sushi", Medium Rare	122°F for 10 to 30 Min (50.0°C)
Medium Rare	132°F for 10 to 30 Min (55.6°C)
Medium	140°F for 10 to 30 Min (60.0°C)

Monkfish

"Sushi", Rare	104°F for 10 to 30 Min (40.0°C)
"Sushi", Medium Rare	118°F for 10 to 30 Min (47.8°C)
Medium Rare	132°F for 10 to 30 Min (55.6°C)
Medium	140°F for 10 to 30 Min (60.0°C)

Octopus

Slow Cook	170°F for 4 to 7 Hours (76.7°C)
Fast Cook	180°F for 2 to 3 Hours (82.2°C)

Red Snapper

"Sushi", Rare	104°F for 10 to 30 Min (40.0°C)
"Sushi", Medium Rare	122°F for 10 to 30 Min (50.0°C)
Medium Rare	132°F for 10 to 30 Min (55.6°C)
Medium	140°F for 10 to 30 Min (60.0°C)

Salmon

"Sushi", Rare	104°F for 10 to 30 Min (40.0°C)
"Sushi", Medium Rare	122°F for 10 to 30 Min (50.0°C)
Medium Rare	132°F for 10 to 30 Min (55.6°C)
Medium	140°F for 10 to 30 Min (60.0°C)

Sardines

"Sushi", Rare	104°F for 10 to 30 Min (40.0°C)
"Sushi", Medium Rare	122°F for 10 to 30 Min (50.0°C)
Medium Rare	132°F for 10 to 30 Min (55.6°C)
Medium	140°F for 10 to 30 Min (60.0°C)

Scallops

Pre-Sear	122°F for 15 to 35 Min (50.0°C)

Scrod

"Sushi", Medium Rare	122°F for 10 to 30 Min (50.0°C)
Medium Rare	132°F for 10 to 30 Min (55.6°C)
Medium	140°F for 10 to 30 Min (60.0°C)

Sea Bass

"Sushi", Rare	104°F for 10 to 30 Min (40.0°C)
"Sushi", Medium Rare	122°F for 10 to 30 Min (50.0°C)
Medium Rare	132°F for 10 to 30 Min (55.6°C)
Medium	140°F for 10 to 30 Min (60.0°C)

Shark

"Sushi", Medium Rare	122°F for 10 to 30 Min (50.0°C)
Medium Rare	132°F for 10 to 30 Min (55.6°C)
Medium	140°F for 10 to 30 Min (60.0°C)

Shrimp

"Sushi" Medium Rare	122°F for 15 to 35 Min (50.0°C)
Medium Rare	132°F for 15 to 35 Min (55.6°C)

Skate

"Sushi", Medium Rare	129°F for 10 to 30 Min (53.9°C)
Medium Rare	132°F for 10 to 30 Min (55.6°C)
Medium	140°F for 10 to 30 Min (60.0°C)

Soft Shell Crab

Standard	145°F for 3 hours (62.8°C)

Sole

"Sushi", Medium Rare	122°F for 10 to 30 Min (50.0°C)
Medium Rare	132°F for 10 to 30 Min (55.6°C)
Medium	143°F for 10 to 30 Min (61.7°C)

Squid

Pre-Sear	113°F for 45 to 60 Min (45.0°C)
Low Heat	138°F for 2 to 4 Hours (58.9°C)
High Heat	180°F for 1 Hour (82.2°C)

Striped Bass

"Sushi", Rare	104°F for 10 to 30 Min (40.0°C)
"Sushi", Medium Rare	122°F for 10 to 30 Min (50.0°C)
Medium Rare	132°F for 10 to 30 Min (55.6°C)
Medium	140°F for 10 to 30 Min (60.0°C)

Sturgeon

"Sushi", Rare	104°F for 10 to 30 Min (40.0°C)
"Sushi", Medium Rare	122°F for 10 to 30 Min (50.0°C)
Medium Rare	132°F for 10 to 30 Min (55.6°C)
Medium	140°F for 10 to 30 Min (60.0°C)

Swordfish

"Sushi", Rare	104°F for 10 to 30 Min (40.0°C)
"Sushi", Medium Rare	122°F for 10 to 30 Min (50.0°C)
Medium Rare	132°F for 10 to 30 Min (55.6°C)
Medium	140°F for 10 to 30 Min (60.0°C)

Tilapia

"Sushi", Rare	104°F for 10 to 30 Min (40.0°C)
"Sushi", Medium Rare	122°F for 10 to 30 Min (50.0°C)
Medium Rare	132°F for 10 to 30 Min (55.6°C)
Medium	140°F for 10 to 30 Min (60.0°C)

Trout

"Sushi", Medium Rare	122°F for 10 to 30 Min (50.0°C)
Medium Rare	132°F for 10 to 30 Min (55.6°C)
Medium	140°F for 10 to 30 Min (60.0°C)

Tuna

"Sushi", Rare	100°F for 10 to 20 Min (37.8°C)
"Sushi", Medium Rare	129°F for 10 to 30 Min (53.9°C)
Medium Rare	132°F for 10 to 30 Min (55.6°C)

Turbot

"Sushi", Medium Rare	129°F for 10 to 30 Min (53.9°C)
Medium Rare	132°F for 10 to 30 Min (55.6°C)
Medium	140°F for 10 to 30 Min (60.0°C)

FRUITS AND VEGETABLES

Acorn Squash	183°F for 1 to 2 Hours (83.9°C)	**Pears**	183°F for 25 to 60 Min (83.9°C)
Apples	183°F for 1 to 2 Hours (83.9°C)	**Pineapple**	167°F for 45 to 60 Min (75.0°C)
Artichokes	183°F for 45 to 75 Min (83.9°C)	**Plums**	167°F for 15 to 20 Min (75.0°C)
Asparagus	183°F for 10 to 30 Min (83.9°C)	**Potatoes**	
Banana	183°F for 10 to 15 Min (83.9°C)	Small	183°F for 30 to 60 Min (83.9°C)
		Large	183°F for 60 to 120 Min (83.9°C)
Beet	183°F for 60 to 90 Min (83.9°C)		
Broccoli	183°F for 30 to 60 Min (83.9°C)	**Pumpkin**	183°F for 45 to 60 Min (83.9°C)
Brussels Sprouts	183°F for 45 to 60 Min (83.9°C)	**Radish**	183°F for 10 to 25 Min (83.9°C)
Butternut Squash	183°F for 45 to 60 Min (83.9°C)	**Rhubarb**	141°F for 25 to 45 Min (60.6°C)
Cabbage	183°F for 60 Min (83.9°C)	**Rutabaga**	183°F for 2 Hours (83.9°C)
Carrot	183°F for 45 to 60 Min (83.9°C)	**Salsify**	183°F for 45 to 60 Min (83.9°C)
Cauliflower		**Squash, Summer**	183°F for 30 to 60 Min (83.9°C)
Florets	183°F for 20 to 30 Min (83.9°C)	**Squash, Winter**	183°F for 1 to 2 Hours (83.9°C)
For Puree	183°F for 2 Hours (83.9°C)		
Stems	183°F for 60 to 75 Min (83.9°C)	**Sunchokes**	183°F for 40 to 60 Min (83.9°C)
Celery Root	183°F for 60 to 75 Min (83.9°C)	**Sweet Potatoes**	
Chard	183°F for 60 to 75 Min (83.9°C)	Small	183°F for 45 to 60 Min (83.9°C)
		Large	183°F for 60 to 90 Min (83.9°C)
Cherries	183°F for 15 to 25 Min (83.9°C)	**Swiss Chard**	183°F for 60 to 75 Min (83.9°C)
Corn	183°F for 15 to 25 Min (83.9°C)	**Turnip**	183°F for 45 to 60 Min (83.9°C)
Eggplant	183°F for 30 to 45 Min (83.9°C)	**Yams**	183°F for 30 to 60 Min (83.9°C)
Fennel	183°F for 30 to 60 Min (83.9°C)	**Zucchini**	183°F for 30 to 60 Min (83.9°C)
Golden Beets	183°F for 30 to 60 Min (83.9°C)		
Green Beans	183°F for 30 to 45 Min (83.9°C)		
Leek	183°F for 30 to 60 Min (83.9°C)		
Onion	183°F for 35 to 45 Min (83.9°C)		
Parsnip	183°F for 30 to 60 Min (83.9°C)		
Pea Pods	183°F for 30 to 40 Min (83.9°C)		
Peaches	183°F for 30 to 60 Min (83.9°C)		

LAMB

Arm Chop
Medium Rare   131°F for 18 to 36 Hours (55.0°C)
Medium   140°F for 18 to 36 Hours (60.0°C)

Blade Chop
Medium Rare   131°F for 18 to 36 Hours (55.0°C)
Medium   140°F for 18 to 36 Hours (60.0°C)

Breast
Medium Rare   131°F for 20 to 28 Hours (55.0°C)
Medium   140°F for 20 to 28 Hours (60.0°C)
Well-Traditional   165°F for 20 to 28 Hours (73.9°C)

Leg, Bone In
Rare   126°F for 1 to 2 Days (52.2°C)
Medium Rare   131°F for 2 to 3 Days (55.0°C)
Medium   140°F for 1 to 3 Days (60.0°C)

Leg, Boneless
Medium Rare   131°F for 18 to 36 Hours (55.0°C)
Medium   140°F for 18 to 36 Hours (60.0°C)

Loin Chops
Rare   126°F for 1 to 2 Hours (52.2°C)
Medium Rare   131°F for 2 to 4 Hours (55.0°C)
Medium   140°F for 2 to 3 Hours (60.0°C)

Loin Roast
Rare   126°F for 1 to 2 Hours (52.2°C)
Medium Rare   131°F for 2 to 4 Hours (55.0°C)
Medium   140°F for 2 to 3 Hours (60.0°C)

Loin, Boneless
Rare   126°F for 1 to 2 Hours (52.2°C)
Medium Rare   131°F for 2 to 4 Hours (55.0°C)
Medium   140°F for 2 to 3 Hours (60.0°C)

Neck
Medium Rare   131°F for 2 to 3 Days (55.0°C)
Medium   140°F for 2 to 3 Days (60.0°C)
Well-Traditional   165°F for 1 to 2 Days (73.9°C)

Osso Buco
Medium Rare   131°F for 1 to 2 Days (55.0°C)
Medium   140°F for 1 to 2 Days (60.0°C)
Well-Traditional   165°F for 1 to 2 Days (73.9°C)

Rack
Rare   126°F for 1 to 2 Hours (52.2°C)
Medium Rare   131°F for 2 to 4 Hours (55.0°C)
Medium   140°F for 1 to 4 Hours (60.0°C)

Rib Chop
Rare   126°F for 1 to 2 Hours (52.2°C)
Medium Rare   131°F for 2 to 3 Hours (55.0°C)
Medium   140°F for 1 to 3 Hours (60.0°C)

Ribs
Medium Rare   131°F for 22 to 26 Hours (55.0°C)
Medium   140°F for 22 to 26 Hours (60.0°C)
Well-Traditional   165°F for 22 to 26 Hours (73.9°C)

Shank
Medium Rare   131°F for 1 to 2 Days (55.0°C)
Medium   140°F for 1 to 2 Days (60.0°C)
Well-Traditional   165°F for 1 to 2 Days (73.9°C)

Shoulder
Medium Rare   131°F for 1 to 2 Days (55.0°C)
Medium   140°F for 1 to 2 Days (60.0°C)
Well-Traditional   165°F for 18 to 36 Hours (73.9°C)

Tenderloin
Rare   126°F for 1 to 2 Hours (52.2°C)
Medium Rare   131°F for 2 to 3 Hours (55.0°C)
Medium   140°F for 1 to 3 Hours (60.0°C)

PORK

Arm Steak
Medium Rare   131°F for 1 to 2 Days (55.0°C)
Medium   140°F for 1 to 2 Days (60.0°C)

Baby Back Ribs
Medium Rare   131°F for 24 to 48 Hours (55.0°C)
Medium   140°F for 12 to 48 Hours (60.0°C)
Well-Traditional 155°F for 12 to 24 Hours (68.3°C)

Back Ribs
Medium Rare   131°F for 24 to 48 Hours (55.0°C)
Medium   140°F for 12 to 48 Hours (60.0°C)
Well-Traditional 155°F for 12 to 24 Hours (68.3°C)

Belly
Low and Slow   140°F for 2 to 3 Days (60.0°C)
In Between   160°F for 18 to 36 Hours (71.1°C)
High and Fast   180°F for 12 to 18 Hours (82.2°C)

Blade Chops
Medium Rare   131°F for 8 to 12 Hours (55.0°C)
Medium   140°F for 8 to 12 Hours (60.0°C)

Blade Roast
Medium Rare   131°F for 1 to 2 Days (55.0°C)
Medium   140°F for 1 to 2 Days (60.0°C)
Well-Traditional 155°F for 1 to 2 Days (68.3°C)

Blade Steak
Medium Rare   131°F for 18 to 36 Hours (55.0°C)
Medium   140°F for 18 to 36 Hours (60.0°C)

Boston Butt
Medium Rare   131°F for 1 to 2 Days (55.0°C)
Medium   140°F for 1 to 2 Days (60.0°C)
Well-Traditional 155°F for 1 to 2 Days (68.3°C)

Butt Roast
Medium Rare   131°F for 18 to 36 Hours (55.0°C)
Medium   140°F for 18 to 36 Hours (60.0°C)
Well-Traditional 155°F for 18 to 36 Hours (68.3°C)

Country Style Ribs
Medium Rare   131°F for 8 to 24 Hours (55.0°C)
Medium   140°F for 8 to 24 Hours (60.0°C)
Well-Traditional 155°F for 12 to 24 Hours (68.3°C)

Fresh Side Pork
Low and Slow   140°F for 2 to 3 Days (60.0°C)
In Between   160°F for 18 to 36 Hours (71.1°C)
High and Fast   180°F for 12 to 18 Hours (82.2°C)

Ground Pork
Medium Rare   131°F for 2 to 4 Hours (55.0°C)
Medium   140°F for 2 to 4 Hours (60.0°C)

Ham Roast
Medium Rare   131°F for 10 to 20 Hours (55.0°C)
Medium   140°F for 10 to 20 Hours (60.0°C)
Well-Traditional 155°F for 10 to 20 Hours (68.3°C)

Ham Steak
Medium Rare   131°F for 2 to 3 Hours (55.0°C)
Medium   140°F for 2 to 3 Hours (60.0°C)

Kebabs
Medium Rare   131°F for 3 to 8 Hours (55.0°C)
Medium   140°F for 3 to 8 Hours (60.0°C)
Well-Traditional 155°F for 3 to 8 Hours (68.3°C)

Leg (Fresh Ham)
Medium Rare   131°F for 10 to 20 Hours (55.0°C)
Medium   140°F for 10 to 20 Hours (60.0°C)
Well-Traditional 155°F for 10 to 20 Hours (68.3°C)

Loin Chop
Medium Rare   131°F for 3 to 5 Hours (55.0°C)
Medium   140°F for 2 to 4 Hours (60.0°C)

Loin Roast
Medium Rare   131°F for 4 to 8 Hours (55.0°C)
Medium   140°F for 4 to 6 Hours (60.0°C)

Picnic Roast
Medium Rare   131°F for 1 to 3 Days (55.0°C)
Medium   140°F for 1 to 3 Days (60.0°C)
Well-Traditional 155°F for 1 to 3 Days (68.3°C)

Pork Chops
Medium Rare   131°F for 3 to 6 Hours (55.0°C)
Medium   140°F for 2 to 4 Hours (60.0°C)

Rib Chops
Medium Rare 131ºF for 5 to 8 Hours (55.0ºC)
Medium   140ºF for 4 to 7 Hours (60.0ºC)

Rib Roast
Medium Rare 131ºF for 5 to 8 Hours (55.0ºC)
Medium   140ºF for 4 to 7 Hours (60.0ºC)

Sausage
Medium Rare 131ºF for 2 to 3 Hours (55.0ºC)
Medium   140ºF for 2 to 3 Hours (60.0ºC)
Well-Traditional155ºF for 2 to 3 Hours (68.3ºC)

Shank
Medium Rare 131ºF for 8 to 10 Hours (55.0ºC)
Medium   140ºF for 8 to 10 Hours (60.0ºC)

Shoulder
Medium Rare 135ºF for 1 to 2 Days (57.2ºC)
Medium   145ºF for 1 to 2 Days (62.8ºC)
Well-Traditional156ºF for 18 to 24 Hours (68.8ºC)

Sirloin Chops
Medium Rare 131ºF for 6 to 12 Hours (55.0ºC)
Medium   140ºF for 5 to 10 Hours (60.0ºC)

Sirloin Roast
Medium Rare 131ºF for 6 to 12 Hours (55.0ºC)
Medium   140ºF for 5 to 10 Hours (60.0ºC)
Well-Traditional155ºF for 10 to 16 Hours (68.3ºC)

Spare Ribs
Medium Rare 131ºF for 24 to 48 Hours (55.0ºC)
Medium   140ºF for 12 to 48 Hours (60.0ºC)
Well-Traditional155ºF for 12 to 24 Hours (68.3ºC)

Spleen
Spleen   145ºF for 1 Hour (62.8ºC)

Tenderloin
Medium Rare 131ºF for 3 to 6 Hours (55.0ºC)
Medium   140ºF for 2 to 4 Hours (60.0ºC)

TURKEY

Breast

"Rare"   136°F for 1 to 4 Hours (57.8°C)

Medium / Typical   140°F - 147°F for 1 to 4 Hours (63.9°C)

Drumstick

Medium Rare   140°F for 3 to 4 Hours (60.0°C)

Ideal   148°F for 4 to 8 Hours (64.4°C)

For Shredding   160°F for 18 to 24 Hours (71.1°C)

Leg

Medium Rare   140°F for 3 to 4 Hours (60.0°C)

Ideal   148°F for 4 to 8 Hours (64.4°C)

For Shredding   160°F for 18 to 24 Hours (71.1°C)

Sausage

White Meat   140°F for 1 to 4 Hours (63.9°C)

Mixed Meat   140°F for 3 to 4 Hours (64.4°C)

Thigh

Medium Rare   140°F for 3 to 4 Hours (60.0°C)

Ideal   148°F for 4 to 8 Hours (64.4°C)

For Shredding   160°F for 18 to 24 Hours (71.1°C)

FAHRENHEIT TO CELSIUS CONVERSION

This guide gives temperatures in both Fahrenheit and Celsius but to convert from Fahrenheit to Celsius take the temperature, then subtract 32 from it and multiply the result by 5/9:

(Fahrenheit - 32) * 5/9 = Celsius

I've listed out the temperatures from 37°C to 87°C which are the most commonly used range in sous vide.

Celsius	Fahrenheit	Celsius	Fahrenheit
37	98.6	64	147.2
38	100.4	65	149.0
39	102.2	66	150.8
40	104.0	67	152.6
41	105.8	68	154.4
42	107.6	69	156.2
43	109.4	70	158.0
44	111.2	71	159.8
45	113.0	72	161.6
46	114.8	73	163.4
47	116.6	74	165.2
48	118.4	75	167.0
49	120.2	76	168.8
50	122.0	77	170.6
51	123.8	78	172.4
52	125.6	79	174.2
53	127.4	80	176.0
54	129.2	81	177.8
55	131.0	82	179.6
56	132.8	83	181.4
57	134.6	84	183.2
58	136.4	85	185.0
59	138.2	86	186.8
60	140.0	87	188.6
61	141.8	88	190.4
62	143.6	89	192.2
63	145.4	90	194.0

SOUS VIDE THICKNESS TIMES

For more cooking by thickness information you can view the equipment section on my website where I have an iPhone thickness ruler and free printable thickness cards.

You can find them on my website here:
MCMEasy.com/Ruler

A Few Notes on the Times

Times were extrapolated from the descriptions in Baldwin's Practical Guide to Sous Vide (http://bit.ly/hGOtjd) and Sous Vide for the Home Cook, as well as Nathan's tables on eGullet and a few other sources. (http://bit.ly/eVHjS3).

The times are also approximate since there are many factors that go into how quickly food is heated. The density of the food matters a lot, which is one reason beef heats differently than chicken. To a lesser degree where you get your beef from will affect the cooking time, and whether the beef was factory raised, farm raised, or grass-fed. Because of this, I normally don't try to pull it out at the exact minute it is done unless I'm in a rush.

The times shown are also minimum times and food can be, and sometimes needs to be, left in for longer periods in order to fully tenderize the meat. If you are cooking food longer, remember that food should not be cooked at temperatures less than 131°F (55°C) for more than 4 hours.

Heat from Refrigerator to Any Temperature

How long it will take to heat an entire piece of meat from 41°F / 5°C to the temperature of the water bath.

Reminder, this food might not be pasteurized at these times and food should not be cooked at temperatures less than 131°F / 55°C for more than 4 hours.

While there are slight differences in the heating time for different temperatures of water baths, the times usually vary less than 5 to 10% even going from a 111°F / 44°C bath to a 141°F / 60.6°C bath, which equates to a difference of 5 minutes every hour. I show the largest value in the chart, so if you are cooking it at a lower temperature you can knock a little of the time off.

Heat from Freezer to Any Temperature

How long it will take to heat an entire piece of meat from 0°F / -18°C to the temperature of the water bath.

Reminder, this food might not be pasteurized at these times and food should not be cooked at temperatures less than 131°F / 55°C for more than 4 hours.

While there are slight differences in the heating time for different temperatures of water baths, the times usually vary less than 5 to 10% even going from a 111°F / 44°C bath to a 141°F / 60.6°C bath, which equates to a difference of 5 minutes every hour. I show the largest value in the chart, so if you are cooking it at a lower temperature you can knock a little of the time off.

Pasteurize from Refrigerator to 131°F / 55°C

This is the amount of time it will take a piece of meat that is 41°F / 5°C to become pasteurized in a 131°F / 55°C water bath.

Pasteurize from Refrigerator to 141°F / 60.6°C

This is the amount of time it will take a piece of meat that is 41°F / 5°C to become pasteurized in a 141°F / 60.6°C water bath.

Heat from Refrigerator to Any Temperature

70mm	6h 25m
65mm	5h 30m
60mm	4h 45m
55mm	4h 0m 0s
50mm	3h 15m
45mm	2h 40m
40mm	2h 10m
35mm	1h 40m
30mm	1h 15m 0s
25mm	0h 50m
20mm	0h 35m
15mm	0h 20m
10mm	0h 8m
5mm	0h 2m 0s

Pasteurize from Refrigerator to 131°F / 55°C

70mm	5 hrs 15 mins
65mm	4 hrs 45 mins
60mm	4 hrs 15 mins
55mm	3 hrs 50 mins
50mm	3 hrs 25 mins
45mm	3 hrs 00 mins
40mm	2 hrs 40 mins
35mm	2 hrs 20 mins
30mm	2 hrs 00 mins
25mm	1 hrs 50 mins
20mm	1 hrs 40 mins
15mm	1 hrs 30 mins
10mm	1 hrs 25 mins
5mm	1 hrs 20 mins

Heat from Freezer to Any Temperature

70mm	7 hrs 40 mins
65mm	6 hrs 40 mins
60mm	5 hrs 35 mins
55mm	4 hrs 45 mins
50mm	4 hrs 00 mins
45mm	3 hrs 10 mins
40mm	2 hrs 30 mins
35mm	2 hrs 00 mins
30mm	1 hrs 30 mins
25mm	1 hrs 00 mins
20mm	0 hrs 40 mins
15mm	0 hrs 25 mins
10mm	0 hrs 10 mins
5mm	0 hrs 02 mins

Pasteurize from Refrigerator to 141°F / 60.6°C

70mm	3 hrs 50 mins
65mm	3 hrs 25 mins
60mm	3 hrs 00 mins
55mm	2 hrs 40 mins
50mm	2 hrs 20 mins
45mm	2 hrs 00 mins
40mm	1 hrs 40 mins
35mm	1 hrs 25 mins
30mm	1 hrs 10 mins
25mm	0 hrs 55 mins
20mm	0 hrs 45 mins
15mm	0 hrs 35 mins
10mm	0 hrs 25 mins
5mm	0 hrs 21 mins

Chicken Thickness Chart

Pasteurize from Refrigerator to 135.5°F / 57.5°C

This is the amount of time it will take a piece of chicken that is 41°F / 5°C to become pasteurized in a 135.5°F / 57.5°C water bath.

Pasteurize from Refrigerator to 141°F / 60.6°C

This is the amount of time it will take a piece of chicken that is 41°F / 5°C to become pasteurized in a 141°F / 60.6°C water bath.

Pasteurize from Refrigerator to 146.3°F / 63.5°C

This is the amount of time it will take a piece of chicken that is 41°F / 5°C to become pasteurized in a 146.3°F / 63.5°C water bath.

Pasteurize from Refrigerator to 150.8°F / 66°C

This is the amount of time it will take a piece of chicken that is 41°F / 5°C to become pasteurized in a 150.8°F / 66°C water bath.

Pasteurize Refrigerator to 135.5°F / 57.5°C

70mm	6h 30m
65mm	6h
60mm	5h 15m
55mm	4h 45m
50mm	4h 15m
45mm	3h 45m
40mm	3h 20m
35mm	3h
30mm	2h 35m
25mm	2h 20m
20mm	2h 5m
15mm	1h 55m
10mm	1h 45m
5mm	1h 40m

Pasteurize Refrigerator to 141°F / 60.6°C

70mm	4h 55m
65mm	4h 20m
60mm	3h 50m
55mm	3h 20m
50mm	2h 55m
45mm	2h 30m
40mm	2h 5m
35mm	1h 45m
30mm	1h 25m
25mm	1h 10m
20mm	0h 55m
15mm	0h 45m
10mm	0h 36m
5mm	0h 31m

Pasteurize Refrigerator to 146.3°F / 63.5°C

70mm	4h 0m 0s
65mm	3h 35m
60mm	3h 10m
55mm	2h 45m
50mm	2h 20m
45mm	2h
40mm	1h 40m
35mm	1h 20m
30mm	1h
25mm	0h 50m
20mm	0h 35m
15mm	0h 23m
10mm	0h 15m
5mm	0h 10m

Pasteurize Refrigerator to 150.8°F / 66°C

70mm	3h 35m 0s
65mm	3h 10m
60mm	2h 45m
55mm	2h 20m
50mm	2h
45mm	1h 40m
40mm	1h 25m
35mm	1h 5m
30mm	0h 50m
25mm	0h 40m
20mm	0h 26m
15mm	0h 20m
10mm	0h 10m
5mm	0h 5m

Heat Fatty Fish to Any Temperature

These times show how long it will take to heat an entire piece of fatty fish from 41°F / 5°C to any typical temperature.

Reminder, this food might not be pasteurized at these times and food should not be cooked at temperatures less than 131°F / 55°C for more than 4 hours.

While there are slight differences in the heating time for different temperatures of water baths, the times usually vary less than 5 to 10% even going from a 111°F / 44°C bath to a 141°F / 60.6°C bath, which equates to a difference of 5 minutes every hour. I show the largest value in the chart, so if you are cooking it at a lower temperature you can knock a little of the time off.

Pasteurize Lean Fish to 131°F / 55°C

This is the amount of time it will take a piece of lean fish that is 41°F / 5°C to become pasteurized in a 131°F / 55°C water bath.

Pasteurize Lean Fish to 141°F / 60.6°C

This is the amount of time it will take a piece of lean fish that is 41°F / 5°C to become pasteurized in a 141°F / 60.6°C water bath.

Pasteurize Fatty Fish to 131°F / 55°C

This is the amount of time it will take a piece of fatty fish that is 41°F / 5°C to become pasteurized in a 131°F / 55°C water bath.

Pasteurize Fatty Fish to 141°F / 60.6°C

This is the amount of time it will take a piece of fatty fish that is 41°F / 5°C to become pasteurized in a 141°F / 60.6°C water bath.

Heat Fatty Fish to Any Temperature

70mm	6 hrs 25 mins
65mm	5 hrs 30 mins
60mm	4 hrs 45 mins
55mm	4 hrs 00 mins
50mm	3 hrs 15 mins
45mm	2 hrs 40 mins
40mm	2 hrs 10 mins
35mm	1 hrs 40 mins
30mm	1 hrs 15 mins
25mm	0 hrs 50 mins
20mm	0 hrs 35 mins
15mm	0 hrs 20 mins
10mm	0 hrs 08 mins
5mm	0 hrs 02 mins

Pasteurize Lean Fish to 131°F / 55°C

70mm	5 hrs 15 mins
65mm	4 hrs 45 mins
60mm	4 hrs 15 mins
55mm	3 hrs 50 mins
50mm	3 hrs 25 mins
45mm	3 hrs 00 mins
40mm	2 hrs 40 mins
35mm	2 hrs 20 mins
30mm	2 hrs 00 mins
25mm	1 hrs 50 mins
20mm	1 hrs 40 mins
15mm	1 hrs 30 mins
10mm	1 hrs 25 mins
5mm	1 hrs 20 mins

Pasteurize Lean Fish to 141°F / 60.6°C

70mm	6 hrs 30 mins
65mm	6 hrs 00 mins
60mm	5 hrs 15 mins
55mm	4 hrs 45 mins
50mm	4 hrs 15 mins
45mm	3 hrs 45 mins
40mm	3 hrs 20 mins
35mm	3 hrs 00 mins
30mm	2 hrs 35 mins
25mm	2 hrs 20 mins
20mm	2 hrs 05 mins
15mm	1 hrs 55 mins
10mm	1 hrs 45 mins
5mm	1 hrs 40 mins

Pasteurize Fatty Fish to 131°F / 55°C

70mm	5 hrs 15 mins
65mm	4 hrs 45 mins
60mm	4 hrs 15 mins
55mm	3 hrs 50 mins
50mm	3 hrs 25 mins
45mm	3 hrs 00 mins
40mm	2 hrs 40 mins
35mm	2 hrs 20 mins
30mm	2 hrs 00 mins
25mm	1 hrs 50 mins
20mm	1 hrs 40 mins
15mm	1 hrs 30 mins
10mm	1 hrs 25 mins
5mm	1 hrs 20 mins

Pasteurize Fatty Fish to 141°F / 60.6°C

70mm	6 hrs 30 mins
65mm	6 hrs 00 mins
60mm	5 hrs 15 mins
55mm	4 hrs 45 mins
50mm	4 hrs 15 mins
45mm	3 hrs 45 mins
40mm	3 hrs 20 mins
35mm	3 hrs 00 mins
30mm	2 hrs 35 mins
25mm	2 hrs 20 mins
20mm	2 hrs 05 mins
15mm	1 hrs 55 mins
10mm	1 hrs 45 mins
5mm	1 hrs 40 mins

INGREDIENT TABLES

You can find out more information about modernist ingredients and techniques through my free detailed guides to modernist cooking.

You can find them:
MCMEasy.com/GettingStarted

INGREDIENT TECHNIQUES

Ingredient	Emulsions	Foams	Gels	Spherification	Thickening
Agar		X	X		
Carrageenan: Iota		X	X	X	X
Carrageenan: Lambda	X	X			X
Carrageenan: Kappa			X		
Gelatin		X	X		
Gellan	X	X	X		
Guar Gum	X				X
Gum Arabic	X	X			X
Konjac	X		X		X
Lecithin	X	X			
Locust Bean Gum			X		X
Maltodextrin					X
Methylcellulose	X	X	X		
Mono and Diglycerides	X	X			X
Pectin	X	X	X		
Pure Cote B790			X		
Sodium Alginate			X	X	
Ultra-Sperse	X	X			X
Ultra-Tex	X	X			X
Versawhip		X			
Xanthan Gum	X	X			X

INGREDIENT TEMPERATURES

When you are trying to determine which ingredient to use, the hydration, setting, and melting temperatures can be very important.

Ingredient	Dispersion	Hydration	Gel Sets	Gel Melts
Agar	Any	100°C / 212°F	40-45°C / 104-113°F	80°C / 176°F
Carrageenan: Iota	Cool	Above 70°C / 158°F	40-70°C / 104-158°F	5-10°C / 9-18°F above setting
Carrageenan: Kappa	Cool	Above 70°C / 158°F	35-60°C / 95-140°F	10-20°C / 18-36°F above setting
Gelatin	Above 50°C / 122°F	Cool	30°C / 86°F	30°C / 86°F - 40°C / 104°F
Lecithin	Any	Any	N/A	N/A
Maltodextrin	Room temperature	N/A	N/A	N/A
Methylcellulose				
Methocel F50	Any	Below 15°C / 59°F	Above 62-68°C / 143-154°F	Below 30°C / 86°F
Methocel A4C	Hot	Below 15°C / 59°F	Above 50-55°C / 122-131°F	Below 25°C / 77°F
Mono and Diglycerides	Above 60°C / 140°F	Any	N/A	N/A
Sodium Alginate	Any	Any	Any	Above 130°C / 266°F
Xanthan Gum	Any	Any	N/A	N/A

Sous Vide and Modernist Resources

For an up to date look at current books, websites, and other modernist cooking resources you can visit the list I keep on my website.

You can find it at:
MCMEasy.com/Resources

Sous vide and modernist cooking are very complex processes and there is much more to learn about them in addition to what has been covered in this book. There is more and more good information available about modernist cooking. Here are some resources to help you continue to learn more.

MODERNIST RESOURCES

My Other Books
All of my books are available from Amazon.com or on my website.

Sous Vide: Help for the Busy Cook
By Jason Logsdon
My book focusing on how to use sous vide around your busy schedule. Full of recipes, tips and tricks to make sous vide work for you.

Sous Vide Grilling
By Jason Logsdon
This book is focused on grilling and BBQ recipes. It includes 95 great recipes covering steaks, burgers, kebabs, pulled pork, and everything in between.

Modernist Cooking Made Easy: Getting Started
By Jason Logsdon
My introductory book to modernist cooking including detailed looks at many of the most popular techniques and ingredients.

Modernist Cooking Made Easy: Party Foods
By Jason Logsdon
Amaze and delight your friends with easy to make modernist dishes that will blow them away!

Modernist Cooking Made Easy: The Whipping Siphon
By Jason Logsdon
A detailed look at the whipping siphon. It covers the three main uses of the siphon: foaming, carbonating, and infusing.

Beginning Sous Vide: Low Temperature Recipes and Techniques for Getting Started at Home
By Jason Logsdon
My main book covering sous vide. It deals a lot with the various equipment options and has over 100 recipes, some of which have been specially adapted for this book.

Recommended Books

Modernist Cuisine: The Art and Science of Cooking
By Nathan Myhrvold

This aims to be the bible of modernist cuisine. It's over 2,400 pages costs $500 and was several years in the making. If you are serious about learning the newly developing modernist techniques then this might be worth the investment.

Modernist Cuisine at Home
By Nathan Myhrvold

A much more accessible version of Modernist Cuisine especially written for the home cook.

Alinea
By Grant Achatz

A beautify, picture filled book with amazing techniques and whimsical dishes.

Ideas In Food
By Aki Kamozawa and H. Alexander Talbot

Delve into the "why" of traditional and modernist cooking.

Texture - A hydrocolloid recipe collection

Compiled by Martin Lersch from Khymos.com, is a great compendium of recipes for many modernist ingredients.

On Food and Cooking
By Harold McGee

This is the ultimate guide to the scientific aspects of cooking. If you like to know why things happen in the kitchen, at every level, you will find this book fascinating.

Cooking for Geeks
By Jeff Potter

If you are interested in the geekier aspects of cooking then this book does a great job. It takes you through the basics of setting up your kitchen all the way up to kitchen hacks and sous vide cooking.

Under Pressure
By Thomas Keller

This book shows you the extent of what is possible through sous vide cooking. The recipes aren't easy, and they require a lot of work but they can provide great inspiration for dishes of your own. If you are interested in expanding your concept of what can be accomplished through cooking then this is a must have.

Websites

Modernist Cooking Made Easy
http://www.modernistcookingmadeeasy.com/
My website is full of recipes, tips, and tricks for modernist cooking. I also have forums and other ways to talk with other passionate cooks.

Hydrocolloids Primer
http://www.cookingissues.com/primers/hydrocolloids-primer/
Dave Arnold and the Cooking Issues website help to clarify some of the uses of and reasons for modernist ingredients.

Apps

I also have apps for the iPhone and iPad available, as well as one for the Android. You can search in the app store for "Molecular Gastronomy" and "Sous Vide" and mine should be near the top, published by "Primolicious".

INGREDIENT AND TOOL SOURCES

Many of the modernist ingredients cannot be picked up at the local grocery store. I have had good luck on Amazon but here are some other good resources to find these ingredients.

Modernist Pantry
https://www.modernistpantry.com
Modernist Pantry has a good selection of ingredients and equipment. I tend to buy most of my ingredients through them.

Molecule-R
http://www.molecule-r.com/
Molecule-R has a good selection of packaged ingredients and tools. Their ingredients tend to be a little more expensive but if you are just getting started then their Cuisine R-Evolution kit can be a good way to get many of the ingredients and tools to get started.

PolyScience (Now Breville)
http://www.cuisinetechnology.com/
PolyScience carries many of the higher-end modernist cooking tools such as the anti-griddle, chamber vacuum sealers, and rotary evaporators.

RECIPE INDEX

I'm always adding more recipes to my website so for more inspiration you can check out the latest dishes:

MCMEasy.com/Recipes

Beef 53

Beef Ribs and Spicy Lime Corn 95
Brat Grinders with Guinness Mustard 120
Chuck Roast Carnitas 87
Chuck Roast with Bacon and Kale 81
Chuck Steak with Fried Brussels Sprouts 66
Chuck Roast with Roasted Vegetables 79
Corned Beef 91
Filet Mignon with Creamy Blue Cheese 56
Flank Steak with Argentinian Chimichurri 61
Flat Iron Steak with Pancetta Asparagus 75
Hamburger with Bacon and Pineapple 125
Hanger Steak with Peach Salsa 71
London Broil Beef Fajitas 77
Meatballs and Spaghetti 127
New York Strip Steak 69
Pastrami Reubens 97
Prime Rib Roast with Horseradish Cream 83
Ribeye with Herb Butter and Broccoli Raab 59
Short Ribs with Feta and Beet Salad 85
Sirloin Steak with Lime-Ginger Slaw 63
Skirt Steak with Bean Sprouts 65
Top Round French Dip Sandwiches 89
Top Round with Orange Sauce 73
Tri-Tip with Roasted Fennel Orange Salad 92

Chicken 130

Chicken Breast Fried 135
Chicken Breast Parmigiana 132
Chicken Thigh Shredded Enchiladas 139
Chicken Thighs with Cheddar Polenta 141
Chicken Wings 137

Creme Brulee

Cinnamon-Vanilla Creme Brulee 225
White Chocolate Creme Brulee 227

Creme Fraiche

Sous Vide Creme Fraiche 223

Duck 130

Duck Breast with Port Reduction 147
Duck Legs Shredded Sesame Noodles 145

Ducle de Leche

Dulce de Leche 229

Eggs 149

13 Minute Egg on Wilted Spinach Salad 155
Chocolate Chip Cookie Dough Balls 157
Scrambled Eggs French-Style 153
Soft Boiled Egg on Cheddar Hash Browns 151

Fish and Shellfish 159

Calamari with Asian-Flavored Vegetables 179
Cod Chowder with Sourdough Croutons 181
Halibut with Honey-Roasted Beets 167
Mi-Cuit Salmon 165
Monkfish in Dashi with Snow Peas 171
Red Snapper Tostadas with Mango Salsa 173
Salmon with Apple and Jalapenos 163
Scallops with Orange and Chile Strips 177
Sea Bass with Mustard Oil 169
Shrimp Cocktail with Chipotle Sauce 161
Tuna Sesame Crusted with Avocado Salad 175

Fruits 182

Apple Bourbon-Maple Chutney 203
Apples with Spiced Cabbage 202
Lemon Confit 194
Lemon Curd 224
Pears Vanilla Poached 205

Ground Beef 119

Hamburger with Bacon and Pineapple 125
Meatballs and Spaghetti 127

References: Recipe Index 264

Infusions 207
Cherry-Infused Rye Old Fashioned 208
Chile Pepper Infused Oil 219
Chile-Tomato Infused Vodka Bloody Mary 211
Orange-Vanilla Vodka Creamsicle 209
Raspberry Infused Vinaigrette 213
Rosemary and Sage Infused Oil 217
Tarragon, Lemon, and Shallot Vinaigrette 215

Lamb 53
Lamb Loin Rogan Josh 100
Rack of Lamb with Quinoa-Mint Salad 101

Modernist Notes
Apple Bourbon-Maple Chutney 203
Apples with Spiced Cabbage 202
Asparagus with Dijon Mustard Vinaigrette 183
Brat Grinders with Guinness Mustard 120
Broccoli with Parmesan and Lemon 185
Chuck Roast Carnitas 87
Chuck Roast with Bacon and Kale 81
Chuck Steak with Fried Brussels Sprouts 66
Country Style Ribs Honey Glazed 104
Duck Breast with Port Reduction 147
Duck Legs Shredded Sesame Noodles 145
Filet Mignon with Creamy Blue Cheese 56
Flank Steak with Argentinian Chimichurri 61
London Broil Beef Fajitas 77
Mi-Cuit Salmon 165
New York Strip Steak 69
Orange-Vanilla Vodka Creamsicle 209
Pork Chops with Frijoles Negros 107
Pork Tenderloin with Pea Pesto 109
Pulled Pork with Pineapple Chutney 111
Rack of Lamb with Quinoa-Mint Salad 101
Raspberry Infused Vinaigrette 213
Rosemary and Sage Infused Oil 217
Salmon with Apple and Jalapenos 163
Sea Bass with Mustard Oil 169

Short Ribs with Feta and Beet Salad 85
Shrimp Cocktail with Chipotle Sauce 161
Sirloin Steak with Lime-Ginger Slaw 63
Sous Vide Yogurt 221
Tarragon, Lemon, and Shallot Vinaigrette 215
Top Round with Orange Sauce 73
Tri-Tip with Roasted Fennel Orange Salad 92
Tuna Sesame Crusted with Avocado Salad 175
Turkey Breast with Cranberry Chutney 143

Pork 103
Country Style Ribs Honey Glazed 104
Meatballs and Spaghetti 127
Pork Chops with Frijoles Negros 107
Pork Loin Roast Prosciutto-Wrapped 115
Pork Rillettes 117
Pork Tenderloin with Pea Pesto 109
Pulled Pork with Pineapple Chutney 111
St. Louis Ribs with Bourbon BBQ Sauce 113

Sausage 119
Brat Grinders with Guinness Mustard 120
Chicken Sausage with Caprese Salad 129
Italian Sausage with Acorn Squash Puree 123

Turkey 130
Turkey Breast with Cranberry Chutney 143

Vegetables 182
Asparagus with Dijon Mustard Vinaigrette 183
Beets Butter-Poached Salad with Pecans 189
Broccoli with Parmesan and Lemon 185
Butternut Squash Salad 195
Cabbage with Apples 202
Carrots Sweet and Spicy Glazed 187
Cherry Tomatoes Poached 193
Corn on the Cob with Basil 191
Fennel Orange-Saffron Confit 192
Potato Dual-Cooked Creamy Puree 198

Potatoes Mashed Rustic Roasted Garlic 199
Sweet Potato Chipotle Salad 201
Turnips Butter Poached 197

Yogurt
Sous Vide Yogurt 221

References: Recipe Index 266

DID YOU ENJOY THIS BOOK?

If you enjoyed this book check out my other books on sous vide and modernist cooking.

Sous Vide: Help for the Busy Cook

Do you take pride in cooking great food for yourself, your family, and friends but are you on the go all day long?

Sous vide has many benefits for people who are busy during the day. Once you understand how to take advantage of these benefits you can get great meals on the table while working around your schedule.

Modernist Cooking Made Easy: Party Foods

This book provides all the information you need to get started amazing your party guests with modernist cooking.

It is all presented in an easy to understand format along with more than 100 recipes that can be applied immediately to your next party.

Modernist Cooking Made Easy: Getting Started

If you are looking for more information about the other modernist techniques then my first book is for you. It will give you the information you need to create gels, foams, emulsions, as well as teach you how to do spherification, thickening, and sous vide cooking. It also has more than 80 easy-to-follow recipes to get you on your way.

Modernist Cooking Made Easy: The Whipping Siphon

This book focuses on presenting the three main uses of the whipping siphon: Foaming, Infusing, and Carbonating. It delivers the information you need to understand how the techniques work and provides you with over 50 recipes to illustrate these techniques while allowing you to create great dishes using them.

All books are available from Amazon.com as a paperback and Kindle book, on iTunes, and on BN.com.

ABOUT THE AUTHOR

Jason Logsdon is a passionate home cook, entrepreneur, and web developer. He helps cooks understand new modernist cooking techniques with easy-to-understand directions and recipes. He has a website and several books on sous vide and modernist cooking that are read by thousands of people every month including *Modernist Cooking Made Easy: Party Foods, Sous Vide: Help for the Busy Cook, Modernist Cooking Made Easy: Getting Started, Sous Vide Grilling, Modernist Cooking Made Easy: The Whipping Siphon*, and *Beginning Sous Vide*. His website is www.ModernistCookingMadeEasy.com and Jason can be reached at jason@modernistcookingmadeeasy.com or through Twitter at @jasonlogsdon_sv.

Made in the USA
San Bernardino, CA
16 December 2019

61545873R00160